CLARE OF ASSISI
EARLY DOCUMENTS

Edited and Translated by

Regis J. Armstrong, O.F.M., Cap.

Preface by Mother Veronica Namoyo, O.S.C.

PAULIST PRESS
New York / Mahwah

Library of Congress Cataloging-in-Publication Data

Clare, of Assisi, Saint, 1194–1253.
   [Works. English. 1988]
   Clare of Assisi : early documents / translated and introduced by
Regis Armstrong.
   p. cm.
   Bibliography: p.
   Includes indexes.
   ISBN 0-8091-3012-2 (pbk.) : $14.95 (est.)
   1. Clare, of Assisi, Saint, 1194–1253. 2. Clare, of Assisi,
Saint, 1194–1253—Correspondence. 3. Christian saints—Italy—
Assisi—Correspondence. 4. Poor Clares. 5. Francis, of Assisi,
Saint, 1182–1226. I. Armstrong, Regis J. II. Title.
BX4700.C6A2 1988
271'.973'024—dc19
[B]   88-25469
                                                   CIP

Published by Paulist Press
997 Macarthur Boulevard
Mahwah, New Jersey 07430

Printed and bound in the
United States of America.

Contents

80641

To my mother,
Virginia Clark Armstrong,
who was always
an unassuming light of faith
making it easier for me to know the way

Preface

We were once asked: Is Saint Clare relevant today, in Africa and other parts of the world? Catherine de Hueck Doherty, the founder of the Madonna Houses, those modern spiritual centers which attract so many young people in North America, claims: it is the poor who pray. This is also the testimony of the Russian pilgrims of centuries past, as well as of the Sufi mystics or the Syrophoenician woman. But it could well be perhaps more than anything else the motto of Clare and her daughters.

To pray: that is to turn toward God in faith and love, to search in silence for the absolute, to be transfigured into this mirror of Christ that Clare holds before us. But to pray is also to repeat the "have mercy on me" of the repentant sinner and to be constantly united to the intercession of the Mother of God: "They have no wine . . . ", no love, no food . . . To pray with the urgency of both love and need, from the essential poverty of a heart devoid of illusions and self-seeking: how can this become obsolete as long as God is known on earth and Christ reveals Him? Clare is universal like Francis because poverty has centered her heart and life on an unchangeable and unique object.

It is not the shoe that falls out of fashion but the added ribbon or buckle. It is not the lamp that becomes strange but its decorations or style; not the Gospel but its commentaries. There is no interpretation or commentary on the Rule of Francis or Clare: they offer us water from the very spring that satisfies the thirst of blacks and browns and whites of the thirteenth or twentieth century alike, wherever there is a thirst for God and a determination to follow Christ.

"It is the poor who pray." Then monasteries should cover Africa and those parts of the world where the poor can always be found, though, of course, there are more "anawim" than monks and nuns! It is prayer that gives strength for moral freedom as well as guidance for other forms of liberation. Will it not be another role for modern Poor Clares in the third world? Solidarity with the poor is one of the Gospel values that has come to light in our days. More than other contemplatives or priests "in charge" of many activities, we may live this solidarity in the simplicity of our life. We go to our modest tasks like the village women; we suffer from the same insecurity; we experience the lack of remedies at the nearby hospital where our illnesses are imperfectly cared for. We struggle to find proteins for our meals and know exhaustion as well as joy after a day in the field. All this we bring to the God of Nazareth. And at the same time in a world where so much is geared to material development, we feel the responsibility of offering "the supplement of soul" that was wished to a world that reaches to the stars but knows no peace.

Perhaps also "a supplement of heart"? If something makes Clare especially relevant to Africa and to the world, it is her stress on community life and the balance she establishes between a "servant abbess" and her adult and consulted daughters and sisters. It is the warmth of relationship that is also our need and our safeguard even if it looks at times to be an almost unattainable ideal. And finally there is in Clare so much joy and optimism! She is like the smiling faces of those naked children and ragged old people we know so well.

The poor are light for dance and song. The sun warms our land and love our hearts, and so we need to end, as Clare ended her life, with a praise of God Who created us for Himself and multiplied us through all the earth.

Mother Veronica Namoyo, O.S.C.
Monastery of Saint Clare
Chelston, Lusaka
Zambia

Foreword

The recent surge of interest in Franciscan spirituality has had the curious effect of revealing how little attention has been given to Saint Clare of Assisi and how poor are the English resources for coming to a deeper awareness of her place not only in Franciscan history but also in that of religious women. Much of what has been translated is scattered throughout various volumes and has been out of print or sadly deficient in providing accurate and thorough renditions of the original.

The documents contained in this book encompass almost all of the writings by or about Clare from 1212, the year of her entrance into the following of Francis, to 1263, the publication of the *Major Life of Saint Francis* by Saint Bonaventure. Only one known document has been set aside: the *Legenda Versificata*, an early biography of the saint in verse form composed by an unknown author and based upon the *Acts of the Process of Canonization*. Since most of its contents are repeated in the *Legend of Saint Clare*, it was judged best to simply present that more popular and important work. However, some of the translations contained in this volume are appearing for the first time in the English language and, it is hoped, will broaden our knowledge of Saint Clare and the Poor Ladies of San Damiano.

One major difficulty in preparing the volume was the manner of presenting these documents. Since they represent such a variety of writings—canonical legislation, personal letters, official sworn testimonies as well as customary medieval hagiography—I decided to follow the suggestion of Sister Chaira Augusta Lainati, O.S.C., who proposed the threefold division presented in this volume: (1) the writings of Clare herself; (2) those dealing with her and the Poor Ladies of San Damiano; and, finally, (3) those dealing with her, Saint Francis and his brothers.

Another difficulty was the ever-increasing literature concerning the role of women, particularly religious women, in the Middle Ages. So much of what has been written about Clare and the Poor Ladies of San Damiano has been examined from the perspective of the Franciscan movement; little attention has been paid to the larger context of women religious of the twelfth and thirteenth centuries. Thus the notes throughout the volume were written in the hope of expanding the horizons of our future studies of Clare.

3

It should be noted that the writings of Saint Clare presented in this volume are essentially the same as those in FRANCIS AND CLARE: COMPLETE WORKS. However, since the publication of that volume, the scholarly work of Marie-France Becker, Jean-François Godet and Thadee Matura, CLAIRE D'ASSISE: ÉCRITS, in 1985, has nuanced the Latin text and provided a different numbering which, it is hoped, will be more widely accepted than that used previously. Furthermore, I have taken the liberty of expressing in verse lines much of the *Legend of Saint Clare* and part of the *Bull of Canonization*. I did so because of the rhythm of the Latin text that seemed at times to be far more poetical than it had been traditionally translated.

A book such as CLARE OF ASSISI: EARLY DOCUMENTS does not come into being without a large number of collaborators to whom I am tremendously indebted. In the first place, the Sisters of Saint Clare deserve the greatest expression of thanks for inspiring and encouraging me in this project, most especially those of the monasteries in Delray Beach, Florida, Kiryu, Japan, and those spread throughout the Philippines. Without the power of their continued prayers and encouragement, this volume could not have been completed. It is an honor for me to have Mother Veronica Namoyo, the former Abbess of the Monastery in Lusaka, Zambia, as the author of the Preface of this volume. By the power of her example, she has eloquently expressed for those who know her the message of Saint Clare. Now she has done so through the written word.

As I reflect upon the various stages of the volume's development, I cannot but remember the important persons who participated on all the various literary levels. I wish to thank especially Canisius Connors, O.F.M., who patiently corrected my translation of the Latin text, as well as Serge Hughes, who critiqued the translation of the Umbrian dialect text of the *Acts of the Process of Canonization*. Despite many pressing obligations and trying circumstances, both men were marvelously generous with their time and offered me invaluable insights and suggestions concerning an accurate and readable translation. Roger Sorrentino reviewed the English translation, made the necessary grammatical corrections, and, with his poetic sense, helped me to refine the text. However, a priceless and indispensable contribution was made by Margaret Carney, O.S.F., who not only added significantly to the footnotes but added the extremely important feminine reading of the translation. Without her help, enthusiasm and knowledge, it would have been impossible to offer such a work. Throughout all these stages, moreover, Patrick Colbourne, O.F.M. Cap., Chiara Anastasia, O.S.C., of the Protomonastery of St. Clare in Assisi and Nancy Celaschi, O.S.F. of the staff of *L'Osservatore Romano*, were constantly available with their observations, suggestions and encouragement.

Finally, I must add a word of special thanks to Edmundo B. Valera, who proved to be my teacher *par excellence* by unknowingly providing me a clearer understanding and love of the vision of Saint Clare. He continually inspired me, patiently challenged me and gently but firmly prodded me, at times at great personal sacrifice. Everyone should be blessed with such a faithful friend and perceptive guide.

CLARE OF ASSISI:
EARLY DOCUMENTS

Introduction

At the close of the twelfth century, Assisi, that small city built on a southwestern spur of Monte Subasio, was caught in an intense struggle for control of the entire Italian peninsula. The Normans, a dying force in the last part of the century, still maintained control of the southern Sicilian States and, periodically, attempted to exert their influence to regain some of their former properties. The German forces of the north, meanwhile, convinced their emperor was entitled to rule as successor of the great emperors of the Holy Roman Empire, repeatedly jockeyed for positions of power. The papacy, at the same time, remained resolute in its desire to expand its influence and, at this particular time, to govern the central Italian states and prevent a union between the forces of the north and the south which threatened to enervate the strength of the Papal States. The Spoleto Valley and, more importantly, Assisi itself were crucial in this struggle to gain control. The principal route from Rome to Ravenna cut directly through the Spoleto Valley making Assisi, with its ideal geographical position, a most desirable possession.

The city, however, suffered not only from these external political pressures. It was divided from within by a feudalism that had never really asserted itself and, as a result, had favored an urban model of society, characterized by the tensions of two conflicting groups or social parties, the *majores* and the *minores*. The ancient Umbrian city was internally torn by a struggle based on a social inequality that widened the gap between the social classes and solidified sharp social barriers. Assisi's twofold division, political as well as social, was not simply a matter of opposing powers and their desire for domination. It was an expression of a profound enmity expressed in terms of a poverty and a subsequent emargination that stood not only opposed to the riches of the other but also participation in both the old and new forms of power, dignity, and social advantage.

Assisi was at the crossroads. The economic structures that for so long governed its way of life were crumbling and with them the political machinery that had vacillated between one power and another was exerting itself in a revolutionary way. Citizens were now expressing themselves in new ways: destroying the city's fortress, once a symbol of domination by foreigners, proclaiming themselves a "Commune," and breaking new gates

9

into the old city walls that new trade routes might be encouraged. Popes as well as emperors were keeping careful watch on the so-called "Commune of Assisi" and were attempting to keep it within their own power and control.

Amidst all these undercurrents of change, the young Francis of Assisi was attracting more and more followers to his "new" Gospel way of life and, perhaps without realizing it, was advancing the profound social, political and economic changes that were already affecting daily life. In place of the hierarchical distinctions of a religious life, monasticism, that mirrored those of feudalism, Francis developed a way of life built upon a Gospel-inspired minority in which poverty, humility and patient suffering formed its foundation. In a society that was torn by such deep division, he proposed the Gospel ideal of brotherhood and a social model in which social differences would not be dictated by riches, power or knowledge. Francis was emerging as a peacemaker rather than an underminer of the social and religious worlds, even though his vision of a Gospel way of life did, in fact, weaken the feudal and monastic social structures both of which had been developed according to a system of inequalities and hierarchies.

Among his followers was a young woman, Clare di Favorone, more than likely one of the favorite daughters of the city. History has traditionally regarded her as *la pianticella*, the little plant, of Saint Francis. This designation of Clare as nothing other than "an offshoot" or the most faithful disciple of Francis has tended to obscure her unique position in Franciscan spirituality. On closer examination, Clare emerges more clearly as one who accepted the charism of Francis, expressed it in her unique feminine way, and, at a period of medieval history in which the role of women was also undergoing change, shattered many of the traditional religious stereotypes. As we study Clare more carefully, she becomes more of a strong, thoroughly convinced and heroic woman who would not let the purity of Francis' charism die despite the enormous forces discouraging her. During the twenty-seven years between the death of Francis and her own, she is the living witness that strongly shapes the consciousness of the Franciscan family and, during that period, unwittingly becomes a creative innovator of the religious life of the Church.

I

Clare was the third of five children born to this somewhat well-to-do family of Assisi. In the *Acts of the Process of Canonization*, Sister Filippa, the third witness, testified under oath to the apprehension of Ortulana, Clare's mother, as the time of her child's birth drew near. Ortulana frequently visited a nearby church, the witness states, and one day heard a response to her prayer for the safe delivery of her child. "O lady," the voice told her, "do not be afraid, for you will joyfully bring forth a clear light that will illumine the world." Within a short time, a female child was born to Ortulana and her husband Favarone, and was named Chiara or Clare, the clear or bright one.

The witnesses in the *Acts of the Process of Canonization* do not hesitate to describe her as a holy, dedicated young woman even before her "conversion." The *Legend*, based on the *Acts* states: "The Spirit worked within and formed her into a most pure vessel. . . . She began to be praised by her neighbors and the report of her goodness was spread about among the townspeople." Docility to her parents, generosity and compassion for the poor, dedication to daily prayer: these are some of the virtues Clare's biographer adds among the qualities of her youth.

Assisi could not have been an ideal environment in which to enjoy the simple joys of youth, especially for the Favarone family. In 1198, when Clare was three or four years old, the excitable Assisians stormed the Rocca Maggiore, the city's fortress inhabited by the family of the Emperor, Frederick Barbarosa, and tore it to the ground as a sign of their intention never again to be dominated by a foreign power. During the successive years, the city's history is pockmarked with the blemishes of one battle after another: family fighting family, city fighting city until the notorious battle of Collestrada in 1202 when the Perugians devastated and humiliated the Assisians. We will never know how much this affected Clare for there is no indication of her family's involvement in those years of strife. But we should place the evidence offered by those who knew her during those years into that turbulent framework.

She must have grown to be a beautiful young woman. The eighteenth witness in the *Acts of the Process of Canonization*, Lord Rainerio de Bernardo of Assisi, says as much and admits to having asked her many times to consent to marriage. But Clare had other things in mind: the preservation of her virginity and, it seems, the embrace of a life of poverty. Even in her youth, her attention was directed elsewhere, to the things of God. Thus, on Palm Sunday, March 18, 1212, when all the young ladies of Assisi customarily dressed in their finest and proudly processed to the Bishop for a palm branch, it was not too surprising that Clare confronted Assisi with the conflict between its social yearnings and its spiritual promise. Rather than approaching the Bishop, Clare remained in her place prompting him to come to her. It was a symbolic gesture suggesting her renunciation of the social conventions of the time with all the vanity and appeal to wealth with which they were imbued and the Bishop's awareness and reverence of the movement of God within her calling her to accept the "palm of martyrdom" in imitation of the suffering Christ.

We cannot determine when and how Clare first met Francis, the popular young man who had turned his back on the military establishment and the business world, but she probably heard him proclaim his message of penance and peace in the piazzas of Assisi. It is certainly possible that Clare heard the young Francis preach in the cathedral of San Rufino in 1210, for her family lived directly adjacent to it. At about this time her uncle had made arrangements for her to marry but Clare refused and, with the help of her servant, Bona di Guelfuccio, made arrangements to meet Francis and receive his advice. "The Father Francis," the *Legend* narrates, "encouraged her to despise the world, showing her by his living speech how dry the hope of the world was and how deceptive its beauty. He whispered in her ears of a sweet espousal with Christ, persuading her to preserve the pearl of her virginal purity for that blessed Spouse Whom Love made man." On that significant Palm Sunday, then, Clare followed the advice of Francis, accepted the palm branch from the Bishop of Assisi, and that evening went secretly to Our Lady of Angels, the Portiuncula, where Francis and his brothers received her commitment to follow them in the pursuit of Gospel life.

Francis and his brothers escorted Clare to the Benedictine monastery of San Paolo delle Abbadesse in Bastia, a short distance from the Portiuncula, where she was guaranteed sanctuary until further arrangements could be made. After her relatives attempted to convince her to return home, Francis moved her to San Angelo di Panzo, a monastery of Beguine recluses, and finally to San Damiano, the first of the little churches Francis had repaired in fulfillment of the Lord's command. Clare remained there until her death in 1253. Within a short period of time, she was joined by others, even her mother, Ortulana, and the "Poor Ladies of San Damiano" became recognized followers of Francis of Assisi.

In her *Rule*, Clare cites a short "form of life" that Francis gave to her and her sisters. It is a simple statement describing the Trinitarian foundations of the life at San Damiano, as well as the close ties that Francis saw binding the Poor Ladies and his brothers. Although there are no other documents of either Francis or Clare that provide more details concerning the daily life of the "Damianites," as they were called, in 1216 Jacques de Vitry, an astute observer of new forms of religious life at that time, described their life in his *Historia orientalis et occidentalis*. He writes:

"The women live near the cities in various hospices. They accept nothing, but live from the work of their hands. In fact, they are very much offended and disturbed because they are honored by the clergy and laity more than they deserve."

Twelve years later, Thomas of Celano, in his *First Life of Saint Francis*, presents a beautiful description of Clare and the community of San Damiano and begins:

> "A noble structure of the most precious pearls arose above her, *whose praise comes not from men but from God* (Rom 2:29), since our limited understanding is not sufficient to imagine it nor our scanty vocabulary to utter it."

Thomas proceeds to praise Clare and her sisters for their steadfast practice of charity, humility, virginity and chastity, abstinence and silence, patience and contemplation. What is remarkable about these paragraphs is their composition during the lifetime of Clare herself who no doubt heard them read aloud with each celebration of the feast of Saint Francis. No doubt Thomas saw her as the living witness of the primitive Franciscan fraternity and the intimate bond between Francis and themselves. Did he perceive of her role as similar to that of Mary, the Mother of the Church, to whom the apostles looked for embodied guidance and knowledge of Jesus after His Ascension? Certainly their positions bear resemblances. For at this very time the friars were beginning to see strong likenesses in the lives of Christ and Francis and to take seriously the theme of the "conformities" between the two. But Thomas makes no reference to the similarity between Mary, the Mother of Jesus, and Clare. We must wait until after her death when the anonymous author of the *Legend* describes Clare in a most beautiful and telling phrase as "the footprint of the Mother of God."

II

In attempting to understand the attractiveness of Clare of Assisi and her sisters in their daily life at San Damiano, we would find it helpful to reflect upon the very foundation upon which they built that life: their intense pursuit of a relationship with God. This is never an easy task when dealing with contemplatives for there are so many basic suppositions that must be taken for granted in the day-to-day life of the enclosure: a profound faith, for example, or an unquenchable desire to grow spiritually. What we might call their "standard of success," moreover, is so totally different from that of more active or pastoral religious, for so much depends on intangible or transparent realities. All this is even more difficult in the case of Clare for the autobiographical reflections of her forty-three years in the enclosure of San Damiano are so few and unassuming. As we have seen, we must rely on her *Testament*, those few but precious insights she offers us in the *Rule*, and the spiritual advice found in her letters to Agnes of Prague. Nonetheless, we have an extremely valuable source of information in those Poor Ladies who testified under oath concerning their daily life with her. What they said comes to us untouched by the hand of a hagiographer who consciously or unconsciously interprets facts through the prism of his own theological view. Thus, putting these sources together—Clare's few writings and the testimony of those sisters who lived with her—we do well to focus on the daily rhythm of Clare's life with her sisters in the confines of San Damiano. In so doing we quite easily perceive the principal currents that carved and shaped her vision: her life of intense prayer, pursuit of an authentic Gospel poverty, and understanding of the Gospel revelation of the Triune life of God as providing the pattern of her daily life with her sisters.

When we look at the Rules governing San Damiano during Clare's life and that which she left to her sisters at her death, we can immediately see that the pace of the monastery's everyday life was established by its life of prayer, especially the Liturgy of the Hours. Both the Rules of Hugolino and Innocent stated specifically: "The offering of the Divine Office to the Lord both day and night should be observed . . . with gravity and modesty." Innocent's *Rule* goes further in suggesting the recitation of the Office of the Blessed Virgin Mary, a popular devotion in this period of history, and the *Legend* states that Clare also recited the *Office of the Cross* composed by Francis. Thus we are given the contours of the typical enclosed religious life which unfolds according to a rhythm of prayer that seven times daily brings one to worship the Lord.

If we are to comprehend the daily life of Clare and the Poor Ladies, we should reflect more fully upon the implications of this hour plan. All of their activities revolved around their pursuit of prayer, the *opus Dei*, the work of God, as the monastic tradition calls it. This dedication to prayer would necessarily have prevented the sisters from undertaking large projects or involving themselves in strenuous or demanding work. Prayer was the principal activity of the day to which each sister untiringly dedicated herself. It would seem, then, that their life of prayer was interrupted by other duties, simple and unassuming as they may have been. This devotion, moreover, had its effects not only on the daily way of life of the Poor Ladies; it also shaped their manner of thinking, reckoning time, and interpreting the flow of history. The tenth witness, for example, comments on the intensity of Clare's prayer at the liturgical hour of Sext when "the Lord was placed on the cross." The same sister also described Clare's abundance of tears at the completion of Compline, the closing prayer of the day in which both the goodness of the Lord and the temptations of the devil are brought to mind. But beyond these observations on the two periods of each day when Clare was deeply moved by thoughts of the suffering of Christ, the sisters unwittingly show us that the liturgical celebrations caused each of them to use certain feasts or seasons as points of reference for events. Thus many of the sisters respond to questions concerning the dates of the miraculous deeds of Clare by simply stating they can only remember its occurrence on or about some liturgical feast. All of which underscores the contemplative tendency to interpret reality in the light of the mysteries of prayer, incorporate daily events into a different time frame, and consider time as yet another gift with which to praise God.

The sisters, however, repeatedly move us beyond this daily liturgical rhythm in their descriptions of Clare's spirit of prayer. Two of the witnesses, as well as the *Bull of Canonization* and the *Legend*, underscore her dedication to praying during both the day and the night. She spent long periods with the Lord before and after the celebration of the hours. The word which the witnesses use continually in their descriptions is "assiduous," that is, constantly giving or applying herself to the practice of prayer. When these passages are placed beside those describing Clare's intensity during the periods, we are given the impression that she used all of her energy to place and give herself totally to the Lord.

The unassuming Clare, of course, tells us very little about her practice of prayer. We must turn to her writings to read between the lines for any clues or insights and, in so doing, discover the crystal clear transparency of her life of prayer. When we consider the *Testament* and the letters to Agnes of Prague as coming from the context of "spiritual direction," we more easily see them as flowing from the depths of her heart. The fact that the same basic approach is found throughout these writings which span a period of more than eighteen years suggests a certain consistency and, therefore, a basic structure in her relationship with God.

In the earliest of her writings, the first letter to Agnes of Prague, Clare provides us the most obvious aspect of her prayer: its never ending fascination with the person of Jesus. Simple as this seems, it underscores the profundity of her understanding of life as a continuous relationship with Christ which expresses itself most beautifully in unceasing prayer. Repeatedly we come across Clare's encouragement to focus on the Lord: " . . . may you totally love Him Who gave Himself totally for your love," " . . . cling to Him Whose beauty all the blessed hosts of heaven unceasingly admire," "Look upon Him Who became contemptible for you." When we read her writings with this increased awareness of the presence of Christ, we are left with the impression that Clare was a woman passionately in love with Him. She offers very few intellectual or practical formulas for making progress in the life of prayer. It is almost as if Clare consciously wanted to teach her sisters that prayer was simply a matter of falling in love, a process that defies plans, methods or well defined approaches. On the contrary, in light of the numerous reflections on the mystery of Christ in her letters to Agnes, she suggests that the development of a life of prayer comes only through focusing our attention on Him.

From this perspective, then, we can appreciate the simple formula that Clare offers Agnes in her second letter: "O most noble Queen, gaze upon [Him], consider [Him], contemplate [Him], as you desire to imitate [Him]." This is, perhaps, the only insight that we have into Clare's method of prayer. *Intuere*, she writes, that is, pay attention, focus your gaze upon the suffering Christ. *Considera*, consider or try to understand the mystery upon which you are reflecting that you may lose yourself in lovingly contemplating, *contemplare*, Him. Yet, all the while, she counsels, you should be desiring to imitate Him, *desiderans imitari*. It is a beautiful formula, profound in its simplicity and reflecting the insights of a woman eager to awaken affection in others for the One she loves.

Were this formula only to appear in the second letter to Agnes of Prague, we might be tempted to interpret it as a simple suggestion of a spiritual directress eager to teach a method of prayer. But Clare repeats it eighteen years later in a much fuller way. "Gaze upon that mirror (Jesus) each day," she writes, "and continually study your face in it, that you may adorn yourself within and without with beautiful robes. . . . Look at the border of that mirror. . . . At the surface of that mirror, consider. . . . Then, in the depth of this same mirror, contemplate. . . . " The elements are the same, although the image of Christ is developed in a marvelously contemplative and feminine way through the concept of the mirror. By combining the dimensions of the mirror with three different periods in the life of Christ, Clare allows us a glimpse into the bond that exists between her practice of prayer and her pursuit of spiritual growth.

While "mirror literature" was quite popular among the religious of the twelfth and early thirteenth centuries, Clare adds significantly to it by developing its christological and feminine qualities. "That Mirror suspended on the wood of the cross," as she refers to Christ, reflected two images: that of the splendor of eternal glory, the transcendent Lord, and that of those creatures who looked upon it. Focusing our gaze upon Christ, therefore, enables us to perceive the Father and, at the same time, to see a reflection of what we are called to be, reflections of His Son. No one had developed that type of imagery before Clare; it was largely overlooked until the fourteenth century. But Clare goes further than suggesting the mirror as an image of Christ; she deliberately offers it as a means of growing in a likeness of Him. "Gaze upon that mirror each day, O Queen and Spouse of Jesus Christ," Clare encourages Agnes, "and continually study your face within it, that you may adorn yourself within and without with beautiful robes. . . . " It is a marvelously practical, down-to-earth piece of feminine advice. Although so many authors before her, most of them monks, had taken the mirror as a starting point of their reflections on the spiritual life, no one had developed it so speculatively and practically as Clare. She gives us, therefore, her profound insights into a way of prayer that flows naturally into everyday life.

That continuous and intense pursuit of a prayer centered on Christ, then, enables us to appreciate more fully Clare's devotion to the practice of poverty. It was the genius of Francis, Clare realized more than most, to see that a life without anything of one's own, *sine proprio*, frees us to enter more profoundly into the mystery of God and His kingdom. "O blessed poverty," she proclaims in her first letter to Agnes of Prague, "who bestows eternal riches on those who love and embrace her! O holy poverty, to those who possess and desire you God promises *the kingdom of heaven* (Mt 5:3) and offers, indeed, eternal glory and blessed life." But more than simply seeing poverty as a means or an aid to deepening the life of prayer, Clare sees it as flowing naturally from that contemplative gazing upon the mystery of Christ, " . . . the God Who was placed poor in the crib, lived poor in the world, and remained naked on the cross." To gaze upon that Mirror, Christ, in other words, is to embrace His state of being without anything of His own. "O God-centered poverty," she writes "whom the Lord Jesus Christ, Who ruled and now rules heaven and earth, *Who spoke and things were made* (cf. Ps 32:9; Ps 148:5), condescended to embrace before else!"

When we look at the writings of Clare, we see how her *Testament* stands out in revealing her profound love of poverty and, at the same time, her desire to preserve it as the foundation of the life of the Poor Ladies. In addition to underscoring Christ as the primary inspiration for this poverty, Clare repeatedly points in the *Testament* to Francis as guiding her and her sisters in understanding its meaning. " . . . I have always been most zealous and solicitous to observe and to have the others observe," she admits, "the holy poverty that we have promised to the Lord and our most holy father Francis." Yet we cannot help being impressed by Clare's ecclesial sense which places this Gospel intuition, brought into focus by the teachings of Francis, firmly within the life of the Church. She describes her endeavor to obtain papal protection for living this poverty and proceeds to beg the Church to help her preserve it. In reading the *Testament*, the words of the Crucified Christ heard by Francis in San Damiano come to mind: "Francis, repair my house which, as you see, is falling to ruin." Did Clare perceive that the 'mandate of San Damiano' had been passed to her and her sisters or that the Poor Ladies were, in fact, called to be faithful reminders of Francis' response? Beyond the reflections of Thomas of Celano whose biographies of Saint Francis clearly suggest these points, we have only to look at Clare's *Testament* to recognize how clearly she understood the role of poverty in the life and mission of the Church.

What is so startling, however, is the severity of Clare's poverty. In both her *Rule* and *Testament* Clare echoes the teachings of Francis especially in his encouragement to live "without anything of one's own." "Let the sisters not appropriate anything, neither a house nor a place nor anything at all," Clare insists; "instead, as pilgrims and strangers in this world who serve the Lord in poverty and humility, let them confidently send for alms." She is not simply writing of a poverty of accidentals, such as clothing or money, even though, with her practical sense, she treats of these things. Her primary concern centers on the refusal of possessions and stable belongings, that is, of the socio-economic foundations considered indispensable in the ecclesiastical world of the time. Without a doubt this insistence comes from the inspiration of Francis, but Clare expresses it concerning an enclosed community and, thereby, implies a far more demanding way of life. To live without any stable form of income or support, without the freedom to go about begging for alms as the friars were doing: these were expressions of a religious life which was unheard of and, undoubtedly, seen as utopian and naively presumptuous. Yet it is precisely this demanding way of poverty that so clearly underscores what is at its very heart: an unflinching confidence, even in the direst circumstances, in the loving providence of God. Clare's expression of poverty is far more dependent upon the generosity of others and is, therefore, thoroughly imbued with faith: faith in the goodness of people, faith in the overwhelming goodness of God.

The ebb and flow of this life "without anything of one's own" frees us from our attachments and gently prompts us to focus our attention on others as day by day we become more dependent upon them. Francis seems to have clearly perceived this not only as he became more aware of the never-ending love of God, but also as he continually and profoundly linked the concepts of poverty and fraternity thereby implying that growth in one augments and enhances the development of the other. This is even more so with Clare whose embrace of such a demanding poverty within the confines of a small enclosed community made her ever more dependent on the generosity of God as she became increasingly sensitive to the needs of others.

The *Testament*, above all, focuses on this aspect of Clare's relationship with God. While in her *Rule* she refers to God as the "Most High Heavenly Father," in the *Testament* she speaks more descriptively of the "Father of mercies" and of His mercy, love and grace. Like Francis, she repeats that it is only through the mercy and love of God, not our merits, that good is accomplished. With great conviction she expresses gratitude for the daily initiative of "the glorious Father of Christ" in bestowing so many gifts upon us. "I give thanks to the Giver of grace," she writes to Agnes of Prague, "from Whom, we believe, every good and perfect gift proceeds." Everything comes from His generosity: the call to following His way, that way which is the Son of God, Francis who gave Clare and her sisters deeper insights into that Way. The God of the *Testament*, Whom Clare recognizes in her poverty as a loving Father, enlightens her heart, places Francis on the path of her life, inspires her to conversion, gives her sisters, leads her to San Damiano, and makes her community grow. He is "the Lord Father" Who has begotten in the Church "the little flock" of the Poor Ladies; He is the "Father of our Lord Jesus Christ" before Whom Clare falls on her knees in thanksgiving and praise.

As we have seen, though, Clare's attention is largely directed to "the Son of God [Who] has been made for us the Way" to the Father and, as such, is the primary inspiration of her life. Once again, we see in her *Testament*, Clare's awareness that Christ continually teaches us the wonder of the Father's love, the ways of simplicity, poverty and humility that make us more receptive of that love, and the "incomparable treasures" and "joys of redemption" that flow from it. Out of her profound love of Christ, Clare writes to Agnes of Prague of a beautiful and sensitive espousal with the Son of God in which poverty is a prerequisite as well as an enhancement. "As a poor virgin," she encourages Agnes, "embrace the poor Christ." Undoubtedly she realized during her journey to the Father that Christ reveals the blessings that come from living "without anything of our own" and that the more thoroughly this is embraced the more effectively it deepens our relationship with Him.

In her poverty, however, Clare came to a greater sensitivity to the workings of the Spirit of the Lord in the unfolding of the Gospel life. From the very beginning of her religious life, she must have known of and been familiar with the central role played by the Holy Spirit. "[Y]ou . . . have taken the Holy Spirit as your spouse," Francis wrote in the *Form of Life* he gave to Clare and her sisters during that early period at San Damiano. The inclusion of this passage in her *Rule* some forty years later, as well as the repetition of Francis's teaching concerning "the Spirit of the Lord and Its holy manner of working," suggests her consciousness of the Holy Spirit as the dynamic principle of the life of the sisters. Three of the witnesses during the *Acts of the Process of Canonization* testify to her speaking of the Triune Life of God right up to the last hours of her life, and, in particular, of the presence of the Holy Spirit in the soul. "Having created you," she said on her deathbed, "He placed the Holy Spirit within you." We can understand, therefore, her awareness of the Spirit's role in filling Francis with joy and enlightenment as he prophesied about the coming of the Poor Ladies, in calling them to a divine espousal, to the perfection of the Gospel, and to the fullness of joy.

While we may marvel at these Trinitarian foundations of her spiritual life, we should not overlook the remarkable ways in which they affected her life among her sisters. It is certainly a proof of the authenticity of her contemplative life that she translated her insights into the Gospel life into the unassuming and transparent language of everyday life in the community of San Damiano.

This can be seen, without a doubt, in the simple, day-to-day pulse of the enclosed community that was so extraordinarily dependent on the attentive care and largesse of the loving Father. Even when confronted with the prospect of hunger, sickness or death, Clare confidently lived each day in peace and tranquility and infused these virtues into her community life. While reading the *Acts of the Process of Canonization*, we cannot help being impressed by the strength of her undaunted faith in the providence of the "Father of mercies" and can more easily, therefore, appreciate her refusal to give in to those who were cautioning her to be more prudent and far-sighted in her embrace of poverty.

The influence of this Trinitarian vision becomes clearer when we reflect upon the ways in which she governed her sisters. The first witness of the *Acts of the Process of Canonization* tells us of the "prayers and insistence of Saint Francis, who almost forced her," that made Clare accept the role of abbess. Although she accepted the title of abbess from the *Rule of Hugolino* which was based on the Benedictine tradition, she understood her role not in a hierarchical sense but in one of subservience characterized by a ministry and service more in keeping with the minority of Christ as Francis himself had done. The title, however, appears only in Clare's *Rule* in which it refers to her successor. In all her other writings she refers to herself as the "handmaid," "mother," or "servant." More than exercising an authority of power or domination, Clare envisions the abbess serving the others through manifesting a maternal tenderness, consoling the afflicted, and being "the last refuge for those who are troubled." "Let the Abbess . . . be so familiar with [the sisters]," she declares in the *Rule*, "that they can speak and act with her as ladies do with their servant. For this is the way it should be: the Abbess should be the servant of all the sisters." Without a doubt, Clare realized there would be tensions in the community, but her advise to the abbess is to be generous and merciful. "She should strive," Clare maintains, " . . . to preside over the others more by her virtues and holy behavior than by her office, so that, moved by her example, the sisters may obey her more out of love than out of fear." We are given, then, the portrait of someone whose manner of governing others is influenced by the example of Christ and totally imbued with the values of the Gospel.

If there is any aspect of her writings and life that most reflects the influence of Clare's Trinitarian vision, it is her emphasis on a freedom that combines flexibility and expansiveness. When her *Rule* is placed beside those of Hugolino and Innocent, the Pauline foundation of her approach—"Where the Spirit of the Lord is present, there is freedom" (2 Cor 3:17)—can be clearly seen. In order to leave the monastery, for example, the *Rule of Hugolino* declared: the sisters "should remain enclosed the whole time of their life . . . they should never be granted any permission or faculty to leave," except to establish a new foundation. Clare, however, states: "[The sister] may not go outside the monastery except for a useful, reasonable, evident, and approved purpose." Silence, in the *Rule of Hugolino*, is perpetual, while in that of Clare is flexible. The prescriptions concerning fasting, although more rigorous in Clare's document, are far more moderate than in Hugolino's. In so many details, we are struck by the obvious sense of freedom and flexibility with which Clare approaches the daily life of the Poor Ladies and are left with the impression that she had a great respect for the workings of the Spirit of the Lord in her sisters.

This is also obvious in her frequent encouragement of the abbess to use "discernment." The word and its derivatives appears sixteen times in Clare's writings, most frequently in her *Rule*. Yet here we have a remarkable example of Clare's awareness that each sister was moved by "divine inspiration," that is, the Spirit of the Lord, to come to San Damiano and recognized that Spirit's presence in her. We can see, therefore, a remarkable sense of reverence and respect in Clare's attitude toward her sisters, one that prompted her to treat them as mature spirit-filled women whose principal desire was to live fully the Gospel life.

In the final analysis, then, our attempts to enter the world of San Damiano in order to understand the attractiveness of Clare will succeed only when we seriously consider her growth in an intense relationship with Christ. For it provided the very strength she needed to follow a way of life that had the Trinitarian pattern provided by the Gospel-oriented Francis as its starting point. Her passionate falling in love with the Lord Jesus Christ, "Whose power is stronger . . . Whose love more tender," encouraged Clare to pursue insights into the Gospel that were gradually translated into her ways of thinking, writing and living. What attracted others to her, then, was her transparency or, to play on the word, her "clarity" in manifesting the Spirit of Gospel Love.

III

Day passes quietly and unobservably into day in the monastic world. Even events bordering on the spectacular lose their time frame and blend unassumingly into the atmosphere of prayer in which all significance centers on the Lord. As proof of the validity of that prayer, the sisters offered themselves to that crucible of daily charity in such a way that their hidden, intense life in community became a manifestation of the Spirit that motivated them. Although the sisters observed the power of Clare's presence, those who were interviewed during the process of canonization were unable to specify days or even years of the deeds of Clare, miraculous as they may have been; what was far more important for them was the statement her life made concerning her holiness.

During Francis' lifetime and after his death, the Poor Ladies continued to flourish in the unassuming enclosure of San Damiano. An unusual document concerning a piece of land, dated June 8, 1238, tells us that the monastery was filled with fifty sisters. By that date, according to some chroniclers, there were at least fifty new foundations spread throughout Italy and large numbers in France, Germany, Bohemia, and Spain. It is difficult to determine the number with any precision, but the number of papal documents written to or about the Poor Ladies suggests their rapid growth drew considerable attention.

We must see this growth of the Poor Ladies, however, in the context of the Fourth Lateran Council in 1215 and its legislation forbidding the establishment of any new religious orders. While Pope Innocent III had continually encouraged new expressions of religious life, the Council restricted his initiatives by demanding that only the approved and well tested religious rules be followed. By the time of the Council, though, the Poor Ladies had become recognized as a religious community and granted a papal privilege of living in an intense poverty. But there is no evidence of the Council acknowledging or approving their way of life. The prescription of the Council, then, directly affected the form of life followed by Clare and her sisters.

As the fame of the San Damiano foundation began to spread and new monasteries were established, the Cardinal Legate of Tuscany and Lombardy, Hugolino dei Conti di Segni, was appointed by Pope Honorius III as their protector. In order to provide a more stable form of living for the Poor Ladies, one that would be in conformity with the directives of the Council, Hugolino gave them a new, detailed and austere Rule based on the *Benedictine Rule*. Two central points, however, were missing from the *Rule:* the pursuit of the Gospel poverty inspired by Francis and dependence on the Friars Minor. And so a struggle began for Clare that was to continue throughout the remainder of her life. Hugolino, no doubt, realized how difficult it was for the Poor Ladies to live the type of poverty they proposed, for it demanded a total dependence on the generosity and dedication of others for their well-being. The Benedictine and Augustinian expressions of religious life envisioned a poverty permitting the sharing of goods as well as the cultivation of appropriate means of support. Clare, on the other hand, took a much more demanding view in which reliance on the bountiful providence of God was at the foundation. It was a far more audacious, confident poverty that rested trustingly on faith. Hugolino, however, officially entrusted with protecting the Poor Ladies, must have felt more confident with the type of material security provided by the more proven expressions of religious life and attempted to persuade Clare to follow them.

Within a year of Hugolino's election to the papacy, the new Pope, Gregory IX, followed the example of Innocent III, and permitted the Poor Ladies to live the intense poverty they desired. The *Acts of the Process of Canonization*, however, make it clear that Gregory was not happy with this concept and attempted to dispense Clare from her promise to follow this ideal. When this failed, he decided to remove the Friars Minor as chaplains to the Poor Ladies. But this only prompted Clare to proclaim a "hunger strike" by refusing to have the Friars as the questors of the sisters. Needless to say, within a short period of time, the Pope once more acceded to her wishes and, on September 17, 1228, granted the Poor Ladies his own written privilege of poverty.

On August 6, 1247, Gregory's successor, Innocent IV, provided a new rule for all the monasteries of the Order of San Damiano and in a papal bull, *Quoties a nobis*, August 23, 1247, bound them to its observance. This second rule was a milder form of that given by Hugolino. This document mitigated fasting obligations and even allowed possessions. There is no trace of Clare's outright resistance to this new rule. The fact remains, however, that it lost its binding force three years later when Innocent declared in another papal bull, *Inter Personas*, June 6, 1250, that no sister could be forced to accept this rule. At about this time, Clare, once more courageous and determined, began to write her own rule based on that of Francis and accepted passages from the earlier rules of Hugolino and Innocent.

Clare thus became the first woman to write a rule for religious women. During a period of forty years her ideals were becoming more clearly defined especially as the Rules of Hugolino and Innocent forced her to reflect upon the uniqueness of her own vision. At this point, the intimacy of her experience of Christ, flowing as it did from the teaching and example of Francis made her more resolute. There has always been a temptation to interpret Clare's *Rule* in light of that of Francis from which it borrows. However, it is a unique document articulating that demanding expression of religious life that she perceived was her calling and, at the same time, a startling sense of individual freedom that was based on Clare's experience of the maturity of her sisters. Clare's insistence on its recognition and acceptance by the Church not simply as a privilege but as a right forged a new understanding of role of charism in the unfolding of the Church's life.

Throughout all these years of struggle, Clare was ill and confined to bed. The *Legend* speaks of her continual illness during a span of twenty-eight years; it does not, however, provide any clues as to its nature. More than likely, the extreme mortification and rigorous penance of Clare's life took a severe toll on her health. It is understandable, in light of the witnesses' comments, that both Francis and Guido, the Bishop of Assisi, intervened and demanded that she mitigate her austere practices. We may well imagine that her sense of loneliness at Francis's death in October of 1226 must have added to her weakened condition. Nevertheless, Clare appears as an inwardly steadfast, determined woman, convinced of the form of life and the charism of poverty that Francis gave to her and insistent on obtaining papal approval in order to protect it.

On September 16, 1252, Cardinal Raynaldus dei Conti di Segni, the Protector of the Poor Ladies, approved Clare's *Rule* in the name of the Pope. But this did not satisfy. She continued to seek the personal approval of Innocent IV, the living sign of the Church's unity. This occurred on August 9, 1253 when the officials of the papal court realized that Clare was dying. On August 10, 1253, the *Rule* was brought to her carrying the seal of Innocent IV and, on the following day, Clare died. The crowning act of her life had just been completed: the ideals that she held so close to her heart had been accepted and ratified by the Church.

Clare's body was taken from San Damiano and placed in the church of San Giorgio where Francis had been buried before his body was transferred to the basilica built in his honor. In 1255, Clare was solemnly declared a saint during ceremonies that were led by her friend and confidant, Cardinal Raynaldus, now Pope Alexander IV who rhapsodized on "this woman, the first of the poor . . . [who] was dwelling in spirit in heaven." Five years later, that little church of San Giorgio became part of a basilica dedicated to another of Assisi's saints, Clare. The preacher on that occasion was the Minister General of the Friars Minor, Brother (later Saint) Bonaventure of Bagnoreggio, whose own understanding of Franciscan spiritual life was being expressed in terms of the "charism of poverty" and the simplicity and clarity it produced in penetrating the mysteries of God.

The Writings of Clare

The patrimony of Clare's writings is quite small. Her *Rule*, four letters to Blessed Agnes of Prague, a *Testament*, *Blessing*, and a letter to a Sister named Ermentrude of Bruges are the only writings which are known to us. The differences between these few writings, however, deserve some of our attention. There are four different styles of writing within them: that of the *Rule* which reflects Clare's awareness of the legal terminology of her time; that of the *Testament* filled as it is with a wealth of autobiographical reflections and insights; that of the letters which is elegant, poetic and marvelously refined; and, finally that of the *Blessing* rich in scriptural texts.

In light of these writings we can certainly raise questions concerning Clare's education, and her use of secretaries. Both the *Acts of the Process of Canonization* and the *Legend* give us little information other than to note Clare's lack of formal education; they do not mention anything of her use of secretaries. Nevertheless there are reasons to conclude that she employed others to help her. The *Rule*, for example, shows such a refined knowledge of religious law that the presence of expert canonists, possibly sent by Cardinal Raynaldus, must be taken for granted. The *Testament*, the most difficult of Clare's writings to translate, contains a constantly changing flow of styles, some of which are smooth and easy to read, while others are not only awkward but ambiguous. Thus we are left the impression that different sisters were involved at various times in its composition. A totally different conclusion is reached in considering Clare's letters to Agnes of Prague. They are filled with an elegance and dignity that can be found in no other of her writings. When we consider that they were written over nineteen years, the consistency of their style immediately strikes us and forces us to ask: if Clare did not write these masterpieces, who did? Finally, there is her *Blessing* which is far more extensive than that of Francis and uses scriptural references not found elsewhere in Clare's writings, prompting some to wonder if this writing is authentic.

Far more important, however, is the question of the sources of her writings. The obvious ones are the Scriptures and the Liturgy, especially the antiphons and responsories of those women who were the great heroines of women religious in the Middle Ages: the Blessed Virgin Mary and Saint Agnes, the Roman martyr. When we consider the principal sources of Clare's inspiration, however, we should not lose sight of the role of the memory in medieval spirituality. We can look in vain for a library in the monastery of San Damiano; there simply was none. Instead the Poor Ladies depended on the Word of God that was liturgically proclaimed to them and celebrated several times throughout each day and night in the Liturgy of the Hours. Since this was her daily nourishment, Clare must have cherished it, memorized it, and kept it in her heart as did the model of her spiritual life, Mary, thus allowing it to form her thought and way of daily life.

Among those texts, though, we notice immediately certain verses that never seem to leave her consciousness. Repeatedly, for example, quotations from the Canticle of Canticles appear. This is not unusual at this period of history which was extraordinarily rich in commentaries and reflections on this mystical love song. What is unusual, however, is Clare's choice of certain verses that appear not only in her support of Agnes of Prague's choice of Christ as her Spouse but also in her embrace of poverty. We might speculate on how frequently Clare reflected on a verse found in Innocent III's Privilege of Poverty: "His left hand is under my head; his right hand will embrace me (Ct. 1:3)." Bernard of Clairvaux had offered this passage to his monks as a stimulus to develop confidence in God's everpresent, tender care and expectation of the wonders of His love that were to come. Clare may well have encouraged her sisters along the same lines, as she does in her fourth letter to Agnes of Prague, since this scriptural passage was so central to their embrace of poverty.

We can also see that Clare quotes the Gospel of Matthew most frequently in her writings and borrows most from the Sermon on the Mount. Although the passages she uses reflect a variety of Jesus' teachings, Clare continually returns to verses on poverty, on the blessedness of those who are poor, on the passing nature of material goods, and on the rewards that come from walking the more difficult and arduous path of renunciation of all things. From this perspective, Clare's writings offer us a meditation on Matthew's theology of the kingdom possessed by those who are truly poor and the testimonies of those sisters who lived with her reveal how the daily community life of San Damiano realized it. Thus, when the scriptural foundations of Clare's understanding are placed beside those of Francis, we see clearly that she not only accepted his teaching but developed it in a different and, in a sense, more profound way.

Writings to and about St. Clare

One of the most curious aspects of the corpus surveyed in the writings in the present volume is its lack of writings by women to or about Clare. It would seem natural that women of this period would have written more about her and her uniqueness in following the teachings of Francis. Yet there are only three writings coming from feminine hands: the letter written to Clare by Agnes of Assisi, her sister; the notification of her death composed by the Poor Ladies of San Damiano; and the mandate of 1238 which more than likely was drawn up by some curial official. Whereas we might not have paid much attention to this lack in the past, our contemporary sensitivity prompts us to look more closely at the variety of writings to and about Clare and to study their contents from a different perspective. Two tendencies stand out immediately in those writings of male origin: their great reverence and respect for Clare, expressed even during her lifetime, and their imposition of masculine constructs without attempting to understand her unique feminine expression of the Franciscan ideal.

Jacques de Vitry, as we saw, was the first to express his admiration for Clare and the Poor Ladies. In 1216 this somewhat itinerant clergyman, intrigued by new religious movements especially of women, encountered what he called the "Lesser Sisters" and wrote positively of his impressions of their poverty and humility, thus becoming the first of a long line of admirers. That same year, Pope Innocent III also must have come to know and admire the community of San Damiano, for shortly before his death he granted Clare that unheard of privilege of poverty. Two years later, another curial official, Cardinal Hugolino dei Conti di Segni, met Clare, brought her and the community of San Damiano to the attention of Pope Honorius III and was shortly thereafter appointed their protector and guide.

From this point of view, however, we might begin to wonder if Clare and her vision were ever fully understood, for Hugolino wrote a rule of life for the Poor Ladies based largely on the *Benedictine Rule* and the large amount of legislation affecting religious life. We cannot find any evidence of Clare's desire to follow an itinerant manner of life such as that of Francis and his brothers; on the contrary, everything points to her acceptance of the enclosure. This aspect of Hugolino's *Rule* was acceptable to her, but, as we have seen, it implied enormous practical problems for Hugolino who saw the poverty proposed by Clare as incompatible with life in the enclosure. Hugolino's failure to appreciate the essential dimension of poverty in the life of the Poor Ladies triggered off that struggle which so absorbed much of Clare's life, the struggle to have the Church officially recognize her expression of Gospel life and the charism of poverty which she perceived as a great gift.

While Francis was alive, Clare no doubt found strength and support for her desires. In the *Testament* she speaks of Francis as "our one pillar [of strength], our one consolation and support," and later, as given them as "a planner, founder, planter and helper in the service of Christ and in those things we have promised to God." Yet we can imagine that Francis stood in awe of Clare's embrace of a poverty that was far more demanding than his own, a poverty dependent on the providence of God, the generosity of others, and the care and attention of the brothers charged with begging for their needs. We might even speculate as to what Francis learned from Clare in his understanding of poverty rather than imagine that she received everything from him. Clare's vision of a life *sine proprio*, without anything of one's own, for example, is certainly more expressive of dependence upon and receptivity of the providence of God. In any case, two writings coming from the last period of Francis' life express his encouragement and even hint at his awareness that, after his death, others would attempt to dissuade Clare and the Poor Ladies from embracing the charism of poverty.

We might wonder about the role of the friars at this time. While Clare was persistent in her struggle to live an authentic poverty, the friars were accepting one dispensation after another, were becoming increasingly entangled in legal interpretations of the meaning of "a life without anything of one's own," and were slipping further from the ideals of Saint Francis. In 1230 Pope Gregory IX had written his famous declaration, *Quo elongati*, which officially interpreted the poverty of Francis in light of the teaching authority of the Church. During that same year, the friars accepted the scholastic distinction between *precept* and *counsel* in order to arrive at legalistic solutions to many of the differing interpretations of what Francis intended. Eleven years later, the *Expositio Quatuor Magistrorum*, a document sponsored by the friars of France, was a further attempt at resolving some of the doctrinal questions that confronted the Order, some of which centered on the issue of poverty.

Thomas of Celano, it is true, had been poetically describing Clare's virtues, as we have seen, but eighteen years later, in his *Second Life of Saint Francis*, he reminded his brothers of their obligations to stay close to her and her sisters. Was Thomas doing this solely out of his concern for the welfare of the Poor Ladies or was he hoping that his brothers would profit from their associations with them? We wonder. Nonetheless, throughout those difficult years after Francis' death, Clare was the one who courageously and forthrightly expressed the Gospel way of poverty for all, even the friars, to see. She did this not by means of long treatises but by the power of her own example and that of her sisters.

One person who remains somewhat overlooked during these years is Cardinal Raynaldus dei Conti di Segni, the nephew of Gregory IX, who succeeded his uncle as Protector of the Poor Ladies. Raynaldus' letter to Clare and her sisters in 1228 expresses many of the same sentiments as those of his uncle. Yet as the years progressed and the need for papal approval became more acute, he obviously acquired a deeper and more comprehensive understanding of Clare's vision.

Upon the death of his uncle, Raynaldus continued as Cardinal Protector of the Poor Ladies during the papacy of Innocent IV. We know little of his role in the composition of Innocent's new rule, but we might speculate about his contributing to its far more Franciscan tone in recognizing, among other things, the role of the Friars Minor as visitators and chaplains.

Raynaldus appears to have been closely in touch with the ideals and aspirations of the Poor Ladies and, at the same time, close to Innocent IV who continually kept him in his entourage. Nevertheless, when Clare rejected this document for its obvious repetition of the same failure seen in Hugolino's Rule, that is, the lack of seeing poverty as the foundation of their lives, Raynaldus must have had an important place in encouraging her to write her own rule and in persuading the Pope to ratify it. Innocent's recognition of this role was recorded for all to see when Raynaldus' document of approval was placed alongside the papal bull, *Solet annuere*, that finally ratified Clare's *Rule*.

A little more than a year after Clare's death, in December, 1254, Raynaldus himself became Pope Alexander IV and as such finalized the steps leading to her canonization. In his Bull of Canonization, *Clara claris praeclara*, he echoes the Exsultet of the Easter Vigil as he praised "this woman . . . [whose] life was an instruction and a lesson to others who learned the rule of living in *this book of life* (Rev 21:27)." "Let Mother Church rejoice," he proclaims, "because she has begotten and reared such a daughter. . . . Let the devout multitude of the faithful be glad because the King and Lord of heaven has chosen their sister and companion as His spouse. . . . Finally, let the multitude of saints *rejoice* because *the nuptials of a* new *royal bride* (Mt 22:2; 25:10) are being celebrated in their heavenly midst."

It is ironic that most of the authors, while praising her and admiring her ideals, never seemed to grasp her role in creating a new form of Franciscan life. While Francis and his brothers were molding an itinerant and/ or eremetical religious life held together by the bonds of brotherhood, Clare and her sisters were living in the confines of the enclosure. Both ways of life were founded on the same pursuit of a demanding personal and communal poverty, but mobility and lack of it were deciding factors in how that poverty would be expressed. The friars traveled easily throughout the world, working or begging to satisfy their needs. The sisters, on the other hand, were totally dependent on the care and generosity of others. Without a doubt many of Clare's contemporaries realized the practical implications of her enclosed-Franciscan ideal of poverty and tried to have her mitigate them. Did they perceive, though, that in her embrace of this demanding way of life she was underscoring what was at the very heart of poverty: a strong, unwavering confidence in the providence of God and the well-being of the Church? While the men were concerned with looking to and providing for the future with prudence and foresight, Clare was valiantly and patiently casting her care upon the Lord and, in so doing, manifesting her profound faith. In a sense, then, the vision of Francis finds in Clare its necessary complement and fulfillment, prompting us to wonder: without the presence and witness of the Poor Ladies would the Franciscan ideal have retained its vitality? To portray Clare, then, as simply "la pianticella," the little plant, of Francis is to do her an injustice. She took the Gospel insights offered by her teacher and recast them in a new, more demanding form, thereby showing us in her clear, transparent way the Spirit of Gospel Love that animated her.

Part I

THE WRITINGS
OF
SAINT CLARE

The First Letter of Saint Clare
to Agnes of Prague (1234)

Agnes of Prague, daughter of King Premsyl Ottokar I of Bohemia and his second wife Queen Constance of the Hungarian Arpad dynasty, was born in 1205. Agnes was engaged at an early age to a son of the duke of Silesia and was sent to that court to live. Her education there was taken care of by Queen, later saint, Hedwig.

When Agnes was only three years old, the young duke died and the princess returned to Prague where she was placed in a Premonstratensian monastery for her education. Shortly after she was engaged to the son of the Emperor Frederick II, the future Henry VII, who was in residence at the court of Duke Leopold of Austria. Agnes was then sent to Austria to live, but, after some time, Agnes was jilted by the young Henry who married the duke's daughter. Once again Agnes returned to Prague where her angry father was preparing to wage war against Leopold, but the princess persuaded her father not to avenge her. She next received offers of marriage from the royal court of England, and then from Frederick II whose wife had died. Her father did not accept any of these offers, however, leaving Agnes free to remain in Prague, devoting herself to charitable works.

At this time she met the Friars Minor who had arrived in the city in 1225. No doubt these friars spoke to her of Clare, the life of the Poor Ladies of San Damiano, and the ideals of Franciscan life. Agnes then set out fulfilling her own plans. In 1232 she obtained property from her brother for the erection of a hospice, which she built and turned over to the administration of the Crosiers of the Red Star. She also obtained land for a convent to house the "Poor Ladies" and a residence to satisfy the needs of the Friars Minor who would act as chaplains. When the building was completed, Agnes wrote to Clare and the Holy See, asking permission to establish the Poor Ladies of San Damiano in Prague and requesting sisters from Italy for the purpose.

In the spring of 1234, during an immense public celebration, Agnes, with seven other young women of the wealthiest noble families of Bohemia and five of the Poor Ladies of Italy entered the new monastery.

The presence of so many passages taken from the solemn consecration of virgins suggests that Saint Clare sent this letter to the Lady Agnes at the time of her embrace of religious life.[1] *Clare poetically encourages Agnes in the choice of Christ as her Spouse and devotes a large part of the letter to a consideration of poverty.*[2] *If this were the only writing of Saint Clare's in existence, it would suffice in revealing not only her profound understanding of poverty, but also her marvelous teaching skills in gently leading "her student," Agnes, to move to an embrace of a "blessed" and "holy" poverty promising eternal riches and beyond to that more mystical or "God-centered" poverty motivated by a simple, profound love of the Lord Jesus Christ.*

Even in this early writing of Saint Clare, her clarity of understanding of the charism of poverty and her remarkable strength in practicing it distinguishes her. She emerges as someone who amplifies and develops his Gospel intuition and, in fact, preserves untarnished what the brothers were in danger of losing. Thus, her first letter to Lady Agnes already establishes Saint Clare as a marvelous contributor to the Gospel spirituality of Saint Francis and not simply his "perfect follower, as many would prefer to consider her."

1. To the esteemed and most holy virgin, Lady Agnes, daughter of the most excellent and illustrious King of Bohemia: 2. Clare, an unworthy servant of Jesus Christ and a *useless* servant (cf. Lk 17:10) of the enclosed Ladies of the Monastery of San Damiano, her subject and servant in all things, presents herself totally with a special reverence that she *attain the glory* of everlasting happiness (cf. Sir 50:5).[3]

3. As I hear of the fame of Your holy conduct and irreproachable life, which is known not only to me but to the entire world as well, *I greatly rejoice and exult in the Lord* (Hab 3:18).[4] 4. I am not alone in rejoicing at such

---

[1] A thorough biography of and detailed bibliography for the life of Agnes of Prague can be found in J. Nemec, *Agnese di Praga* (Sta. Maria degli Angeli: Edizioni Porziuncola, 1982).

[2] Cf. supra.

[3] An immediate similarity can be seen here between Saints Francis and Clare in her choice of images to describe herself as an "unworthy" and "useless" servant (cf. R.J. Armstrong, "The Prophetic Implications of the Admonitions," *Laurentianum* 26 (1985): pp. 396–464. In this sentence St. Clare uses two different Latin words: *famula*, a woman who was part of the family or a personal domestic servant of a lord or master, and *ancilla*, someone who was "at the service" of others as a maid or servant. Cf. infra RegC1 × 5, note 51. Cf. M. Goodish, "The Ancilla Dei: The Servant as Saint in the Late Middle Ages," *Women of the Medieval World*, eds. Julius Kirschner and Suzanne F. Wemple (Oxford: Basil Blackwell, 1985), 119–136.

[4] Throughout this first letter, St. Clare uses the polite or formal manner of address: You (*Vos*), Your (*Vester*), etc., that is, the second person plural form. In the other three letters she adopts a more familiar style.

great news, but [I am joined by] all who serve and seek to serve Jesus Christ. 5. For, though You, more than others, could have enjoyed the magnificence and honor and dignity of the world and could have been married to the illustrious emperor with splendor befitting You and His Excellency, 6. You have rejected all these things and have chosen with Your whole heart and soul a life of holy poverty and destitution.⁵ 7. Thus You took a spouse of a more noble lineage, Who will keep Your virginity ever unspotted and unsullied, the Lord Jesus Christ.

8. "When You have loved [Him], You are chaste;
   when you have touched [Him], You become more pure;
   when you have accepted [Him], You are a virgin.

9. Whose power is stronger,
   Whose generosity more abundant,
   Whose appearance more beautiful,
   Whose love more tender,
   Whose courtesy more gracious.

10. In Whose embrace You are already caught up;
    Who has adorned Your breast with precious stones
        and has placed priceless pearls on Your ears
11. and has surrounded You with sparkling gems
        as though blossoms of springtime
        and placed on Your head *a golden crown
        as a sign of Your holiness.*"⁶

---

⁵Historians do not agree on the identity of the emperor (*Caesar*, the Latin word employed by St. Clare). Most probably he was Emperor Frederick II, widower from 1228, since a contemporary historian, Albert of Stade, states plainly in his Chronicle: "The same year, on the feast of Pentecost, the sister of the King of Bohemia, Lady Agnes, at the prompting of the Friars Minor, entered the Order of the Poor Ladies of the Rule of the Blessed Francis at Prague, rejecting for Christ's sake the Emperor Frederick who had earlier asked for her in marriage."

⁶Cf. Sir 45:12. For the most part these lines (8–11) are taken from the ancient legend of St. Agnes, the Roman Martyr, which was incorporated not only into the antiphon and responsories of the liturgy of her feast but also into those of the liturgical consecration of a virgin. By characterizing the state of virginity with phrases from the life of St. Agnes with its emphasis of glory, rapture and inviolable innocence, the consecration liturgy—and, in this instance, St. Clare—presented her as an appropriate model to imitate. Cf. M. Teresa Tavormina, "Of Maidenhood and Maternity: Liturgical Hagiography and the Medieval Ideal of Virginity," *American Benedictine Review* 31 (December 1980): pp. 384–399. For precise liturgical references, cf. R.J. Armstrong, I.C. Brady, *Francis and Clare: The Complete Works* (Paulist Press: New York, 1982), p. 191.

12. Therefore, most beloved sister, or should I say, Lady, worthy of great respect: because You are *the spouse and the mother and the sister* of my Lord Jesus Christ (cf. 2 Cor 11:2; Mt 12:50),[7] 13. and have been beautifully adorned with the sign of an undefiled virginity and a most holy poverty: Be strengthened in the holy service which You have undertaken out of a burning desire for the Poor Crucified, 14. Who for the sake of all of us *took upon Himself* the Passion of the Cross (Heb 12:2), delivered us from the power of the Prince *of Darkness* (Col 1:13) to whom we were enslaved because of the disobedience of our first parent, and so *reconciled us* to God the Father (2 Cor 5:18).

15. O blessed poverty,
     who bestows eternal riches
          on those who love and embrace her!
16. O holy poverty,
          God promises *the kingdom of heaven*
               and, in fact, offers eternal glory and a blessed life
          to those who possess and desire you![8]

17. O God-centered poverty,
     whom the Lord Jesus Christ
          Who ruled and now rules heaven and earth,
          Who spoke and things were made,
               condescended to embrace before all else![9]

18. *The foxes have dens,* He says, *and the birds of the air have nests, but the Son of Man,* Christ, *has nowhere to lay His head* (Mt. 8:20), *but bowing His head gave up His spirit* (Jn 19:30).

19. If so great and good a Lord, then, on coming into the Virgin's womb, chose to appear despised, needy, and *poor* in this world (cf. 2 Cor 8:9), 20. so that people who were in utter poverty, want and absolute need of heavenly nourishment might become rich in Him by possessing the

---

[7]This is clearly a biblical image which is frequently used by St. Francis to describe the relationships flowing from the presence of the Holy Spirit in the soul (cf. *The First Version of the Letter to the Faithful* 17; *The Second Version of the Letter to the Faithful* 50). St. Clare uses the formula twice more in her third and fourth letters (III LAg 1; 4 LAg 4). For an excellent treatment of this theme, see Optatus Van Asseldonk, "The Holy Spirit in the Writings and Life of Saint Clare," *Greyfriars Review* 1 (September 1987), 93–105.

[8]Cf. Mt 5:3.

[9]Cf. Ps 32:9; 148:5. The Latin word *pia* is translated here as "God-centered" since the English equivalent, "pious" or "compassionate," does not contain the richness of the thought of this highly esteemed medieval virtue. For an interpretation, cf. R.J. Armstrong, I.C. Brady, *Francis and Clare: The Complete Works* (Paulist Press: New York, 1982), p. 192, n. 8.

kingdom of heaven, 21. *be* very *joyful and glad* (cf. Hab 3:18)! Be filled with a remarkable happiness and a spiritual joy! 22. Because, since contempt of the world has pleased You more than its honors, poverty more than earthly riches, and You have sought to store up greater *treasures in heaven* rather than on earth, 23. *where* rust does not consume *nor moth destroy nor thieves break in and steal* (cf. Mt 6:20), *Your reward is very rich in heaven!* (Mt 5:12). 24. And You have truly merited to be called *a sister, spouse and mother* (cf. 2 Cor 11:2; Mt 12:50) of the Son of the Most High Father and of the glorious Virgin.

25. You know, I believe, that *the kingdom of heaven* is promised and given by the Lord only *to the poor* (cf. Mt 5:3) for she who loves temporal things loses the fruit of love. 26. Such a person *cannot serve God and money,*[10] for *either the one is loved and the other hated,* or *the one* is served and *the other despised* (cf. Mt 6:24).

27. You also know that one who is clothed cannot fight another who is naked, because she is more quickly thrown who gives her adversary a chance to get hold of her;[11] 28. and that one who lives in the glory of earth cannot rule with Christ in heaven.

Again [You know] that it is easier for *a camel to pass through the eye of a needle than for a rich person to enter the kingdom of heaven* (Mt 19:24). 29. Therefore, You have cast aside Your garments, that is, earthly riches, that You might not be overcome by the one fighting against You [and] You might enter the kingdom of heaven through *the straight path* and *the narrow gate* (cf. Mt 7:13–14).

30. What a great and praiseworthy exchange:
to leave the things of time for those of eternity,
to choose the things of heaven for the goods of earth,
to receive the hundred-fold in place of one,
and *to possess* a blessed eternal *life!*[12]

---

[10]Literally, "Mammon" according to the biblical text.

[11]Cf. Gregory the Great, *Homilia in Evangelia* II, 32, 2 (PL 76, 1233b). This image is used in the Divine Office, Common of a Martyr outside of Paschal Time, Matins, III Nocturn, as well as in Matins, IX Lesson, of the Feast of the Stigmata of Saint Francis. It can also be found in Thomas of Celano, *First Life of Saint Francis*, 15: "Behold, how he wrestles naked with his naked adversary, and having put off everything that is of this world, he thinks only *about the things of the Lord* (1 Cor 7:35)." *St. Francis of Assisi: Omnibus of Sources*, ed. Marion A. Habig (Chicago: Franciscan Herald Press, 1973), p. 241.

[12]Cf. Mt 19:29. The theme of the "exchange" or *commercium* forms the basis of a theological reflection on poverty by an unknown author entitled the *Sacrum commercium St. Francisci cum Domina Paupertate* (Florence: Ad Aquas Claras, 1929; English translation found in *St. Francis of Assisi: Omnibus of Sources*, ed. Marion A. Habig [Chicago: Franciscan Herald Press, 1973], 1531–1596). It is generally accepted as coming from an early period of Franciscan literature, some claim as early as 1227.

31. Because of this I have resolved, as best I can, to beg Your Excellency and Your holiness by my humble prayers in the mercy of Christ, to be strengthened in His holy service, 32. and to progress from good to better, from virtue to virtue (cf. Ps 83:8), that He Whom You serve with the total desire of Your soul may bestow on You the reward for which You so long.

33. I also beg You in the Lord, as much as I can, to include in Your *holy prayers* (cf. Rm 15:30) me, Your servant, though *useless* (cf. Lk 17:10), and the other sisters with me in the monastery, who are all devoted to You, 34. that by their help we may merit the mercy of Jesus Christ, and together with You may merit to enjoy the everlasting vision.

35. Farewell in the Lord. And *pray for me* (cf. 1 Th 5:25).

The Second Letter of Saint Clare
to Agnes of Prague (1235)

The obvious changes in tone suggest not only a later date but also some external circumstances that may have impeded the Lady Agnes from pursuing her ideals. An early manuscript of this letter is entitled "Concerning Strong Perseverance in a Good Proposal," thus suggesting an important reason for its composition: Saint Clare's encouragement to persevere in the embrace of poverty.

The letter was definitely written during the generalate of Br. Elias (1234–1239) since he is mentioned as minister general.[1] However it may well have been inspired by the papal decree of May 18, 1235, Cum relicta saeculi, in which Gregory IX attempted to provide some sort of material support for Lady Agnes and her companions in the monastery in Prague.[2] In 1235 Pope Gregory IX informed Agnes of his decision to unite economically and administratively the hospice and monastery in Prague to guarantee the support of the entire enterprise. Finally, in 1237, to Agnes' great satisfaction, after lengthy negotiations, that provision was retracted in the papal bull, Omnipotens Deus, and the direction of the hospice was entrusted to the Confraternity of the Crosiers of the Red Star who were simultaneously recognized as a religious Order.

Saint Clare's repeated reference to the pursuit of perfection seems based on this papal document. However, she underscores what the Pope does not seem to understand: the necessity of following the radical poverty of the Poor Christ. In this light, she always provides an insight into her understanding of how perseverance can best be achieved in this pursuit: through continuous contemplation of the Poor Christ.

---

[1]Br. Elias of Assisi, after being Francis' vicar from 1221 to 1227, became the minister general from 1232 to 1239 when he was dismissed by Pope Gregory IX because of pressure from the brothers. For further information, see L. Di Fonzo, "Élic d'Assise," *Dictionnaire d'Histoire et de Géographie Ecclésiastiques* 15 (1963), c. 167–183; G. Odoardi, "Elia d'Assisi," *Dizionario degli Istituti di Perfezione* 3 (1976), c. 1094–1110; D. Berg, "Elias von Cortona. Studien zu Leben und Werk des zweiten General Ministers im Franziskanerorden," *Wissenshaft und Weischeit* 41 (1978), pp. 102–126.

[2]Cf. Gregory IX, "Cum relicta saeculi," *Bullarium Franciscanum* I, p. 156.

1. To the daughter *of the King of kings*, the servant *of the Lord of lords* (Rev 19:16), the most worthy Spouse of Jesus Christ, and, therefore, the most noble Queen, Lady Agnes: 2. Clare, *the useless* (Lk 17:10) and unworthy servant of the Poor Ladies: greetings and perseverance in a life of the highest poverty.[3]

3. I give thanks to the Giver of grace *from Whom*, we believe, *every good and perfect gift proceeds* (Jas 1:17), because He has adorned you with such splendors of virtue and illuminated you with such marks of perfection, 4. that, since you have become such a diligent imitator *of the Father of all perfection* (Mt 5:48), you might be made perfect and His eyes do not see anything imperfect in you.[4]

5. This is that perfection with which the King himself will take you to Himself in the heavenly bridal chamber where He is seated in glory on a starry throne,[5] 6. because you have despised the splendor of an earthly kingdom and considered of little value the offers of an imperial marriage. 7. Instead, as someone zealous for the holiest poverty, in a spirit of great humility and the most ardent charity, you have held fast *to the footprints* (1 Pt 2:22) of Him to Whom you have merited to be joined as a Spouse.

8. But since I know that you are adorned with many virtues, I will spare my words and not weary you with needless speech, 9. even though nothing seems superfluous to you if you can draw some consolation from it. 10. But because *one thing is necessary* (Lk 10:42), I bear witness to that one thing and encourage you, for love of Him to Whom you have offered yourself as *a holy* and pleasing *sacrifice* (Rm 12:1), 11. that, like another Rachel (cf. Gen 29:16),[6] you always remember your resolution and be conscious of your beginning.

What you hold, may you [always] hold,
What you do, may you [always] do and never abandon.
12. But with swift pace, light step,
    unswerving feet,

---

[3]This opening greeting is in marked contrast from that of the first letter and suggests the underlying theme of this letter. While Francis only uses the word *paupertas* sixteen times in his writings, Clare does so forty-one times throughout hers and most frequently with the adjectives: *sancta* or *sanctissima* (16 times), *summa* or *altissima* (5), *beata* (3), *pia* (1) and *stupenda* (1).

[4]This is the only instance in which the image of "the Father of all perfection" is used in the writings of either Francis or Clare.

[5]A reference to the Liturgy of the Hours for the feast of the Assumption of the Blessed Virgin Mary, August 14, Lauds, II Antiphon.

[6]The figure of Rachel should be examined in the context of the medieval tradition that considered her as representing the withdrawn life of prayer, asceticism and contemplation. Cf. Paul-Marie Guillaume, *Rachel et Lia*, DSAM (Paris 1987).

so that even your steps stir up no dust,[7]
13. may you go forward
    securely, joyfully, and swiftly,
    on the path of prudent happiness,
14. not believing anything,
    not agreeing with anything
        that would dissuade you from this resolution
        or that would place a stumbling block for you on the way,[8]
    so that you may offer *your vows to the Most High*[9]
        in the pursuit of that perfection
        to which the Spirit of the Lord has called you.[10]

15. In all of this, follow the counsel of our venerable father, our Brother Elias, the Minister General, that you may walk more securely in the way of the commands of the Lord (Ps 118:32).[11] 16. Prize it beyond the advice of the others and cherish it as dearer to you than any gift. 17. If anyone would tell you something else or suggest something that would hinder your perfection or seem contrary to your divine vocation, even though you must respect him, do not follow his counsel.[12]

18. But as a poor virgin,
        embrace the poor Christ.
19. Look upon Him Who became contemptible for you,
        and follow Him, making yourself contemptible in this world
        for Him.

---

[7]Cf. Gregory the Great, *Dialogues*, Prologue (PL 77:152A). This exhortation is also used by Thomas of Celano, *First Life of St. Francis*, n. 71: "[Francis'] greatest concern was to be free from everything of this world lest the serenity of his mind be disturbed even for an hour by the taint of anything which was mere dust." Thomas of Celano, *First Life, Saint Francis of Assisi: Omnibus of Sources*, ed. Marion Habig (Chicago: Franciscan Herald Press, 1973), p. 288.

[8]Cf. Rm 14:13.

[9]Cf. Ps 49:14.

[10]Clare articulates the dynamic principle of the spiritual life, the Spirit of the Lord, and echoes the teaching of Francis, cf. R.J. Armstrong, I.C. Brady, *Francis and Clare: The Complete Works* (Paulist Press: New York, 1982): *The Admonitions*, p. 26, n. 1; *The Form of Life Given to Saint Clare and Her Sisters*, p. 44, n. 1; and *The First Version of the Letter to the Faithful*, p. 63, n. 3. For further commentary, see Optatus Van Asseldonk, "The Holy Spirit in the Writings and Life of Saint Clare," *Greyfriars Review* 1 (September 1987), 93–105.

[11]Cf. supra p. 39, note 1.

[12]Is St. Clare making a veiled reference to the letter of May 18, 1235, *Cum relicta saeculi*, in which Pope Gregory IX permitted Agnes to accept the possessions and revenues for the support of her monastery (Cf. *Bullarium Franciscanum* I, p. 156)? In any event, she is echoing a final counsel of St. Francis for the Poor Ladies: " . . . keep most careful watch that you never depart from this (most holy life and poverty) by reason of the teaching or advice of anyone" (cf. Ult Vol 3).

20. Your Spouse, though *more beautiful than the children of men* (Ps 44:3), became, for your salvation, the lowest of men, was despised, struck, scourged untold times throughout His entire body, and then died amid the suffering of the Cross.

O most noble Queen,
gaze upon [Him].
consider [Him]
contemplate [Him],
as you desire to imitate [Him].[13]

21. If you suffer with Him, *you will reign with Him.*[14]
[If you] weep [with Him], you shall rejoice with Him;
[If you] *die with Him* on the cross of tribulation,[15]
    you shall possess heavenly mansions *in the splendor of the saints*[16]

22.   and, *in the Book of Life* your *name* shall be called glorious among men.[17]

23. Because of this you shall share always and forever the glory of the kingdom of heaven in place of earthly and passing things, and everlasting treasure instead of those that perish, and you shall live forever.

24. Farewell, most dear Sister, yes, and Lady, because of the Lord, your Spouse. 25. Commend me and my sisters to the Lord in your fervent prayers, for we rejoice in the good things of the Lord that He works in you through His grace. 26. Commend us truly to your sisters as well.

---

[13]These may well be considered steps of prayer: gazing upon (*intuere*) the poor crucified Christ, considering (*considera*), and contemplating (*contemplare*) Him. Throughout all these expressions of prayer, the desire to imitate the poverty of Christ is present. The same formula also appears in a more complete way in Clare's *Fourth Letter to Agnes of Prague* 15–23.

[14]Cf. Rm 8:17.

[15]Cf. 2 Tim 2:12.

[16]Cf. Ps. 109:3.

[17]Cf. Phil 4:3; Rev 3:5

The Third Letter of Saint Clare
to Agnes of Prague (1238)

One of the principal reasons for this letter is a papal decree issued by Pope Gregory IX on February 9, 1237, Licet velut ignis, which imposed upon all the monasteries of the Order of San Damiano total abstinence from meat "in imitation of the Cistercians."¹ No doubt this directive caused confusion among the Poor Ladies and prompted an inquiry from Agnes of Prague since it was contrary to the practice at San Damiano. The advice contained in lines 29–41 of this letter addressed this concern.

Clare, on her part, however, seems to be writing to Agnes because of the papal bull, Pia credulitate tenentes, of April 15, 1238, in which the Pope accepted Agnes' renunciation of the Hospice of St. Francis to dedicate herself and her sisters to a life of contemplation free from temporal concerns.² Thus this third letter presents marvelous insights into Clare's understanding of the enclosure, a life of extremely demanding poverty, and her mission in the Church.

1. To the lady [who is] most respected in Christ and the sister loved more than all [other] human beings, Agnes, sister of the illustrious king of Bohemia, but now *the sister and spouse* of the Most High King of heaven (cf. Mt 12:50; 2 Cor 11:2):³ 2. Clare, the most lowly and unworthy handmaid of Christ and servant of the Poor Ladies: the joys of redemption *in the Author of Salvation* (Heb 2:10) and every good thing that can be desired.

3. I am filled with such joys at your well-being, happiness, and marvelous progress through which, I understand, you have advanced in the path you have undertaken to win *a* heavenly *prize* (cf. Phil 3:14). 4. And I sigh with so much more exultation in the Lord as I have known and believe that you supply most wonderfully what is lacking both in me and in the

---

¹Cf. *Bullarium Franciscanum* I, 209–210.
²Cf. *Bullarium Franciscanum* I, 236–237.
³In the First Letter, Agnes is greeted as the daughter of the King of Bohemia, Ottokar I, also known as Premislaus II, who had died some years earlier (December 15, 1230). The reference to her illustrious brother, Wenceslaus III, king from December, 1230, to September, 1253, accentuates the greater dignity Agnes possesses as "sister and spouse" of the Most High Lord.

other sisters in following the footprints of the poor and humble Jesus Christ.

5. Truly I can rejoice—and no one can rob me of such joy—6. since, having at last what under heaven I have desired, I see that, helped by a special gift of wisdom from the mouth of God Himself and in an awe-inspiring and unexpected way, you have brought to ruin the subtleties of our crafty enemy, the pride that destroys human nature, and the vanity that infatuates human hearts. 7. [I see, too] that by humility, the virtue of faith, and the strong arms of poverty, you have taken hold of that *incomparable treasure hidden in the field* of the world and of the human heart (cf. Mt 13:44), with which you have purchased that by Whom all things have been made from nothing.[4] 8. And, to use the words of the Apostle himself in their proper sense, I consider you *a co-worker of God* Himself (cf. 1 Cor 3:9; Rm 16:3) and a support of the weak members of His ineffable Body.

9. Who is there, then, who would not encourage me to rejoice over such marvelous joys? 10. Therefore, dearly beloved, may you too *always rejoice in the Lord* (Phil 4:4). 11. And may neither bitterness nor a cloud [of sadness] overwhelm you, o dearly beloved Lady in Christ, joy of the angels and crown of your sisters!

12. Place your mind before the mirror of eternity!
Place your soul *in the brilliance of glory!*[5]
13. Place your heart *in the figure of the* divine *substance!*[6]
And *transform* your entire being *into the image*
of the Godhead Itself through contemplation.[7]

14. So that you too may feel what His friends feel
as they taste *the hidden sweetness*
that God Himself has reserved from the beginning
for those who love Him.[8]

15. And, after all who ensnare their blind lovers
in a deceitful and turbulent world
have been completely sent away,

---

[4]This is a difficult text to translate since Clare uses the neuter pronoun, *illud.*

[5]Here Clare introduces a theme, the mirror of contemplation, which becomes more prominent in her *Fourth Letter to Agnes of Prague.* For a fuller understanding of this important aspect of twelfth and thirteenth century spiritual literature cf. R. J. Armstrong, "Clare of Assisi: The Mirror Mystic," *The Cord* July–August, 1985, 195–202.

[6]Cf. Heb 1:3.

[7]Cf. 2 Cor 3:18.

[8]Cf. Ps 30:20; 1 Cor 2:9.

you may totally love Him
Who gave Himself totally for your love,[9]

16. Whose beauty the sun and the moon admire,
Whose rewards and their preciousness and greatness
are without end;
17. I am speaking of Him
Who is the Son of the Most High,
Whom the Virgin brought to birth
and remained a virgin after His birth.

18. May you cling to His most sweet Mother who gave birth to a Son whom the heavens could not contain.[10] 19. And yet she carried Him in the little enclosure of her holy womb and held Him on her virginal lap.

20. Who would not dread the treacheries of the enemy of humanity who, through the arrogance of momentary and deceptive glories, attempts to reduce to nothing that which is greater than heaven itself? 21. Indeed, it is now clear that the soul of a faithful person, the most worthy of all creatures because of the grace of God, is greater than heaven itself, 22. since the heavens and the rest of creation cannot contain their Creator and only the faithful soul is His dwelling place and throne, and this only through the charity that the wicked lack. 23. [He Who is] the Truth has said: *Whoever loves me will be loved by My Father, and I too shall love him, and We shall come to him and make Our dwelling place with him* (Jn 14:21, 23).

24. As the glorious Virgin of virgins carried [Him] materially, 25. so you, too, *by following in* her *footprints* (cf. 1 Pet 2:21), especially [those] of poverty and humility, can, without any doubt, always carry Him spiritually in your chaste and virginal body, 26. holding Him by Whom you and *all things are held together* (Wis 1:7), possessing that which, in comparison with the other transitory possessions of this world, you will possess more securely. 27. How many kings and queens of this world let themselves be deceived, 28. for, even though their pride may reach the skies and their heads touch the clouds, in the end they are as forgotten as a dungheap!

29. Now concerning those matters that you have asked me to clarify

---

[9]This passage is reminiscent of Francis' *Letter to the Entire Order* 29: " . . . hold back nothing of yourselves for yourselves so that He Who gives Himself totally to you may receive you totally." Cf. R.J. Armstrong, I.C. Brady, *Francis and Clare: The Complete Works* (Paulist Press: New York, 1982), p. 58.

[10]For the liturgical allusions found in lines 16, 17 and 18, cf. R.J. Armstrong, I.C. Brady, *Francis and Clare: The Complete Works* (Paulist Press: New York, 1982), p. 201, notes 7, 8, and 9.

for you: 30. which are the specific feasts our most glorious Father Saint Francis urged us to celebrate in a special way by a change of food—feasts of which, I believe, you already have some knowledge—I propose to respond to your love.

31. Your prudence should know, then, that except for the weak and the sick, for whom [Saint Francis] advised and admonished us to show every possible discernment in matters of food,[11] 32. none of us who are healthy and strong should eat anything other than Lenten fare, either on ferial days or on feast days. 33. Thus, we must fast every day except Sundays and the Nativity of the Lord, on which days we may have two meals. 34. And on ordinary Thursdays everyone may do as she wishes, so that she who does not wish to fast is not obliged. 35. However, we who are well should fast every day except on Sundays and on Christmas.

36. During the entire Easter week, as the writing of Saint Francis tells us, and on the feasts of the Blessed Virgin Mary and of the holy Apostles, we are not obliged to fast, unless these feasts occur on a Friday. 37. And, as I have already said, let us who are well and strong always eat Lenten fare.[12]

38. But *our flesh is not bronze nor is our strength that of stone* (Jb 6:12). 39. No, we are frail and inclined to every bodily weakness! 40. I beg you, therefore, dearly beloved, to refrain wisely and prudently from an indiscreet and impossible austerity in the fasting that you have undertaken. 41. And I beg you in the Lord to praise the Lord by your very life, to offer the Lord your *reasonable service* (Rm 12:1) and your *sacrifice* always *seasoned with salt* (Lev 2:13).

42. May you do well in the Lord, as I hope I myself do. And remember me and my sisters in your prayers.

---

[11]Clare frequently employs the notion of discernment in her writings, e.g. *III Letter to Agnes of Prague* 40; *Rule* II 10, 16, 19; IV 23–24; V 3; VII 5, 8, 11, 20; IX 18; XI 1; XII 5; *Testament* 63. Cf. O. Van Asseldonk, "Chiara, donna di divina discrezione cristiana," *L'Italia Francescana* July–October 1987, 485–494.

[12]It is interesting to note that Pope Gregory IX rescinded his prescription in his directive, *Pia meditatione pensantes*, May 5, 1238 (cf. *Bullarium Franciscanum* I, 240–241). Clare made the practice of fast and abstinence described here part of her Rule, cf. *Rule* III 8–11. For further information on fasting in general, cf. R. Bell, *Holy Anorexia* (Chicago: University of Chicago Press, 1985); C.W. Bynum, *Holy Feast & Holy Fast: The Religious Significance of Food to Medieval Women* (Berkeley: University of California Press, 1987); P. Deseille, "Jeûne," *Dictionnaire de Spiritualité* 8 (1974), cc. 1164–1175.

The Fourth Letter
to Blessed Agnes of Prague (1253)

Almost fifteen years had passed since the composition of the third letter when Clare began this last letter to Agnes. Her own blood-sister, Agnes, who had been in the monastery of Montecelli, had returned to San Damiano to be with her sister, no doubt, during her last days. Thus the letter was written sometime during those days in 1253 when the two sisters were again reunited.

Of the four letters, many consider this as the most beautiful not only because of its powerful affective expressions, but also because of the uplifting eschatological tone that permeates nearly every paragraph. Moreover, this letter offers us some insights into Clare's life of contemplative prayer by returning to that "formula of prayer" suggested in her second letter to Agnes of Prague and the image of the mirror found in the third letter.

1. To her who is half of her soul and the special shrine of her heart's deepest love, to the illustrious Queen and Bride of the Lamb, the eternal King: to the Lady Agnes, her most dear mother, and, of all the others, her favorite daughter, 2. Clare, an unworthy servant of Christ and a *useless* handmaid (Lk 17:10) of His handmaids in the monastery of San Damiano of Assisi: 3. health and [a prayer] that she may sing *a new song* (Rev 14:3) with the other most holy virgins before the throne of God and the Lamb and *follow the Lamb wherever He may go* (Rev 14:4).[1]

4. O mother and daughter, spouse of the King of all ages, if I have not written to you as often as your soul—and mine as well—desire and long for, do not wonder 5. or think that the fire of love for you glows with less delight in the heart of your mother. 6. No, this is the difficulty: the lack of messengers and the obvious dangers of the roads. 7. Now, however, as I write to your love, I rejoice and exult with you *in the joy of the Spirit* (1 Thes 1:6), O spouse of Christ, 8. because, since you have totally abandoned the vanities of this world, like the other most holy virgin, Saint Agnes, you have been marvelously espoused to *the spotless Lamb, Who takes away the sins of the world* (1 Pt 1:19; Jn 1:29).

---

[1] The Latin text makes a play on the Latin word *agnus*, lamb, and the name of Agnes suggesting the close relationship that united the Lamb of God, Christ, and Agnes herself.

9. Happy, indeed, is she
 to whom it is given to share in this sacred banquet
 so that she might cling with all her heart
 to Him
 10. Whose beauty all the blessed hosts of heaven unceasingly admire
 11. Whose affection excites
  Whose contemplation refreshes,
  Whose kindness fulfills,
 12. Whose delight replenishes,
  Whose remembrance delightfully shines,
 13. By Whose fragrance the dead are revived,
  Whose glorious vision will bless
   all the citizens of the heavenly Jerusalem:
 14.   which, *since it is the splendor of* eternal *glory,*[2] is
    the brilliance of eternal light
    and the mirror without blemish.[3]

15. Gaze upon that mirror each day, O Queen and Spouse of Jesus Christ, and continually study your face within it, 16. that you may adorn yourself within and without with beautiful robes, 17. covered, as is becoming the daughter and most chaste bride of the Most High King, with the flowers and garments of all the virtues. 18. Indeed, blessed poverty, holy humility, and inexpressible charity are reflected in that mirror, as, with the grace of God, you can contemplate them throughout the entire mirror.[4]

19. Look at the border of this mirror, that is, the poverty of Him Who was placed in a manger and wrapped in swaddling clothes.[5]

20. O marvelous humility!
 O astonishing poverty!
21. The King of angels,

---

[2]Cf. Heb 1:3.
[3]Cf. Wis 7:2.
[4]Cf. supra, p. 44 note 5.
[5]The three dimensions of the medieval mirror that Clare mentions in this passage are difficult to translate. This is particularly so since Clare mixes these images with three periods in the life of Christ. The medieval mirror was a thin disk of bronze that was slightly convex on one side. Its border, therefore, reflected an image in an obscure way. Parts of the surface would do the same. Only certain in-depth parts of the mirror reflected an image clearly. Cf. R. J. Armstrong, "Clare of Assisi: The Mirror Mystic," *The Cord* July–August, 1985, 195–202.

the Lord of heaven and earth,
is laid in a manger!

22. Then, at the surface of the mirror, consider the holy humility, the blessed poverty, the untold labors and burdens that He endured for the redemption of the whole human race. 23. Then, in the depth of this same mirror, contemplate the ineffable charity that led Him to suffer on the wood of the Cross and to die there the most shameful kind of death.

24. Therefore,
> that Mirror,
>> suspended on the wood of the Cross,
>> urged those who passed by to consider, saying:
>> 25. *"All you who pass by the way,*
>>> *look and see if there is any suffering*
>>> *like my suffering!"*[6]
26. Let us respond
>> with one voice,
>> with one spirit,
>> to Him crying and grieving Who said:
>> *"Remembering this over and over*
>> *leaves my soul downcast within me!"*[7]

27. From this moment, then, O Queen of our heavenly King, let yourself be inflamed more strongly with the fervor of charity. 28. As you further contemplate His ineffable delights, eternal riches and honors, 29. and sigh for them in the great desire and love of your heart, may you cry out:

30. *Draw me after you,*
>> *we will run in the fragrance of your perfumes,*[8]
>> O heavenly Spouse!
31. I will run and not tire,
>> until *You bring me into the wine-cellar,*[9]
32.   until Your *left hand is under my head*

---

[6] Cf. Lam 1:12. In much the same way, we find Francis continually inviting his brothers to respond to this invitation of Christ Crucified; cf. *Office of the Passion* VI 1.

[7] Cf. Lam 3:20.

[8] Cf. Cant 1:3. Insights into these passages should be sought in the rich spirituality of the twelfth and thirteenth centuries which delighted in commenting on the Canticle of Canticles, e.g., Bernard of Clairvaux, William of Saint Thierry. For an excellent discussion of this aspect, see Jean Leclercq, *Monks and Love in Twelfth-Century France: Psycho-Historical Essays* (Oxford: Oxford at Clarendon Press, 1979).

[9] Cf. Cant 2:4.

and Your *right hand will embrace me* happily,[10]
[and] *You will kiss me with the* happiest *kiss of Your mouth.*[11]

33. In this contemplation, may you remember your poor little mother,
34. knowing that *I have inscribed* the happy memory of you *on the tablets of my heart* (Prov 3:3), holding you dearer than all others.

35. What more can I say? Let the tongue of the flesh be silent when I seek to express my love for you; and let the tongue of the Spirit speak, 36. because the love that I have for you, O blessed daughter, can never be fully expressed by the tongue of the flesh, and even what I have written is an inadequate expression.

37. I beg you to receive my words with kindness and devotion, seeing in them at least the motherly affection that in the fire of charity I daily feel toward you and your daughters, to whom I warmly commend myself and my daughters in Christ. 38. On their part, these daughters of mine, especially the most prudent virgin Agnes, our sister, recommend themselves in the Lord to you and your daughters.

39. Farewell, my dearest daughter, to you and to your daughters until we meet at the throne *of the glory of the great God* (Tit 2:13), and desire [this] for us.

40. Inasmuch as I can, I recommend to your charity the bearers of this letter, our dearly beloved Brother Amatus, *beloved of God and men* (Sir 45:1), and Brother Bonaugura. Amen.[12]

---

[10]Cf. Cant 2:6. It is also helpful to remember that this passage also appears in the Privilege of Poverty given to Clare by Pope Innocent III and Gregory IX; cf. infra. pp. 83–84.

[11]Cf. Cant 1:1.

[12]Cf. R.J. Armstrong, I.C. Brady, *Francis and Clare: The Complete Works* (Paulist Press: New York, 1982), p. 206, n. 10.

Letter of Saint Clare
to Ermentrude of Bruges

Luke Wadding, the Irish friar who meticulously examined the documents of the early Franciscan tradition, writes in the Annales Minorum, *1257, n. 20, that Saint Clare wrote two letters to Ermentrude of Bruges, who had founded several monasteries in Flanders where the sisters sought to live according to the way of life of the Poor Ladies of San Damiano.*[1] *However, Wadding presents only one text, which appears to be a summary of both letters; he does not indicate what manuscript or text he had at hand. Modern scholarship with all that is available to it has never been able to corroborate Wadding's findings and has continually called this text into doubt.*[2] *Nonetheless, since the sixteenth century, it has been consistently presented as part of the patrimony of Clare and, as such, it is presented here.*

1. To her very dear sister, Ermentrude: Clare of Assisi, a lowly servant of Jesus Christ, greetings and peace!
2. I have learned, O most dear sister, that, with the help of God's grace, you have fled the mire of the world. 3. I rejoice and congratulate you because of this and, again I rejoice that you are walking courageously on the path of virtue with your daughters.

4. Be faithful, dearly beloved, till death
   to Him to Whom you have promised yourself,
   for *you shall be crowned* by Him with the garland *of life.*[3]

---

[1]Cf. L. Wadding, *Annales Minorum*, a. 1257, nn. 8–27. Cf. D.DeKok, O.F.M., "De Origine Ordinis S. Clarae in Flandris," *Archivum Franciscanum Historicum* 7 (1914): 234–246; A. Heyesse, "Origo et progressus Ordinis S. Clarae in Flandria," *Archivum Franciscanum Historicum* (1944): 165–201.

[2]Cf. M.F. Becker, J.F. Godet, T. Matura, *Claire D'Assise: Écrits* (Paris: Les Éditions du Cerf, 1985), 18–19; E. Grau, L. Hardick, *Leben und Schriften der hl. Klara von Assisi*, 3rd ed. (Werl-West, 1960), 24.

[3]Cf. Jb 1:12.

5. Our *labor* here is brief,
    the reward eternal;
    may the excitements *of the world,*
    fleeing like a shadow,[4]
    not disturb you.

6. May the false delights of the deceptive world
    not deceive you.
    Close your ears to the whisperings of hell
    and bravely oppose its onslaughts.

7. Gladly endure whatever goes against you
    and do not let your good fortunes lift you up:
    for these things destroy faith and those demand it.

8. *Offer* faithfully what *you have vowed to God*
    and He shall reward you.[5]

9. Look to heaven that invites us, O dearly beloved,
    and *take up the cross* and *follow* Christ
    Who goes before us,[6]

10. for through Him
    we shall enter into His glory
    after *many* different *trials.*[7]

11. *Love God*
    and Jesus, His Son, Who was crucified for us sinners,
    from the depths of your heart,
    and never let the thought of Him leave your mind.[8]

12. Meditate constantly on the mysteries of the cross
    and the agonies *of His mother standing at the foot of the cross.*[9]

13. *Pray and* always *be vigilant.*[10]

---

[4]Cf. Wis 10:17; Eccl 18:22; Jb 14:2.
[5]Cf. Ps 75:12.
[6]Cf. Lk 9:23.
[7]Cf. Acts 14:22; Lk 24:26.
[8]Cf. Dt 6:5; 11:1; Lk 10:27; 1 Cor 16:22.
[9]Cf. Jn 19:25.
[10]Cf. Mt 26:41.

14. *The work* you have begun well, *complete* immediately
and *the ministry* you have assumed,
fulfill in holy poverty and sincere humility.[11]

15. Do not be afraid, daughter.
God, Who is *faithful in all His words*
and holy in all His deeds,
will pour His blessings upon you and your sisters;[12]

16. and He will be your helper and the best consoler;
He is our redeemer and our eternal reward.

17. *Let us pray* to God *for one another*,
for by carrying *each other's burden* of charity in this way
we will easily *fulfill the law of Christ*.[13]

   Amen.

The Testament
of Saint Clare (1247–1253)

Of all the writings of Clare, the Testament is certainly the most autobiographical, filled as it is with personal and Franciscan remembrances that marvelously reveal the charism of Clare.[1] *Yet the document cannot be fully understood without seeing it in light of Clare's struggle to have her Rule, her own interpretation of the Form of Life left to her and the Poor Ladies by Saint Francis, approved by the Pope. No doubt she wrote this Testament as a statement of the essential values she perceived in the daily life of San Damiano. It was her farewell message, her "last will" that would guide her sisters after her death.*

In the past, scholars cast doubts on the authenticity of the Testament. Their arguments sprang from the weaknesses of the manuscript tradition which only sporadically presents a complete edition of the text, and from the changes of style in the work itself. The sisters of Saint Clare, however, have never accepted the doubts of the scholars and have persistently relied on the Testament as a principal source of their tradition. Recent scholarship has authenticated their intuitions by presenting solid manuscript evidence, especially those of Uppsala, Messina and Urbino, and advancing the proposition of various stages of composition or rewriting during the life of Clare herself.[2]

1. In the name of the Lord! Amen.

2. Among the other gifts that we have received and do daily receive from our benefactor, *the Father of mercies* (2 Cor 1:3), and for which we must express the deepest thanks to the glorious Father of Christ, 3. there is our vocation, for which, all the more by way of its being more perfect and greater, do we owe the greatest thanks to Him. 4. Therefore the Apostle [writes]: "Know your vocation" (1 Cor 1:26). 5. The Son of God has been

---

[1] For further treatment of the Testament of St. Clare, see C.L. Lainati, "Il Testamento di Santa Chiara," *Dizionario Francescano* (Padova: Edizioni Messaggero Padova, 1983), cc. 1827–1846; "Il Testamento di Santa Chiara," *Forma Sororum*, XXIII (1986): 196–220.

[2] An excellent treatment of the complex manuscript tradition surrounding the Testament as well as proof of its authenticity can be found in M.F. Becker, J.F. Godet, T. Matura, *Claire d'Assise: Ecrits* (Paris: Les Éditions du Cerf, 1985), pp. 21–27.

made for us *the Way* (cf. Jn 14:6), which our blessed father Francis, His true lover and imitator, has shown and taught us by word and example.

6. Therefore, beloved sisters, we must consider the immense gifts that God has bestowed on us, 7. especially those that He has seen fit to work in us through His beloved servant, our blessed father Francis, 8. not only after our conversion but also while we were still [living among] the vanities of the world. 9. In fact, almost immediately after his conversion, when he had neither brothers nor companions, 10. while he was building the church of San Damiano, where he was totally visited by divine consolation and impelled to completely abandon the world, 11. through the great joy and enlightenment of the Holy Spirit, the holy man made a prophecy about us that the Lord later fulfilled.[3]

12. For at that time, climbing the wall of that church, he shouted in French to some poor people who were standing nearby: 13. "Come and help me in the work [of building] the monastery of San Damiano, 14. because ladies will again dwell here who will glorify *our heavenly Father* (cf. Mt 5:16) throughout His holy, universal Church by their celebrated and holy manner of life."[4]

15. We can consider in this, therefore, the abundant kindness of God to us. 16. Because of His mercy and love, He saw fit to speak these words through His saint about our *vocation and choice* (cf. 2 Pt 1:10) through His saint. 17. And our most blessed father prophesied not only for us, but also for those who would come to this [same] holy vocation to which the Lord has called us.

18. With what eagerness and fervor of mind and body, therefore, must we keep the commandments of our God and Father, so that, with the help of the Lord, we may return to Him an increase of His *talent* (cf. Mt 25:15–23)! 19. For the Lord Himself has placed us not only as a form for others in being an example and mirror, but even for our sisters whom the Lord has called to our way of life as well, 20. that they in turn might be a mirror and example to those living in the world. 21. Since the Lord has called us to such great things that those who are to be a mirror and example to others may be reflected in us, 22. we are greatly bound to bless and praise God and be all the more strengthened to do good in the Lord. 23. Therefore, if

---

[3]Clare beautifully underscores her understanding that Francis' vision of founding the community of the Poor Ladies preceded the establishment of his fraternity.

[4]Cf. *Legenda Trium Sociorum* 24 (ed. T. Desbonnets), *Archivum Franciscanum Historicum* 67 (1974), 38–144; infra, pp. 262–263. An interesting nuance of this citation of Francis' prophecy is the author's addition of the words *"futura est,"* which are missing in Clare's Testament. Clare suggests that San Damiano was, indeed, a monastery in the past. Further information on the significance of this change can be found in M. Bigaroni, "San Damiano-Assisi. La Chiesa prima di San Francesco," *Atti Accademia Properziana del Subasio* VI 7 (1983): 49–87.

we live according to the form mentioned above, we shall *leave* others a noble *example* (cf. 2 Mac 6:28, 31) and gain, with very little effort, *the prize* of eternal happiness (cf. Phil 3:14).[5]

24. After the most high heavenly Father saw fit in His mercy and grace to enlighten my heart, that I should do penance according to the example and teaching of our most blessed father Francis,[6] 25. a short while after his conversion, I, together with a few sisters whom the Lord had given me after my conversion, willingly promised him obedience,[7] 26. as the Lord gave us the light of His grace through his wonderful life and teaching. 27. When the blessed Francis saw, however, that, although we were physically weak and frail, we did not shirk deprivation, poverty, hard work, trial, or the shame or contempt of the world—28. rather, we considered them as great delights, as he had frequently examined us according to the example of the saints and his brothers—he greatly rejoiced in the Lord. 29. And moved by compassion for us, he bound himself, both through himself and through his Order, to always have the same loving care and special solicitude for us as for his own brothers.[8]

30. And thus, by the will of God and our most blessed father Francis, we went to dwell in the Church of San Damiano, 31. where, in a little while, the Lord, through His mercy and grace, made our number increase so that He would fulfill what He had foretold through His saint. 32. In fact, we had stayed in another place [before this], but only for a short while.[9]

33. Afterwards he wrote a form of life for us, especially that we always persevere in holy poverty. 34. While he was living he was not content to encourage us with many words and examples to the love of holy poverty and its observance, but he gave us many writings that, after his death, we would in no way turn away from it, 35. as the Son of God never wished to abandon this holy poverty while He lived in the world. 36. And our most blessed father Francis, having imitated His footprints, never departed either in example or in teaching from this holy poverty that he had chosen for himself and his brothers.

---

[5]Once again we find the theme of the mirror that has already been accentuated in the *Third* and *Fourth Letters to Agnes of Prague*. In this instance, however, Clare refers to the sisters themselves as mirrors obliged to reflect that which they gaze upon to others. Cf. R. J. Armstrong, "Clare of Assisi: The Mirror Mystic," *The Cord* July–August, 1985, 195–202.

[6]The phrase "enlighten my heart" may be a reference to Francis' *Prayer before the Crucifix* 1.

[7]This is a reference to the creation of the juridical bond of obedience which Clare accentuates at the beginning of her Rule; cf. *Rule of St. Clare* I 4.

[8]Cf. *Rule of St. Clare* VI 2; *First Letter to Agnes of Prague* 17; also II Cel 204.

[9]Cf. *Legend of St. Clare* 8, 10 in which the authors refers to Clare's residency at the monastery of San Paolo in Bastia and that of Sant'Angelo in Panzo near Assisi. Cf. pp. 197–198.

37. Therefore, I, Clare, a handmaid of Christ and of the Poor Sisters of the Monastery of San Damiano—although unworthy—and the little plant of the holy father, consider together with my sisters so lofty a profession and the command of such a father 38. and also the frailty of some others that we feared in ourselves after the passing of our holy father Francis, who was our pillar [of strength] and, after God, our one consolation and support. 39. Time and again we willingly bound ourselves to our Lady, most holy Poverty, that after my death, the sisters, those present and those to come, would never turn away her.

40. And as I have always been most zealous and solicitous to observe and to have the others observe the holy poverty that we have promised to the Lord and our holy father Francis, 41. so, too, the others who will succeed me in office should be always bound to observe holy poverty with the help of God and have it observed by the other sisters. 42. Moreover, for greater security, I took care to have our profession of the most holy poverty that we promised our father strengthened with privileges by the Lord Pope Innocent, during whose pontificate we had our beginning, and by his other successors, 43. that we would never nor in any way turn away from her.[10]

44. For this reason, on bended knees and bowing low with both [body and soul],[11] I commend all my sisters, both those present and those to come, the holy Mother the Roman Church, the supreme Pontiff, and, especially, the Lord Cardinal who has been appointed for the Order of Friars Minor and for us, 45. that out of love of the God Who was placed poor in the crib, lived poor in the world, and remained naked on the cross, 46. [our Protector] may always see to it that his little flock (cf. Lk 12:32), which the Lord Father has begotten in His holy Church by the word and example of our blessed father Francis by following the poverty and humility of His beloved Son and His glorious Virgin Mother, 47. observe the holy poverty that we have promised to God and our most blessed father Saint Francis. May he always encourage and support them in these things.

48. And as the Lord gave us our most blessed father Francis as a founder, planter, and helper in the service of Christ and in those things we have promised to God and to our blessed father, 49. who while he was living was always solicitous in word and in deed to cherish and take care of us, his plant, 50. so I commend and leave my sisters, both those present and those to come, to the successor of our blessed Father Francis and to the entire Order, 51. that they may always help us to progress in serving God

---

[10] A reference to the *Privilege of Poverty* granted by Pope Innocent III in 1216 and renewed by his successors; cf. infra pp. 83–84; 103–104.

[11] A difficult expression to translate "*utroque homine inclinato.*" It is also used by Thomas of Celano in his *First Life of Saint Francis* 45, 101 to indicate the interior person and the exterior person, that is, that which is visible in a person and that which is not.

more perfectly and, above all, to observe more perfectly most holy poverty.

52. If the sisters spoken of ever leave and go elsewhere, let them be bound, after my death, wherever they may be, to observe that same form of poverty that we have promised God and our most blessed father Francis.[12]

53. Nevertheless, let both [the sister] who is in office,[13] as well as the other sisters, exercise such care and farsightedness that they do not acquire or receive more land about the place than extreme necessity requires for a vegetable garden. 54. But if, for the integrity and privacy of the monastery, it becomes necessary to have more land beyond the limits of the garden, no more should be acquired than extreme necessity demands. 55. This land should not be cultivated or planted but remain always untouched and undeveloped.

56. In the Lord Jesus Christ, I admonish and exhort all my sisters, both those present and those to come, to strive always to imitate the way of holy simplicity, humility and poverty and [to preserve] the integrity of our holy way of living, 57. as we were taught from the beginning of our conversion by Christ and our blessed father Francis. 58. May *the Father of mercies* (cf. 2 Cor 1:3) always spread the fragrance of a good name from them (cf. 2 Cor 2:15), both among those who are far away as well as those who are near, not by any merits of ours but by the sole mercy and grace of His goodness. 59. And loving one another with the charity of Christ, may the love you have in your hearts be shown outwardly in your deeds 60. so that, compelled by such an example, the sisters may always grow in love of God and in charity for one another.

61. I also beg that [sister] who will be in an office of the sisters to strive to exceed the others more by her virtues and holy life than by her office, 62. so that, stimulated by her example, they obey her not so much because of her office as because of love. 63. Let her also be discerning and attentive to her sisters as a good mother is to her daughters, 64. and let her take care especially to provide for them according to the needs of each one out of the alms that the Lord shall give.[14] 65. Let her also be so kind and available

---

[12]In fact, only four years after the death of Clare, the Sisters left San Damiano and took up residence in the area of the little church of San Giorgio where Clare, like Francis before her, had been buried. This is the site of the present day basilica and protomonastery of St. Clare.

[13]That is, the abbess. It should be noted that Clare never uses this word, abbess, in her Testament, suggesting that, although she accepted it for the composition of her Rule, she probably preferred the title of "servant" or "handmaid," as we can see in her letters to Agnes of Prague.

[14]This is an echo of Francis' counsel in "The Canticle of Exhortation to St. Clare and her Sisters" 14; cf. infra. p. 251.

that they may safely reveal their needs 66. and confidently have recourse to her at any hour, as they see fit both for themselves and their sisters.

67. Let the sisters who are subjects, however, keep in mind that they have given up their own wills for the sake of the Lord. 68. Therefore I want them to obey their mother of their own free will as they have promised the Lord, 69. so that, seeing the charity, humility and unity they have toward one another, their mother might bear all the burdens of her office more easily, 70. and, through their way of life, what is painful and bitter might be changed into sweetness.

71. And because *the way* and path *is difficult and the gate* through which one passes and enters *to life is narrow, there are both few who* walk it and enter through *it* (cf. Mt 7:14). 72. And if there are some who walk that way for a while, there are very few who persevere on it. 73. But how blessed are those to whom it has been given *to walk* that way and *to persevere till the end* (cf. Ps 118:1; Mt 10:22).

74. Let us be very careful, therefore, that, if we have set out on the path of the Lord, we do not at any time turn away from it through our own fault or negligence or ignorance, 75. nor that we offend so great a Lord and His Virgin Mother, and our blessed father Francis, the Church Triumphant and even the Church Militant. 76. For it is written: *"Those who turn away from your commands are cursed"* (Ps 118:21).

77. For this reason I *bend my knee to the Father of our Lord Jesus Christ* (cf. Eph 3:14) that, through the supporting merits of the glorious and holy Virgin Mary, His Mother, and of our most blessed father Francis and all the saints, 78. the Lord Himself, Who has given a good beginning, will also give the increase and *final perseverance* (cf. 2 Cor 8:6, 11). Amen.

79. So that it may be better observed, I leave you this writing, my very dear and beloved sisters, those present and those to come, as a sign of the blessing of the Lord and of our most blessed father Francis and of my blessing, your mother and servant.

Rule of Saint Clare (1253)

The last years of Clare's life were characterized by her struggle to have her vision of religious life approved by the Church. In order to understand her Rule for the Poor Ladies, it is helpful to read those which preceded it, those of Cardinal Hugolino and Pope Innocent IV, which were based on the Benedictine Rule and the canonical legislation of the twelfth and early thirteenth centuries. Clare's insistence on her own Rule no doubt came from years of attempting to live the vision Francis inspired in her within the limits of these documents, imposed as they were by men who did not comprehend the uniqueness of her vision. It is remarkable that Clare became the first woman to write a religious rule and, in so doing, inaugurated a totally new epoch for women in the life of the Church.[1]

Although it had been overlooked among the relics of Clare until 1893, the original document with the papal bull of Innocent IV is still preserved in the Protomonastery of Saint Clare in Assisi. The manuscript contains two phrases handwritten by the Pope: "Ad instar fiat! S. (So be it!)" and "Ex causis manifestis michi et protectorii mon[asterii] fiat ad instar. For reasons known to me and the protector of the monastery, so be it!" The first of these is the formula of approval given by Innocent IV who uses the first letter of his baptismal name, Sinibaldo, as his signature; the second is a clause explaining the uniqueness of the document. In the margin of the papal bull, someone else has written: "Hanc beata Clara tetigit et obsculata (!) est pro devotione pluribus et pluribus vicinis. Blessed Clare touched and kissed this many times out of devotion."

---

[1]Background information on the Rule of St. Clare may be found in the Introduction to this volume, cf. supra, pp. 22–24. For recent studies on the Rule of St. Clare, see E. Grau, "Die Schriften der Heiligen Klara und die Werke Ihrer Biographen," *Movimento Religioso Femminile e Francescanesimo nel Secolo XIII* (Assisi: Società Internazionale di Studi Francescani, 1980), 205–213; M.F. Becker, J.F. Godet, T. Matura, *Claire d'Assise: Écrits* (Paris: Les Editions du Cerf, 1985), 19–21; P. van Leeuwev, "Clare's Rule," *Greyfriars Review* I (September 1987), 65–77. For a general treatment of the historical context of the founding of the Poor Sisters see: R. Brooke and C.N.L. Brooke, "St. Clare," *Medieval Women*, ed. D. Baker (Oxford: Basil Blackwell, 1978), 275–288. Also: B. Bolton, "*Vitae Matrum: A Further Aspect of the Frauenfrage*," ibidem, pp. 253–273.

1. Innocent, Bishop, Servant of the servants of God, to his beloved daughters in Christ, Clare, Abbess, and the other sisters of the monastery of San Damiano in Assisi: health and apostolic blessing.

The Apostolic See is accustomed to accede to the pious requests and to be favorably disposed to grant the praiseworthy desires of its petitioners.[2] Thus, we have before Us your humble request that We confirm by our Apostolic authority the form of life that Blessed Francis gave you and which you have freely accepted. According to [this form of life] you should live together in unity of mind and heart and in the profession of the highest poverty.[3] Our venerable brother, the Bishop of Ostia and Velletri, has seen fit to approve this way of life, as the Bishop's own letters on this matter define more fully, and We have taken care to strengthen it with our Apostolic protection. Attentive, therefore, to your devout prayers, We approve and ratify what the Bishop has done in this matter and confirm it in virtue of our Apostolic authority and support it in this document.[4] To this end we include herein the text of the Bishop, word for word, which is the following:

2. Raynaldus by divine mercy Bishop of Ostia and Velletri, to his most dear mother and Daughter in Christ, the Lady Clare, Abbess of San Damiano in Assisi, and to her sisters, both present and to come, greetings and a fatherly blessing.

Beloved daughters in Christ, we approve your holy way of life in the Lord and we desire with fatherly affection to impart our kind favor upon your wishes and holy desires, because you have rejected the splendors and pleasures of the world and, following the footprints of Christ Himself (cf. 1 Pt 2:21) and His most holy Mother, you have chosen to live bodily enclosed and to serve the Lord in the highest poverty that, in freedom of soul, you may be the Lord's servants. Acceding to your pious prayers, by the authority of the Lord Pope as well as our own, we, therefore, confirm forever for all of you and for all who will succeed you in your monastery this form of life and we ratify by the protection of this document the manner of holy

---

[2] The papal document, *Solet annuere*, August 9, 1253, confirms "the form of life that Blessed Francis" gave to St. Clare and her sisters but only for the monastery of San Damiano in Assisi.

[3] Here Pope Innocent combines the charism of "unity of mind and heart" with that of "the profession of the highest poverty." This double aspect is seen as the foundation for the form of life that St. Clare and her sisters have embraced.

[4] In winning this papal approval, St. Clare became the first woman in the Church to receive such recognition for her legislation. Cf. Peter Dronke, *Women Writers of the Middle Ages: A Critical Study of Texts from Perpetua (203) to Marguerite Porete (1310)* (Cambridge: Cambridge University Press, 1984) 230–332.

unity and highest poverty which your blessed Father Saint Francis gave you for your observance in word and writing. It is as follows:

[Chapter One:
In the Name of the Lord Begins
the Form of Life of the Poor Sisters][5]

1. The form of life of the Order of the Poor Sisters[6] that Blessed Francis established is this: 2. to observe the Holy Gospel of our Lord Jesus Christ, by living in obedience, without anything of one's own, and in chastity.[7]
3. Clare, the unworthy servant of Christ and the little plant of the most blessed Francis, promises obedience and reverence to the Lord Pope Innocent and his canonically elected successors, and to the Roman Church. 4. And, just as at the beginning of her conversion, together with her sisters she promised obedience to the Blessed Francis, so now she promises his successors to observe the same obedience inviolably,[8] 5. And the other sisters shall always be obliged to obey the successors of Blessed Francis and Sister Clare and the other canonically elected Abbesses who succeed her.[9]

[Chapter Two:
Those Who Wish to Accept This Life
and How They Are To Be Received]

1. If, by divine inspiration, anyone should come to us desiring to accept this life, the Abbess is required to seek the consent of all the sisters; 2. and if the majority have agreed, she may receive her, after having ob-

---

[5]The original text of the Rule does not contain divisions into chapters with separate titles. These are of later origin but retained here to facilitate reading, although a richer interpretation of the document's theology can be discovered without them.

[6]In addition to asserting at once that St. Francis directly "established" the Order, St. Clare also makes use of the original title, "Poor Sisters." Her choice of the term "sisters" (*sorores*) instead of "nuns" (*monache*) expresses a determination to inculcate values of minority and fraternity. By the time of St. Bonaventure, the title "Sisters of Saint Clare" had become current (cf. Sermon 11, *Opera Omnia* IX, 576). In the Rule of Pope Urban IV (1263), the official title was given: "the Order of Saint Clare." Cf. Jean-François Godet, "Lettura della Forma di Vita," *Vita Minorum* 3 (Maggio-Giugno, 1985), 239–240.

[7]Cf. Reg Inn 1. St. Clare does not include a specific formula of profession. Cf. Sr. Margaret Mary, "Evolution of the Teaching on Commitment by Monastic Vow: from Cluny to the End of the 19th Century," *Cistercian Studies* 12 (1977), 41–65. There is no formula for profession in the *Rule of Clare*, as there is in the previous rules of Hugolino and Innocent IV.

[8]Reg Inn 12.

[9]It is worth noting that St. Clare affirms the bond that links her community to the Friars Minor having lived through the terms of five Ministers General and at a time in which the friars were experiencing significant difficulties in their own interpretation of poverty.

tained the permission of the Lord Cardinal Protector.[10] 3. If she judges [the candidate] acceptable, [the Abbess] should carefully examine her, or have her examined, concerning the Catholic faith and the sacraments of the Church. 4. And if she believes all these things and is willing to profess them faithfully and to observe them steadfastly to the end; 5. and if she has no husband, or if she has [a husband] who has already entered religious life with the authority of the Bishop of the diocese and has already made a vow of continence,[11] and if there is no impediment to her observance of this life, such as advanced age or ill-health or mental weakness, 6. let the tenor of our life be thoroughly explained to her.[12]

7. If she is suitable, let the words of the holy Gospel be addressed to her that she should go and sell all that she has and take care to distribute the proceeds to the poor (cf. Mt 19:21). 8. If she cannot do this, her good will suffices. 9. Let the Abbess and the sisters take care not to be concerned about her temporal affairs, so that she may freely dispose of her possessions as the Lord may inspire her. 10. However, if some counsel is required, let them send her to some discerning and God-fearing men, according to whose advice her goods may be distributed to the poor.

11. Afterwards, once her hair has been cut off round her head and her secular clothes set aside, she may be permitted three tunics and a mantle.[13] 12. Thereafter, she may not go outside the monastery except for a useful, reasonable, evident, and approved purpose.[14] 13. When the year of pro-

---

[10]Whereas the friars, in keeping with their itinerant life-style, received candidates individually at first (RegNB II 1) and then through the provincials (RegB II 1), Clare prudently requires consultation of all sisters of the community and the permission of the Cardinal Protector. This is the first of several instances in which she expresses great confidence in the sisters' ability to share the responsibility for major decisions.

[11]Neither the Rule of Hugolino nor that of Innocent IV deals with the admission of a woman who was married. *Quum autem vir* of Innocent III, December 9, 1198, made provision for dispensations allowing married partners the freedom to embrace a continent state of life by mutual consent. Cf. K. Esser, *Anfänge und ursprungliche Zeilsetzungen des Ordens de Minderbruder* (Leiden, 1966) 17, n. 1.

[12]Whereas the previous texts (RegHug 4, RegInn 1) require explaining "the hard and austere realities" of religious life to the novice, Clare simply asks that "the tenor of our life" be taught. This delicacy in communicating the free acceptance of a new vocation is dictated by her awareness that each new sister is a gift of God (cf. *Testament* 25).

[13]RegHug 9. Clare summarizes the prescriptions of the Rule of Hugolino. The form of tonsure and the veil signified religious consecration. The tunics, which could be worn simultaneously for warmth, signified penance.

[14]There is a marked difference between Clare's norms for permission to leave the monastery and those of the previous texts (RegHug 4; RegInn 1). Clare's balance between flexibility and acceptance of the monastic enclosure is a complex problem. Recent contributions to the literature on the subject include: C.A. Lainati, "The Enclosure of St. Clare and the First Poor Clares in Canonical Legislation and in Practice," *The Cord* 28 (1978) 4–15 and 47–

bation is ended, let her be received into obedience, promising to observe perpetually our life and form of poverty.

14. No one is to receive the veil during the period of probation. 15. The sisters may also have little mantles for convenience and propriety in serving and working. 16. In fact, the Abbess should with discernment provide them with clothing according to the diversity of persons, places, seasons and cold climates, as it shall seem expedient to her by necessity.[15]

17. Young girls who are received into the monastery before the age established by law should have their hair cut round [their heads]; and, putting aside their secular clothes, they should be clothed in a religious garb, as the Abbess sees fit.[16] 18. However, when they reach the age required by law, they may make their profession clothed in the same way as the others. 19. The Abbess shall carefully provide a Mistress from among the more discerning sisters of the monastery both for these and the other novices. 20. She shall form them diligently in a holy way of life and proper behavior according to the form of our profession.

21. The same form described above should be observed in the examination and reception of the sisters who serve outside the monastery.[17] 22. These sisters may wear shoes. 23. No one may live with us in the monastery unless she has been received according to the form of our profession.[18]

24. I admonish, beg, and exhort my sisters to always wear cheap garments out of love of the most holy and beloved Child Who was wrapped in such poor little swaddling clothes and laid in a manger and of His most holy Mother.

60; R. Manselli, "La Chiesa e il francescanesimo femminile nel secolo XIII," *Movimento religioso feminile e francescanesimo nel secolo XIII: Atti del convegno internazionale di studi francescani* (Assisi: 1980) 239–261.

[15]The word "discernment" and its derivative recurs in Clare writings. An examination of these texts reveals that one learns discernment from the Spirit of the Lord and that it is at once an enemy of the superfluous and the sister of charity. It understands the necessities of each sister.

[16]RegHug 9. It would appear that these young girls were aspirants who were accepted and who were given some form of subsistence and/or education.

[17]The role of the "serving sisters" was to provide a prudent means of contact with the townspeople whose good will supported the monastery. Not only did they perform the external business communications of the monastery, but they also witnessed to the richness of the Gospel life within it (cf. Reg Cl IX 11–16).

[18]In the Middle Ages it was common for monasteries to become refuges for woman of noble families who could not marry. Often these women lived a secular life-style within the monastery retaining servants and creating social situations that warred against poverty and recollection. Cf. J. Leclercq, "Il Monachesimo Femminile nei Secoli XII e XIII," *Movimento Religioso Femminile e Francescanesimo nel Secolo XIII* (Assisi: 1980), 79–83.

[Chapter Three:
The Divine Office and Fasting,
Confession and Communion]

1. The sisters who can read shall celebrate the Divine Office according to the custom of the Friars Minor.[19] 2. They may have breviaries for this, but they should read it without singing. 3. Those who, for some reasonable cause, occasionally are not able to recite their hours by reading them, may, like the other sisters, say the Our Father's.

4. Those who do not know how to read shall say twenty-four *Our Father*'s for Matins; five for Lauds; seven for each of the hours of Prime, Terce, Sext, and None; twelve, however, for Vespers; seven for Compline. 5. Let them also say for the dead seven *Our Father*'s with the *Requiem aeternam* at Vespers; twelve for Matins, 6. because the sisters who can read are obliged to recite the Office of the Dead. 7. When a sister of our monastery shall have departed this life, however, they should say fifty Our Father's.

8. The sisters shall fast at all times.[20] 9. They may eat twice on Christmas, however, no matter on what day it happens to fall. 10. The younger sisters, those who are weak, and those who are serving outside the monastery may be mercifully dispensed as the Abbess sees fit. 11. But the sisters are not bound to corporal fasting in time of manifest necessity.[21]

12. They shall go to confession, with the permission of the Abbess, at least twelve times a year. 13. They shall take care not to introduce other talk unless it pertains to the confession and the salvation of souls. 14. They should receive Communion seven times [a year], that is, on Christmas, Thursday of Holy Week, Easter, Pentecost, the Assumption of the Blessed Virgin, the feast of Saint Francis, and the Feast of All Saints. 15. The Chaplain may celebrate inside [the enclosure] in order to give Communion to the sisters who are in good health or to those who are ill.[22]

---

[19]Cf. R.J. Armstrong, I.C. Brady, *Francis and Clare: The Complete Works* (Paulist Press: New York, 1982), p. 214, n. 9; H. Grundmann, "Litteratus-illiteratus. Der Wandel einer Bildungsnorn von Altertum zum Mittelalter," *Archivum fur Kulturgeschichte* 40 (1958), 1–65; L. Hardick, "Gedanken zu Sinn and Tragweite des Begriffes 'Clerici'," *Archivum Franciscanum Historicum* 50 (1957), 7–26.

[20]RegHug 7

[21]Cf. R.J. Armstrong, I.C. Brady, *Francis and Clare: The Complete Works* (Paulist Press: New York, 1982), p. 214, n. 10; also, Ernest Gilliat-Smith, *St. Clare of Assisi: Her Life and Legislation* (New York: E.P. Dutton & Co. 1914), 153–156.

[22]Clare, like Francis, is implementing the program of the Fourth Lateran Council for a renewal of liturgical life. Its goal, in part, was to overcome negative effects of a deficient theology that was keeping the faithful from reception of the Eucharist due to an exaggerated sense

[Chapter Four:
The Election and Office of the Abbess:
The Chapter, and the Officials and the Discreets]

1. The sisters are bound to observe the canonical form in the election of the Abbess.[23] 2. They should quickly arrange to have the Minister General or the Minister Provincial of the Order of Friars Minor present. 3. Let him dispose them, through the Word of God, to perfect harmony and the common good in the election that is to be held.[24] 4. No one should be elected who is not professed. 5. And if a non-professed is elected or somehow given them, she should not be obeyed unless she first professes our form of poverty.[25]

6. At her death the election of another Abbess shall take place. 7. If at any time it should appear to the entire body of sisters that she is not competent for their service and common welfare, the sisters are bound as quickly as possible to elect another as abbess and mother according to the form described above.[26]

8. Whoever is elected should reflect upon the kind of burden she has undertaken and to Whom *she must render an account* of the flock committed to her (cf. Mt 12:36). 9. She should strive as well to preside over the others more by her virtues and holy behavior than by her office, so that, moved by her example, the sisters may obey her more out of love than out of fear. 10. Let her avoid particular friendships, lest by loving some more than others she cause scandal among all. 11. Let her console those who are afflicted. 12. Let her also be the last refuge for those who are troubled, lest the sickness of despair overcome the weak should they fail to find in her the remedies for health.[27]

13. Let her preserve common life in everything, especially in whatever

---

of sin. Cf. Jean-François Godet, "Lettura della Forma di Vita," *Vita Minorum* 3 (Maggio-Giugno, 1985), 239–240.

[23]Neither of the preceding texts contains this precise synthesis of juridical matters. We see herein Clare's ability to combine legal precision with insistence on a spirit of mutual responsibility of all members.

[24]In The Rule of Innocent 12 power to confirm the community's election resided in the Minister General of the Friars Minor. Clare, however, indicates a pastoral, not a juridical role for the Minister during the chapter of elections.

[25]Cf. supra note 18.

[26]As Francis had made provision for cases of incompetence (cf. *RegB* VII 4), so Clare does here. Otherwise the presumption is that the office is held for life.

[27]This section on the model abbess recalls both the *Rule of St. Benedict* 64:7–8, 15 and the *Second Life of St. Francis*, 185, by Thomas of Celano.

pertains to the church, the dormitory, refectory, infirmary, and clothing. 14. Let her vicaress be bound to serve in the same way.[28]

15. The Abbess is bound to call her sisters together at least once a week in the Chapter, 16. where both she and her sisters should humbly confess their common and public offenses and negligences. 17. Let her consult with all her sisters there concerning whatever pertains to the welfare and good of the monastery, 18. for the Lord frequently reveals what is best to the least [among us].[29]

19. Let no heavy debt be incurred except with the common consent of the sisters and by reason of manifest necessity, and let this be done by the procurator. 20. Let the Abbess and her sisters, however, be careful that nothing is deposited in the monastery for safekeeping; 21. for such practices often give rise to troubles and scandals.

22. Let all who hold offices in the monastery be chosen by the common consent of all the sisters to preserve the unity of mutual love and peace. 23. Let at least eight sisters be elected from the more discerning ones in the same way, whose counsel the Abbess should be always bound to use in those matters which our form of life requires. 24. Moreover, the sisters can and should, if it seems useful and expedient, remove the officials and discreets and elect others in their place.[30]

[Chapter Five:
Silence, the Parlor, and the Grille]

1. Let the sisters keep silence from the hour of Compline until Terce, except those who are serving outside the monastery. 2. Let them also continually keep silence in the church, the dormitory, and the refectory, only while they are eating.[31] 3. They may speak discreetly at all times, however,

---

[28]The Latin verb used here (*servare*) indicates a spirit of vigilance regarding the spirit of the life of the community. There has been a tendency to interpret it in the sense of demanding correct observance (*observare*) of common life or correct behavior on the part of the abbess and vicaress. Cf. R.J. Armstrong, I.C. Brady, *Francis and Clare: The Complete Works* (Paulist Press: New York, 1982), p. 216, n. 14.

[29]Neither text of Francis' Rules, nor the Rules of Hugolino or Innocent described this form of chapter. The public confession of faults was an ancient monastic custom that strengthened personal fidelity to the rule of life. The inclusion of "the least among us" in the discussion of community business seems to be a direct quote from the Benedictine Rule; cf. 3:3. However, Clare substitutes "the least" for Benedict's "young" thus underscoring the Gospel teaching found in Matthew 11:25–30. Cf. R.J. Armstrong, I.C. Brady, *Francis and Clare: The Complete Works* (Paulist Press: New York, 1982), p. 216, n. 15.

[30]The function of the discreets is innovative with respect to the previous Rules.

[31]The refectory obviously did at least double, if not triple, duty, often serving as a Chapter room, work room, etc.

in the infirmary for the recreation and service of the sick. 4. Nevertheless, they can communicate always and everywhere, briefly and in a low tone of voice, whatever is necessary.

5. The sisters may not speak in the parlor or at the grille without the permission of the Abbess or her Vicaress. 6. Let those who have permission not dare to speak in the parlor unless they are in the presence and hearing of two sisters. 7. Let them not presume to go to the grille, moreover, unless there are at least three sisters present [who have been] appointed by the Abbess or her Vicar from the eight discreets who were elected by all the sisters for the council of the Abbess. 8. Let the Abbess and her Vicaress be themselves bound to observe this form of speaking. 9. [Let the sisters speak] very rarely at the grille and, by all means, never at the door.[32]

10. Let a curtain be hung inside the grille which may not be removed except when the Word of God is preached or when a sister is speaking with someone. 11. Let the grille have a wooden door which is well provided with two distinct iron locks, bolts, and bars, 12. so that it can be locked, especially at night, by two keys, one of which the Abbess should keep and the other the sacristan. 13. Let it always be locked except when the Divine Office is being celebrated and for the reasons given above. 14. Under no circumstance whatever, may a sister speak to anyone at the grille before sunrise or after sunset. 15. Let there always be a curtain on the inside of the parlor, which may not be removed.

16. No one may speak in the parlor during the Lent of Saint Martin and the Greater Lent, 17. except to a priest for Confession or for some other manifest necessity, which is left to the prudence of the Abbess or her Vicaress.[33]

[Chapter Six:
The Lack of Possessions]

1. After the Most High Heavenly Father saw fit by His grace to enlighten my heart to do penance according to the example and teaching of our most blessed Father Saint Francis, shortly after his own conversion, I, together with my sisters, willingly promised him obedience.[34]

---

[32]Clare not only maintains the strictures of the canonical discipline found in the Rules of Hugolino and Innocent; she goes beyond them. The grille referred to separated the nuns' choir from the church. The parlor grille was required first in the Rule of Innocent. She maintains the requirement of witnesses for conversations with visitors; cf. RegHug 6, 11; RegInn 3.

[33]See supra, note 14.

[34]At this point, Clare inserts in three chapters the heart of the "life and poverty" of Jesus Christ that is the cornerstone of the Order. This section of the Rule possesses a dramatically

2. When the Blessed Father saw we had no fear of poverty, hard work, trial, shame, or contempt of the world, but, instead, regarded such things as great delights, moved by compassion he wrote a form of life for us as follows:

3. "Because by divine inspiration you have made yourselves daughters and servants of the Most High King, the heavenly Father, and have taken the Holy Spirit as your spouse, choosing to live according to the perfection of the holy Gospel, 4. I resolve and promise for myself and for my brothers to always have that same loving care and solicitude for you as [I have] for them."[35]

5. As long as he lived he diligently fulfilled this and wished that it always be fulfilled by his brothers.

6. Shortly before his death he once more wrote his last will for us that we—or those, as well, who would come after us—would never turn aside from the holy poverty we had embraced. He said:

7. "I, little brother Francis, wish to follow the life and poverty of our most high Lord Jesus Christ and of His holy mother and to persevere in this until the end; 8. and I ask and counsel you, my ladies, to live always in this most holy life and poverty. 9. And keep most careful watch that you never depart from this by reason of the teaching or advice of anyone."

10. Just as I, together with my sisters, have ever been solicitous to safeguard the holy poverty which we have promised the Lord God and blessed Francis, 11. so, too, the Abbesses who shall succeed me in office and all the sisters are bound to observe it inviolably to the end: 12. that is to say, by not receiving or having possession or ownership either of themselves or through an intermediary, 13. or even anything that might reasonably be called property, 14. except as much land as necessity requires for the in-

---

different autobiographical tone than occurs again in the *Testament*. This particular chapter comes directly from Clare and forms the heart of the Rule, thus providing a principal font for this new form of life in the Church.

[35]Clare secures her Rule by reproducing literally the *Form of Life* and the *Last Will* written by Francis for the Poor Ladies. She also establishes the claim to the continuing support of the Friars Minor that is promised there.

tegrity and proper seclusion of the monastery, 15. and this land may not be cultivated except as a garden for the needs of the sisters.[36]

[Chapter Seven:
The Manner of Working]

1. Let the sisters to whom the Lord has given the grace of working work faithfully and devotedly after the Hour of Terce at work that pertains to a virtuous life and the common good. 2. They must do this in such a way that, while they banish idleness, the enemy of the soul, they do not extinguish the Spirit of holy prayer and devotion to which all other things of our earthly existence must contribute.[37]

3. At the Chapter, in the presence of all, the Abbess or her Vicaress is bound to assign the work of her hands that each should perform. 4. Let the same be done if alms have been sent by someone for the needs of the sisters, so that a prayer may be offered for them in common. 5. Let all such things be distributed for the common good by the Abbess or her vicaress with the advice of the discreets.[38]

[Chapter Eight:
The Sisters Shall Not Acquire Anything
as Their Own; Begging Alms; The Sick Sisters]

1. Let the sisters not appropriate anything, neither a house nor a place nor anything at all; 2. instead, as pilgrims and strangers in this world who serve the Lord in poverty and humility, let them confidently send for alms.[39] 3. Nor should they be ashamed, since the Lord made Himself poor

---

[36]This "solicitude" was first manifested in 1216 when St. Clare asked for and received from Pope Innocent III the Privilege of Poverty; cf. infra pp. 83–84. For an important general treatment of the problem of economic and pastoral support for medieval religious women see Brenda Bolton, "Mulieres Sanctae," originally published in *Studies in Church History*, vol 10, pp. 77–85, edited by Derek Baker. Published for the Ecclesiastical History Society by Basil Blackwell, London, and Barnes and Noble, New York, in 1973. This is a key reference in this regard.

[37]Echoing Francis' *Later Rule* V 1–2, Clare describes work as a normal means of subsistence and a concrete way of practicing poverty and inculcating a spirit of minority. This passage indicates the existence of a monastic style of horarium. The *Process of Canonization* describes Clare as never idle, but given over to her spinning even when ill; cf. *Process* I 11.

[38]The use of the chapter as the place for assignments and distribution of goods was to prevent favoritism.

[39]The medieval pilgrimage was a major expression of a life of penance. Thus, even though the Poor Sisters remained enclosed in San Damiano, the renunciation of financial security and its consequent reliance upon daily work and alms created a spirit of pilgrim-like insecurity for the sisters.

in this world for us. 4. This is that summit of the highest poverty which has established you, my dearest sisters, heiresses and queens of the kingdom of heaven; it has made you poor in the things [of this world] but exalted you in virtue. 5. Let this be your portion which leads into the land of the living (cf. Ps 141:6). 6. Clinging totally to this, my most beloved sisters, do not wish to have anything else forever under heaven for the name of our Lord Jesus Christ and His most holy mother.[40]

7. Let no sister be permitted to send letters or to receive or give away anything outside the monastery without the permission of the Abbess.[41] 8. Let it not be permitted to have anything that the Abbess has not given or allowed. 9. Should anything be sent to a sister by her relatives or others, let the Abbess give it to the sister. 10. If she needs it, the sister may use it; otherwise, let her in all charity give it to a sister who does need it. 11. If, however, money is sent to her, the Abbess, with the advice of the discreets, may provide for the needs of the sister.[42]

12. Concerning the sick sisters, let the Abbess be strictly bound to inquire diligently, by herself and through other sisters, what their illness requires both by way of counsel as well as food and other necessities.[43] 13. Let her provide for them charitably and kindly according to the resources of the place. 14. [Let this be done] because all are bound to serve and provide for their sisters who are ill just as they would wish to be served themselves if they were suffering from any illness. 15. Let each one confidently manifest her needs to the other. 16. For if a mother loves and nourishes her child according to the flesh, should not a sister love and nourish her sister according to the Spirit even more lovingly?[44]

---

[40]Clare transcribed the *Later Rule* VI 1–6 from Francis but added the image of Mary whose lowliness was exalted (cf. Lk 1:48–49). The life of the sisters is not accepted for ascetical motives, but solely for the sake of the Poor Christ and His Mother and in union with all who suffer marginalization and want.

[41]Inspection of correspondence was imposed by the *Rule of Pope Urban IV* (October 18, 1263).

[42]The Latin text uses "*pecunia*" or currency used for ordinary transactions (petty cash) as opposed to "*denarii*" used for costlier purchases. By using the former term Clare places a limit on the offerings that may be received. See E. Grau, "Die Geldfrage in der Regel der hl. Klara und in der Regel der Minderbrüder," *Chiara d'Assisi. Rassegna del Protomonastero* 1 (1953), 115–119; abridged version in *Franziskanische Studien* 35 (1953), 266–269; also L. Hardick, "Denaro," *Dizionario Francescano* (Padova: Edizioni Messagero Padova, 1983), cc. 329–342. Clare makes provision for the different economic situation of a community of enclosed women who are totally dependent on alms.

[43]Cf. RegHug 8; RegInn 5.

[44]These lines on care of the sick show how Clare assimilated the instructions of Francis (*RegNB* X; *RegB*VI 7–9; *CantExh* 4, 5). Aside from the influence of previous texts we know that women in the Middle Ages played a significant role in the practice of the healing arts and

17. Those who are ill may lay on sacks filled with straw and may use feather pillows for their head; 18. those who need woolen stockings and quilts may use them.

19. When the sick sisters are visited by those who enter the monastery, they may answer them with brevity, each responding with some good words to those who speak to them. 20. But the other sisters who have permission [to speak] may not dare to speak to those who enter the monastery unless in the presence and hearing of the two sister-discreets assigned by the Abbess or her Vicaress. 21. Let the Abbess and her Vicaress, as well, be bound to observe this manner of speaking.

[Chapter Nine:
The Penance To Be Imposed on the Sisters Who Sin;
The Sisters Who Serve outside the Monastery]

1. If any sister, at the instigation of the enemy, has sinned mortally against the form of our profession, 2. and, if after having been admonished two or three times by the Abbess or other sisters, she does not amend, let her eat bread and water on the floor before all the sisters in the refectory for as many days as she shall have been obstinate. 3. If it seems advisable to the Abbess, let her be subjected to even greater punishment. 4. Meanwhile, as long as she remains obstinate, let the prayer be that the Lord will enlighten her heart to do penance. 5. The Abbess and her sisters, however, should beware not to become angry or disturbed on account of anyone's sin, for anger and disturbance prevent charity in oneself and in others.[45]

6. If it should happen—may it never be so—that an occasion of trouble or scandal should arise between sister and sister through a word or gesture, 7. let she who was the cause of the trouble, before offering her gift of prayer to the Lord, not only prostrate herself humbly at once at the feet of the other and ask pardon, 8. but also beg her simply to intercede for her to the Lord that He might forgive her.[46] 9. Let the other sister, mindful of that word of the Lord—"If you do not forgive from the heart, neither will your heavenly Father forgive you" (cf. Mt 6:15; 18:35)—10. generously pardon her sister every wrong she has done her.

---

abbesses were expected to be skilled in this area. Cf. Margaret Wade Labarge, *Women in Medieval Life* (London: Hamish Hamilton, 1986), p. 171.

[45]Clare, like Francis, follows the consideration of physical illness with one on spiritual maladies. The basis is the Gospel mandate of fraternal correction (Mt 18:15). While to modern sensibilities this punishment may seem excessive, it was actually moderate in contrast to existing monastic practices that called for scourging or imprisonment.

[46]Clare applies the evangelical teaching found in Matthew 5:23ff; 6:14. See also *Rule of St. Benedict* 71:8.

11. Let the sisters who serve outside the monastery not linger outside unless some manifest necessity requires it. 12. Let them conduct themselves virtuously and say little, so that those who see them may always be edified. 13. Let them strictly beware of having suspicious meetings and dealings with others. 14. They may not be godmothers of men or women lest gossip or trouble arise because of this.[47] 15. Let them not presume to repeat the gossip of the world inside the monastery. 16. Let them be strictly bound not to repeat outside the monastery anything that was said or done within which could cause scandal.[48]

17. If anyone should innocently offend in these two matters, let it be left to the prudence of the Abbess to mercifully impose a penance on her. 18. But if a sister does this through a vicious habit, let the Abbess, with the advice of her discreets, impose a penance on her according to the nature of the fault.[49]

[Chapter Ten:
The Admonition and Correction of the Sisters]

1. Let the Abbess admonish and visit her sisters, and humbly and charitably correct them, not commanding them anything that is against their soul and the form of our profession.[50] 2. Let the sisters, however, who are subjects, remember that they have renounced their wills for God's sake. 3. Let them, therefore, be firmly bound to obey their Abbess in all the things they have promised the Lord to observe and which are not against their soul and our profession.

4. Let the Abbess, on her part, be so familiar with them that they can speak and act with her as ladies do with their servant. 5. For this is the way it should be: the Abbess should be the servant of all the sisters.[51]

---

[47]Cf. *Decretum Gratiani*, II p., c. XIV, q.1, c.8.

[48]It is obvious that Clare did not consider the "serving sisters" as inferior to the enclosed sisters; cf. supra note 17. Like the mother figure in Francis' *Rule for the Hermitages*, these sisters are the custodians of the recollection of their enclosed co-sisters.

[49]The words "vicious habit" seem severe, thus creating the assumption that Clare legislates from the base of difficult experience.

[50]While following the general structure of Francis' *Later Rule* X, Clare makes changes appropriate to the "form of life" of a stable, monastic community. What does not change is the core concept of loving obedience and authority exercised as a service (cf. Mt 20:25–27; Francis' *Salutation of the Virtues* 3).

[51]The Latin "*ancilla*" used here, as well as in RegCl I 3; VI 6, was the common term for a female servant and implied socially inferior status. When used in religious literature it assumed the symbolic meaning of a cloistered woman who freely chose a subordinate position as an act of humility. Cf. M. Goodish, "The Ancilla Dei: The Servant as Saint in the Late Middle Ages," *Women of the Medieval World*, eds. Julius Kirschner and Suzanne F. Wemple (Oxford: Basil Blackwell, 1985), 119–136.

6. In fact, I admonish and exhort the sisters in the Lord Jesus Christ to beware of all pride, vainglory, envy, avarice, care and anxiety about this world, detraction and murmuring, dissension and division. 7. Let them be always eager to preserve among themselves the unity of mutual love which is the bond of perfection.[52]

8. Let those who do not know how to read not be eager to learn. 9. Let them rather devote themselves to what they should desire to have above all else: the Spirit of the Lord and His holy manner of working,[53] 10. to pray always to Him with a pure heart, and to have humility, patience in difficulty and infirmity, 11. and to love those who persecute, blame, and accuse us, 12. for the Lord says: *Blessed are those who suffer persecution for the sake of justice, for theirs' is the kingdom of heaven* (Mt 5:10). 13. But *whoever perseveres to the end will be saved.*

[Chapter Eleven: The Custody of the Enclosure]

1. Let the portress be mature in her manner of acting, discerning, and of a suitable age. Let her remain in an open cell without a door during the day.[54]

2. Let a suitable companion be assigned to her who may take her place in everything whenever necessary.

3. Let the door be well secured by two different iron locks, with bars and bolts, 4. so that, especially at night, it may be locked with two keys,

---

[52]Clare adds to the text of Francis' *Later Rule* X 7 a double warning against "detraction and murmuring, dissension and division." Thus she re-emphasizes a fundamental value of the Rule and life of the Poor Sisters, "the unity of mutual love."

[53]This expression is found in three texts of St. Francis (Adm I 1; I EpFid 3; ReB X 8). Thus Francis sees in the Holy Spirit the Spirit of Christ enabling all who accept the Gospel to follow in His footsteps. Cf. R.J. Armstrong, I.C. Brady, *Francis and Clare: The Complete Works* (Paulist Press: New York, 1982), p. 26, n. 1; p. 63, n. 3; p. 144, n. 23). Clare not only appropriates the sentiments of Francis, she follows the structural form of his text. In the Later Rule this passage is followed by the chapter admonishing the brothers against entering the monasteries of nuns. Clare follows this passage with the resumption of her treatment of the enclosure which she interrupted after introducing the topic in Chapter V.

[54]The strictness of Clare's legislation of the enclosure exceeds even that of previous norms for the Cistercians and Premonstratensians. Following the Fourth Lateran Council and the death of Pope Innocent III, the general trend toward rigid legislation regarding the enclosure became the general standard. Hugolino, the future Pope Gregory IX, was one of the advocates of this program. Clare's experience as abbess was clearly stamped by ultimate acceptance of this view. Cf. B. Bolton, "*Vitae Matrum:* A Further Aspect of the Frauenfrage," *Medieval Women*, ed. D. Baker (Oxford: Basil Blackwell, 1978), pp. 253–273; R. Brooke and C.N.L. Brooke, "St. Clare," *ibidem*, 284–87.

one of which the portress may have, the other the Abbess. 5. Let it never be left without a guard and securely locked with one key.[55]

6. Let them most diligently take care to see that the door is never left open, except when this can hardly be conveniently avoided. 7. Let it never be opened to anyone who wishes to enter, except to those who have been given permission by the Supreme Pontiff or our Lord Cardinal. 8. The sisters may not allow anyone to enter the monastery before sunrise or to remain within after sunset, unless a manifest, reasonable, and unavoidable cause demands otherwise.[56]

9. If a bishop has permission to offer Mass within the enclosure, either for the blessing of an Abbess or for the consecration of one of the sisters as a nun or for any other reason, let him be satisfied with both as few and virtuous companions and assistants as possible.[57]

10. Whenever it is necessary for other men to enter the monastery to do some work, let the Abbess carefully post a suitable person at the door, 11. who may only open it to those assigned for work and to no one else.[58] 12. Let the sisters be extremely careful at such times not to be seen by those who enter.

[Chapter Twelve: The Visitator, the Chaplain, and the Cardinal Protector]

1. Let our Visitator always be taken from the Order of the Friars Minor according to the will and command of our Cardinal.[59] 2. Let him be the kind of person who is well known for his integrity and good manner of living. 3. His duty shall be to correct any excesses against the form of our profession, whether these be in head or in the members. 4. Taking his

---

[55]RegHug 13.

[56]Clare, as is her habit, places a responsibility to make wise choices upon the shoulders of her sisters, even in this serious situation. This is above all a typical example of Clare's Gospel flexibility.

[57]Solemn ceremonies such as those mentioned here created great influxes of guests into the monasteries of the time. Clare, mindful of simplicity and poverty, legislates a simple entourage for such events. For an example of such instances see Sally Thompson, "The Problem of the Cistercian Nuns in the Twelfth and Early Thirteenth Centuries," *Medieval Women* (Oxford: Basil Blackwell 1978), 229.

[58]Cf. RegHug 10; RegInn 9.

[59]The first Visitator of the Poor Ladies was a Cistercian, Ambrose, who held that position from 1218 to 1219. He was followed by Brother Filippo Lungo, a Friar Minor, and then by a secular, Brunetus, in 1224. No doubt the prescription to have a Friar Minor as Visitator came from Clare's personal experience of a Visitator who did not understand the Franciscan ideal. Cf. Livarius Oliger, O.F.M., "De Origine Regularum Ordinis Sanctae Clarae," *Archivum Franciscanum Historicum* (1912): 181–209.

stand in a public place, that he can be seen by others, let him speak with several and with each one concerning the matters that pertain to the duty of the visitation as he sees best.

5. We ask as a favor of the same Order a chaplain and a clerical companion of good reputation, of prudent discernment and two lay brothers, lovers of a holy and upright way of life, 6. in support of our poverty, as we have always mercifully had from the aforesaid Order of Friars Minor, 7. in light of the love of God and our blessed Francis.[60]

8. Let the chaplain not be permitted to enter the monastery without a companion. 9. When they enter, let them remain in an open place, in such a way that they can always see each other and be seen by others. 10. They may enter the enclosure for the confession of the sick who cannot go to the parlor, for their Communion, for the Last Anointing and the Prayers of the Dying.

11. Suitable and sufficient outsiders may enter, moreover, according to the prudence of the Abbess, for funeral services and on the solemnity of Masses for the Dead, for digging or opening a grave, or also for making arrangements for it.[61]

12. Let the sisters be strictly bound to always have that Cardinal of the Holy Roman Church, who has been delegated by the Lord Pope for the Friars Minor, as Governor, Protector, and Corrector,[62] 13. that always submissive and subject at the feet of that holy Church and steadfast in the Catholic faith, we may always observe the poverty and humility of our Lord Jesus Christ and of His most holy Mother and the Holy Gospel we have firmly promised. Amen.

Given at Perugia, the sixteenth day of September, in the tenth year of the Pontificate of Lord Pope Innocent IV.[63]

Therefore, no one is permitted to destroy this document of our confir-

---

[60]In *Quo Elongati*, September 28, 1230, Pope Gregory IX forbade the friars to enter the monastery without special permission. This was the occasion for Clare's sending the friars away in protest (cf. *Bullarium Franciscanum* I, 70; *Legend of St. Clare* 37). The struggle over the form of relationship between the friars and sisters culminated in 1296 with the bull *Quasdam litteras* in which Boniface VIII reconfirmed that of Pope Innocent IV in 1246, *Licet olim quibusdam*, which insisted that the Friars Minor assume certain responsibilities toward the Poor Ladies (cf. *Bullarium Franciscanum* IV, 396; I, 420).

[61]Cf. RegInn 7, 8.

[62]Hugolino was the Cardinal Protector of the Poor Ladies of San Damiano until his election as Bishop of Rome, March 19, 1227. He was succeeded by Cardinal Raynaldus, who later became his successor as Bishop of Rome, December 12, 1254.

[63]The first date given is September 16, 1252, that is, the date of the approval by the Cardinal Protector, Raynaldus dei Conti di Segni. Cf. *Rule of St. Clare*, Prologue 2.

mation or oppose it recklessly. If anyone shall presume to attempt this, let him know he will incur the wrath of Almighty God and His holy Apostles Peter and Paul.

Given at Assisi, the ninth day of August, in the eleventh year of our Pontificate.[64]

---

[64]The second date is August 9, 1253, on which day Pope Innocent IV gave his approval to Clare's Rule through the bull *Solet annuere*. Clare died two days later.

Blessing (1253)

The Legend of Saint Clare, 45, describes the last hours of the saint's life and tells how she blessed the sisters of San Damiano as well as those of the other monasteries and those who would come in the future. This is possibly the source of the special blessing that has been traditionally attributed to Saint Clare. However, there is also evidence of a blessing that Saint Clare sent to Blessed Agnes of Prague, another sent to Ermentrude of Bruges, and a third to all the sisters. The earliest known text of the blessing is found in a manuscript that is dated at about 1350; this source contains a Middle High German translation of it associated with the Fourth Letter to Agnes of Prague.[1] A Latin text, associated with Ermentrude of Bruges, comes from a much later period, the seventeenth century,[2] while another text addressed to all the sisters is found in various languages in manuscripts of different dates.[3] The tradition of the Poor Clares has always cherished this text as a precious remembrance of their foundress which echoes that blessing given by Saint Francis to Brother Leo while they were on La-Verna.[4]

1. *In the name of the Father and of the Son and of the Holy Spirit* (Mt 28:19).
2. *May the Lord bless* you *and keep you.*
3. *May He show His face* to you *and be merciful* to you.
4. *May He turn His countenance* (cf. Num 6:24–26) to you, my sisters

---

[1]Cf. Walter W. Seton, "Some New Sources for the Life of Blessed Agnes of Prague, including some Chronological Notes and a New Text of the Benediction of Saint Clare," *Archivum Franciscanum Historicum* 7 (1914), 185–197; idem, "The Oldest Text of the Benediction of Saint Clare of Assisi," *Revue d'Histoire Franciscaine* 2 (1925), 88–90; C.M. Borkowski, "A Second Middle High German Translation of the Benediction of Saint Clare," *Franciscan Studies* 36 (1976), 99–104.

[2]Cf. D. DeKok, "De origine Ordinis S. Clarae in Flandria," *Archivum Franciscanum Historicum* 7 (1914), 244–245.

[3]Cf. U.d'Alençon, "Le plus ancien texte de la bénédiction, du privilège de la pauvreté et du testament de sainte Claire d'Assise," *Revue d'histoire Franciscaine* 1 (1924), 469–482; D. Ciccarelli, "Contributi alla recensione degli scritti di S. Chiara," *Miscellanea Francescana* 70 (1979), 353–355; D. DeKok, "S. Clarae Benedictionis textus neerlandici," *Archivum Franciscanum Historicum* 40 (1947), 290–291.

[4]Cf. St. Francis of Assisi, *Francis and Clare: The Complete Works*, ed. R.J. Armstrong and I.C. Brady (New York: Paulist Press, 1982), 99–100.

and daughters, and give peace to you, 5. and to all others who come and remain in your company as well as to others now and in the future, who have persevered in every other monastery of the Poor Ladies.

6. I, Clare, a servant of Christ, a little plant of our most holy Father Francis, a sister and mother of you and the other poor sisters, although unworthy, 7. beg our Lord Jesus Christ through His mercy and the intercession of His most holy Mother Mary and blessed Michael the Archangel and all the holy angels of God, of our blessed father Francis, and all men and women saints, 8. that the heavenly Father give you and confirm for you this most holy blessing *in heaven* and *on earth* (cf. Gen 27:28). 9. On earth, may He multiply you in His grace and His virtues among His servants and handmaids in His Church Militant. 10. In heaven, may He exalt you and glorify you among his men and women saints in His Church Triumphant.

11. I bless you during my life and after my death, as I am able, out of all the blessings 12. with which *the Father of mercies has* and does *bless* His sons and daughters *in heaven* and on earth (2 Cor 1:3; cf. Eph 1:3) 13. and a spiritual father and mother have blessed and bless their spiritual sons and daughters. Amen.

14. Always be lovers of your souls and those of all your sisters. 15. And may you always be eager to observe what you have promised the Lord.

16. May the Lord always be *with you* (cf. 2 Cor 13:11; Jn 12:26; 1 Th 4:17) and may you always be with Him. Amen.

Part II

WRITINGS
CONCERNING SAINT CLARE ALONE
AND THE POOR LADIES

The Privilege of Poverty
of Pope Innocent III (1216)

After the Fourth Lateran Council, November 1215, that decided not to permit new religious rules, Saint Clare was obliged to adopt the Rule of Saint Benedict.[1] In the following year, however, Pope Innocent III, who had already approved the primitive form of life of Saint Francis, granted her request for a privilege of poverty. The Pope granted this unique and unheard of privilege sometime between the conclusion of the Council in 1215 and his death on July 16, 1216, permitting the Poor Ladies to live as a community without property, something that was entirely new and unheard of for a monastic foundation. Thus the Pope approved the poverty Saint Clare desired to follow after the example of Saint Francis and his brothers and which formed the foundation of her expression of the Franciscan charism.[2]

1. Innocent, Bishop, Servant of the servants of God, to his beloved daughters in Christ, Clare and the other servants of Christ of the Church

---

[1]Cf. Fourth Lateran Council, Decree 13: "In order to avoid an excessive diversity of Orders in the Church of God causing serious confusion, we prohibit with force from now on the founding of an Order. But if someone wishes to seek conversion in the life of an Order, let him take one of the accepted Orders. Likewise if someone wishes to renew an already established house of an Order, let him adopt the Rule and attitude of one of the approved Orders. Moreover we forbid anyone from assuming the position of a monk in several houses and also an abbot from exercising authority over several houses." Cf. *Conciliorum oecumenicorum decreta* (Freiburg, 1962): 218.

[2]The authenticity of the *Privilege of Poverty* approved by Innocent III has long been doubted due to its poor manuscript tradition. The only text was that of the *Firmamenta Trium Ordinum* (Paris 1512), V, fol.5r. Some scholars have maintained its authenticity despite the evidence of strong contrary arguments; cf. Z. Lazzeri, "Il 'Privilegium Paupertatis' concesso da Innocenzo II e che cosa fosse in originale," *Archivum Franciscanum Historicum* 11 (1918): 270–276; P. Sabatier, "Le Privilège de la pauvreté," *Revue d'Histoire Franciscaine* 1 (1924): 1–54; E. Grau, "Das Privilegium paupertatis Innocenz III," *Franziskanische Studien* 31 (1949): 337–349; E. Grau, "Das Privilegium paupertatis der hl. Klara. Geschicte und Bedeutung," *Wissenschaft und Weisheit* 38 (1975): 17–25. The recent edition of M.F. Becker, J.F. Godet, and T. Matura, *Claire D'Assise: Écrits* (Paris: Les Éditions du Cerf, 1985), 14, claims the existence of three ancient manuscripts which confirm the positions of these scholars. The translation which is presented here is based on the text published in this latest work.

of San Damiano in Assisi, professing the regular life, both those in the present, as well as those in the future for ever:

2. As is evident, you have renounced the desire for all temporal things, desiring to dedicate yourselves to the Lord alone. 3. Because of this, *since you have sold all things and given them to the poor* (cf. Lk 18:22), you propose not to have any possessions whatsoever, clinging in all things to the footprints of Him, *the Way, the Truth, and the Life* (Jn 14:6), Who, for our sake, was made poor. 4. Nor does a lack of possessions frighten you from a proposal of this sort; 5. *for the left hand* of the heavenly Spouse *is under your head* (cf. Ct 2:6) to support the weakness of your body, which you have placed under the law of your soul through an ordered charity. 6. Finally, He Who *feeds* the birds *of the heavens* (cf. Mt 6:26) and clothes *the lilies of the field* (cf. Mt 6:28) will not fail you in either food or clothing, until He ministers to you in heaven, when His *right hand* especially *will* more happily *embrace you* (cf. Ct 8:3) in the fullness of His [beatific] vision. 7. Therefore, we confirm with our apostolic authority, as you requested, your proposal *of most high poverty* (cf. 2 Cor 8:2), granting you by the authority of this letter that no one can compel you to receive possessions.

8. And if any woman does not wish to, or cannot observe a proposal of this sort, let her not have a dwelling place among you, but let her be transferred to another place.

9. Therefore, we decree that it may not be permitted to anyone to disturb you and your church rashly or to burden you with any kind of vexation. 10. If, therefore, any one, either an ecclesiastic or a secular, knowing this document of our confirmation and constitution, rashly attempts to oppose it, after the second or third warning—unless he has corrected his fault through an appropriate [act of] satisfaction—let him lose the dignity of his power and honor, know that he is subject to the divine judgement for the iniquity perpetrated, excluded from the most sacred Body and Blood of God and the Lord Jesus Christ, our Redeemer, and be subject to a severe punishment at the last judgement.

11. May the peace of our Lord Jesus Christ, however, be with all of you and with those who, in the same place, preserve a love in Christ, so that they may both receive the fruit of their good work here and, before the demanding Judge, discover the rewards of eternal peace.

Letter of Pope Honorius III
to Cardinal Hugolino (1217)

*The following document, the first among those papal documents con-
cerned with the followers of Saint Francis, is the response of Pope Honorius III to a letter written by Cardinal Hugolino dei Conti di Segni who
had in 1217 become Papal Legate for Lombardy and Tuscany, and appar-
ently for the Umbrian and Spoleto Valleys.*[1]

*Born in 1170, Hugolino was related to Pope Innocent III whose ser-
vice he entered after studies in Paris and Bologna. There is evidence that
his spiritual formation was influenced by the Cistercians and resulted in
his great interest in religious movements of the time. When we examine
the letters or documents written by Hugolino in 1216 and 1217, the pos-
sibility of his association with Jacques de Vitry remains strong. This could
explain his interest in the newly developing feminine religious foundations
and, hence, the Poor Ladies whose monasteries were beginning to appear
throughout his territories.*[2]

*The following letter is important in the papal legislation that these
new monasteries were exempt from the jurisdiction of the Bishops and
placed directly under that of the Pope. In effect, this meant that Hugolino,
as the plenipotentiary of Innocent III, became responsible for these con-
vents.*

Honorius, Bishop, servant of the servants of God, sends greetings and
the Apostolic blessing to our brother [Hugolino], Bishop of Ostia and Legate of the Apostolic See.

Your letter which was delivered to us holds that very many virgins
and other women desire to flee the pomp and wealth of this world and make
some homes for themselves in which they may live not possessing anything
under heaven except these homes and the oratories to be constructed for

---

[1] The original Latin text can be found in *Bullarium Franciscanum* I, 1011.

[2] There is abundant material concerning Cardinal Hugolino dei Conti di Segni. See
Guido Levi, *Registri dei Cardinali Ugolino d'Ostia e Ottaviano degli Ubaldini* (1890); "Documenti
ad illustrazione del Registro del Cardinale Ugolino d'Ostia," *Archivo d. R. Società Romana di
Storia Patria XII* (Roma 1899), 241–326; J. Vosius, *Gesta et monumenta Gregorii IX cum scholiis*
(Romae 1586).

them. Because of the instability of worldly prosperity, a nobility seems to promise a prosperous state of life in their world, as He Who breathes where He wills inspires them to flee from the face of the globe, after they drink the wine of compunction and receive an evidently revealed sign. Since for this purpose, foundations are being offered to you by many people in the name of the Church of Rome, some of the people wish to reserve for themselves the improvement, establishment and abandonment of these foundations, and are not afraid, thereby, of impeding the salutary resolutions of these women. Therefore, Your Fraternity has requested that we take care to provide for them with paternal solicitude.

Wishing, therefore, to impart our Apostolic favor upon the pious desires of these women in such a way that they may attain the result of their petition, and that both the Bishops of the diocese and others in whose parishes these women set up their homes, may not have a just reason for complaint, we command you through the authority of this letter to receive, legally as property, the foundations of this kind in the name of the Church of Rome and to ordain that the churches built in these places be solely under the jurisdiction of the Apostolic See. This is so that no Bishop or any other ecclesiastic or secular person is able to claim any right for himself, as long as these women be without possessions, tithes and wills from which damage may accrue to the Ordinaries of the places and to other prelates of churches. If in the future it happens that they do not have possessions, or the other things mentioned above, we do not want these Bishops, or the others, to be defrauded canonically under the pretext of such an exemption.

Given at the Lateran on the twenty-seventh of August in the third year of our pontificate.

The Rule of Cardinal Hugolino (1219)

In his letter to Pope Honorius III, August 27, 1218, Cardinal Hugolino, Papal Legate in Tuscany and Lombardy, described communities of the second order, that is, of religious women, who were living in those territories. Many stood in need of both spiritual and administrative assistance which the corresponding male orders were reluctant or unable to supply. The Premonstratentians, for example, had withdrawn from pastoral assistance to their communities of second order women in 1200, the Cistercians in 1212. Furthermore, many women, inspired by the preaching of the Mendicant Friars Preachers and the Friars Minor, had formed communities based on the ideals of Saint Dominic or Saint Francis. Eventually these communities were neglected because the friars were itinerant and, hence, reluctant to establish fixed residences in or near these communities.

The following year, 1219, Hugolino received authority from the Pope to correct this situation and, in doing so, saw the need to provide a more stable rule or form of life for the Damianites, as they were called. The following document, the Rule of Cardinal Hugolino, was provided by him for the Poor Ladies of San Damiano sometime after August 27, 1218, since there is no mention of a Rule in the Pope's letter.[1] Within the following year, however, four ecclesial documents can be found addressed to the Damianite monasteries of Monticello (27 July 1219), Monte Lucio in Perugia (29 July 1219), Santa Maria extra Portam de Caniullia in Siena (29 July 1219), and Santa Maria de Grataiola in the diocese of Luca (30 July 1219). In three of these documents, Cardinal Hugolino writes of a form of life that the nuns received from him which was based on the Rule of Saint Benedict.[2]

The text that follows is most helpful in providing many insights into St. Clare's desire to have her own Rule with its insistence upon poverty and mutual charity officially recognized by the Church.[3]

---

[1]Cf. L. Oliger, "De Origine Regularum Ordine S. Clarae," *Archivum Franciscanum Storicum* V (1912): 181–209, 413–447.

[2]Cf. *Bullarium Franciscanum*, ed. J. Sbaralea (Roma, 1759): I 3, 4, 13.

[3]The translation contained in this volume follows the Latin text presented in *Escritos de santa Clara y documentos contemporaneos*, ed. I Omaechevarria, (Madrid: Biblioteca de autores christianos: 1970).

1. Gregory, Bishop, servant of the servants of God, to his beloved daughters in Christ, health and apostolic benediction.

When that which is just and becoming is asked of us, both order and the rigor of impartiality demand that it be brought to its due conclusion through the solicitude of our office. Therefore, beloved daughters in Christ, agreeing in a grateful spirit with your just requests, we have decided to incorporate in this letter the *Form and Manner of Living* which we delivered to all the Poor Cloistered Nuns when in a lesser rank we were performing the duties of Legate in parts of Tuscany and Lombardy. We confirm this *Form and Manner of Living* by our apostolic authority and we strengthen it with the protection of this present document, desiring that it always be inviolably observed in your monastery. The tenor of this life is as follows:

2. Every true Religion and approved institute of life endures by certain rules and requirements, and by certain disciplinary laws. Unless each sister has diligently striven to observe a certain correct rule and discipline for living, she will deviate from righteousness to the degree that she does not observe the guidelines of righteousness. She runs the risk of falling at the point where, in virtue of her free choice, she neglected to set for herself a sure and stable foundation for making progress. Therefore, beloved daughters in Christ, because you have chosen under the inspiration of divine grace to travel the hard and narrow path that leads to life, and to lead a poor life in order to gain eternal riches, we have decided that the form and the observance of this way of life should be briefly set down, in order that each one of you may know what she should do and what she should avoid, lest excusing herself perhaps because of ignorance she dangerously presume what is not allowed and prohibited, or lest she little by little through laxity and detestable sloth more dangerously neglect what has been condemned. Therefore, in virtue of obedience we strictly enjoin each and every one of you, and we command that you humbly and devotedly accept this form of life, fully explained below, which we are sending you, and that you and those who follow you strive to observe it inviolably for all time.

3. So that the order of your life, firmly built and established on Christ after the manner of and in imitation of those who have served the Lord without complaint and have crowned the beginning of their blessed and holy way of life with the most blessed conclusion of perseverance, may be able to grow into a holy temple in the Lord and by following the footsteps of the saints may be able to reach the reward of such a high vocation directly and happily, we give you the *Rule of Saint Benedict* to be observed in all things which are in no way contrary to that same *Form of Life* that was

given to you by us and by which you have especially chosen to live.[4] This *Rule of Saint Benedict* is known to embody the perfection of virtue and the greatest discretion. It has been devoutly accepted from the very beginning by the holy Fathers and venerably approved by the Roman Church.[5]

4. Therefore, it is proper and it is a duty that all those women who, after condemning and abandoning the vanity of the world, have resolved to embrace and hold to your Order, should observe this law of life and discipline, and remain enclosed the whole time of their life.[6] After they have entered the enclosure of this Order and have assumed the religious habit, they should never be granted any permission or faculty to leave [this enclosure], unless perhaps some are transferred to another place to plant or build up this same Order.[7] Moreover, it is fitting that, when they die, both ladies as well as servants who are professed, they should be buried within the enclosure.

The hard and austere realities, through which according to the Religion one is led to God and which must necessarily be observed, must be

---

[4]For a summary of the controversies concerning the relationship between St. Clare and the Benedictine Rule, L. Oliger, "De Origine Regularum Ordine S. Clarae," *Archivum Franciscanum Historicum* V (1912): 181–184, 203–205. The Rule of Saint Benedict was given to the community as a necessary juridical basis in light of Canon 13 of the IV Lateran Council. In a letter to Agnes of Prague, Pope Innocent IV maintained that it was never binding upon the sisters except in regard to "obedience, renunciation of ownership, and perpetual chastity." Cf. *Bullarium Franciscanum*, ed. J. Sbaralea (Rome, 1759): I, 316; *Annales Minorum*, III ed. (Florence: Ad Aquas Claras: 1931): 1243, n. 28, iii, 96. See also L. DeSeilhac, O.S.B., "L'utilisation de la Règle de saint Benoît dans les monastères feminins," *Atti del 7 Congresso Internazionale di studi sull'alto medioevo*, Spoleto 1982, 527–545; also J. Leclercq, O.S.B. "Femminile, monachesimo," *Dizionario degli Istituti di perfezione* 3 (1976), 1446–1451. Concerning the expression "Form of Life" see *Rule of St. Clare* and *Testament*, supra pp. 54–77.

[5]For an excellent summary of the evolution of the legislation governing enclosure see, Jane Tibbets Schulenberg, "Strict Active Enclosure and Its Effects on the Female Monastic Experience (ca. 500–1100)," *Medieval Religious Women, Volume One: Distant Echoes*, eds. John A. Nichols and Lillian Thomas Shank (Kalamazoo: Cistercian Publications, 1984), 51–86.

[6]The themes raised in this statement—"condemning and abandoning the world," "law of life and discipline," and "strict enclosure"—touch on the very nature of the monastic enclosure. For an excellent treatment of this subject, see R. Manselli, "La Chiesa e il francescanesimo feminile nel secolo XIII," *Movimento religioso femminile e francescanesimo nel secolo XIII* (Assisi: Società Internazionale di Studi Francescani, 1980), 239–261; also J.T. Schulenberg, ibid.

[7]While enclosure was observed in varying degrees in earlier periods, the thirteenth century witnessed a codification of legislation of which the Rule of Hugolino for the Poor Ladies was typical. Cf. J. Leclercq, "Il monachesimo femminile nei secoli XII e XIII," *Movimento religioso femminile e francescanesimo nel secolo XIII* (Assisi: Società Internazionale di Studi Francescani, 1980), 61–99. The enclosure described in Hugolino's text prefigures the type that became generally enforced in 1298 with the Bull *"Periculoso"* of Pope Boniface VIII. The Council of Trent reinforced these provisions in 1563.

explained to all who wish to enter this Religion and are received, before they actually enter and change their garb, lest ignorance be their excuse later on. One should not be received who proves to be less than sufficiently fit for the observance of this life because of age, a sickness or a mental deficiency. Therefore, any occasion for receiving such a person should be cautiously and diligently avoided, even if at some time for a reasonable cause a dispensation has to be given to someone.

All those received into the enclosure should, according to custom, quickly put aside their secular clothes and, if they are old enough to understand, they should make their profession within a few days to the Abbess.[8] This should also be observed as far as the servants are concerned.[9]

5. Concerning the offering of the Divine Office to the Lord both day and night, let it be observed that those who know how to read the Psalms should celebrate the regular Office.[10] If they also know how to sing, it is permissible for them to celebrate the Office and praise the Lord of all by singing at the prescribed Hours. This they should do with the greatest gravity and modesty, with humility and great devotion, so that those listening to them may be edified for salvation. Those who do not know the Psalms should strive, according to custom, to recite the *Lord's Prayer* devoutly to their Creator during these hours.

If there are some young or even older ones who are humble and capable of learning, the Abbess, if she sees fit, may appoint a capable and discreet mistress for them to teach them to read.

6. Let a continuous silence be kept by all at all times, so that it is not allowed either for one to talk to another or for another to talk to her without permission, except for those on whom some teaching office or duty has been enjoined, which cannot be fittingly discharged in silence.[11] Permis-

---

[8]This was not the custom of the Benedictine communities where a period of formation was envisioned prior to profession.

[9]In addition to those living in the community who were too young to be professed there were also others who were *conversi* (penitents) or servants who dedicated themselves to the service of the Church or Monastery. Cf. D. Knowles, "Gilbertini e Gilbertine," *Dizionario degli Istituti di Perfezione* IV (Roma: 1977) 1178–1182.

[10]The ladies of San Damiano differed from other communities in this regard. The second order of Premonstratensians, for example, recited the Divine Office in a low voice while the clerics sang it. Among the second order Humiliati, the brothers and sisters came together in small chapels to listen as the chaplains recited the Office. Cf. L. Zanoni, *Gli Umiliati nei loro rapporti con l'eresia, l'industria della lana, ed i communi nei secoli XII e XIII* (Roma: 1970): 103.

[11]For further insights into the monastic tradition of silence see: Ambrose G. Wathen, *The Meaning of Silence in the Rule of St. Benedict* (Kalamazoo: Cistercian Studies 22, 1973). Note especially the conclusions, p. 228. Also the introduction to Robert A. Barakat, *The Cistercian Sign Language: A Study in Non-Verbal Communication* (Kalamazoo: Cistercian Publications 22, 1975) pp. 11–27. For a comparison with the practices of Cistercian nuns of the period, cf. Una Monoca Certosina, "Certosine," *Dizionario degli Istituti di Perfezione* II, (Roma: 1975): 773–775.

sion may be given to these to speak about those things which pertain to their office or duty, where, when, and how the Abbess sees fit.

When some religious or secular person of whatever dignity seeks to speak to one of the ladies, let the Abbess be notified first.[12] If she gives permission, let the lady have at least two others appointed by the Abbess to accompany her to the parlor, who will listen to all that is said to her and what she says to others.

Let this be observed firmly by all, the sick as well as the healthy, so that they speak together neither among themselves nor with others unless there are at least three persons present. The exceptions to this are those who, as stated above, are assigned to various offices and duties, and those who need privacy of speech to a priest in confession and to a Visitator concerning the common life and the regular observance of discipline. However, even this should not be done unless there are at least two persons sitting not far away who can see those confessing or talking and likewise be seen by them. Even the Abbess herself should diligently guard this law of speaking, so that all matter for detraction may be removed. However, when she finds it expedient, she can speak privately or publicly at competent hours with her sisters about those things that need expression.

7. The Sisters are held to the following observance of fasting: they should fast daily at all times, abstaining likewise on Wednesdays and Fridays outside of Lent from fruit or vegetables and wine, unless a principal feast of some saint occurs and should be celebrated on those days. If fruit or fresh vegetables are available on these Wednesdays and Fridays, they should be served to sustain the sisters. But they should fast on bread and water for four days a week during the greater Lent, and for three days a week during the Lent of Saint Martin. They may also do this of their own free will on all solemn vigils. However, the very young sisters or the old and those who are altogether debilitated physically or mentally should not be permitted to observe this law of fast and abstinence. They should be mercifully dispensed in regard to food and fasting according to their debility.

8. Let the greatest care and diligence be afforded the sick. The sick should be served kindly and solicitously in a spirit of charity according to what is possible and appropriate both in the food which their sickness requires as well as in other necessary things. Those who are sick should have their own place, if this is ever possible, where they may remain separated from the healthy, so that their well-being and quiet may not be disturbed or dissipated. Those who are not burdened with a very serious illness may

---

[12]The preferred term in this *Rule of Hugolino* is *domina* (lady) in contrast to *soror* (sister) in the *Rule of Saint Clare*.

lie upon straw-pallets and have a feather pillow. But those who are gravely sick may lie upon mattresses, if they can be conveniently found. But all the sick may have woolen slippers which are soled if it can be done. These they can keep and wear, when it is necessary.

9. The following should be observed regarding clothing: each one may have two tunics and a mantle besides a hair shirt or a woven one if they have it, or one of sackcloth. They may also have scapulars of smooth, religious cloth or of woven cloth, if they wish, which are of fitting width and length as the nature and size of each one demands. They should be clothed in these when they are working or doing something which they can not fittingly do wearing a mantle. If they wish to have the scapulars together with the mantles, or even wish to sleep in them, they are not prohibited from doing so. They can be without them sometimes, if it seems fitting to the Abbess, when perhaps because of excessive heat or the like they are too heavy for the sisters to wear. If this precept about wearing the scapular seems too burdensome or troublesome for some to the extent that they can not be inclined or induced to accept it, the Abbess may dispense with it. But those who accept the scapular are acting much more uprightly and are much more pleasing to us, and we believe that they are much more pleasing to God as well.[13]

Let them sleep on planks of wood. If they wish and it seems fitting to the Abbess, these planks may be covered with a mat or a piece of cloth filled with a little straw or hay or something of the kind which is in keeping with their Religion and which can be found in that place. They may also have pillows of straw or hay. They may also have woolen blankets or bedspreads, if wool can easily be acquired.

Their hair should be cut in a circle. No sister should be tonsured, unless an evident physical infirmity demands it.

10. Concerning the entrance of persons into the monastery, we firmly and strictly decree that an Abbess or her sisters may never permit any religious person or secular of whatever dignity to enter the monastery. This is allowed to no one except to whom or concerning whom permission has been granted by the Supreme Pontiff or by us, or following us by him to whom, as to us, the Lord Pope has especially entrusted the concern and special care over you.

You should take solicitous care that, when a Cardinal or a Bishop of the Roman Church, who has been especially designated for you, has passed from this life, you always ask from the Lord Pope another from his brother-

---

[13]The exhortation to wear the scapular implies some lack of agreement between the Cardinal and the sisters as to its use.

bishops, to whom you ought to have special recourse through a Visitator or your own messenger, when a necessity arises.

Excused from the above law of entrance into the monastery are those on whom it is incumbent to enter in order to do some necessary work.

But even if one of the Cardinals sometime comes to a monastery of this Order and would like to enter, he should be received with reverence and devotion, but he should be asked to be accompanied by one or two suitable companions. Any other prelate, to whom permission is ever given to enter, may be content with only one religious and suitable companion. If, by chance, permission is ever given to some Bishop to celebrate Mass within the enclosure for the blessing of an abbess or for consecrating some sister as a nun or for some other reason, let him be content with as few and as virtuous companions and assistants as he can. Let this permission be rarely given to anyone.

No one, whether healthy or sick, should speak with anyone except in the manner mentioned above. Particular caution should be taken that those, to whom permission has been given to enter the monastery, be such in their words and character, in their life and manners, that they edify those who see them and thus are incapable of generating matter for true scandal.

11. When they have their own chaplain, let him be religious in life and manner, and possess a good reputation.[14] He should not be too young, but of a suitable age. When this chaplain sees that one of the sisters, who is gripped by a serious bodily illness, is coming to her end and she finds it necessary to confess her sins or receive the Sacrament of the Body of the Lord, he may enter the enclosure clothed in a white stole and maniple. After he has heard her confession and has given her the Sacrament of the Body of the Lord, he should leave, dressed as he entered, and not delay there any longer. Let him also conduct himself in this way at the commendation of her soul. He may not enter the enclosure to conduct the obsequies at the grave; this duty should be fulfilled in the chapel. Nevertheless, if the Abbess sees fit that he should enter for these obsequies, let him enter in the manner described above, and after the burial let him leave without delay. If, however, it is necessary for someone to enter to dig or open a grave, or certainly to close it afterwards, it is licit for him or anyone else who is upright and suitable to enter for this purpose. But

---

[14]The chaplain is distinct from the Visitator and need not have been a friar. He administered to some of the sacramental needs of the sisters. A friar could not be their confessor only in grave need. In her *Rule* Clare makes a specific request regarding the composition of the friars attached to the monastery (cf. XII 5) and also changes the prescriptions concerning the chaplain (cf. XII 6–8).

for the rest let him not presume to enter the monastery. When some sister wishes to speak to him about confession, let her speak to him through the speaking-grille, and let him listen to her there.

Let no one speak through the iron grille through which they receive Communion or listen to the Office, except when permission is sometimes given to someone for a reasonable cause or when necessity demands it. But this should happen very rarely. Cloth should be placed on the inside of these iron grilles in such a way that no sister is able to see anything in the chapel outside. Let them have wooden doors with iron bars and a key, so that they remain closed and not be opened except for the reasons mentioned above, or for the purpose of listening at times to the Word of God to be proposed in the chapel by a fitting person who must be approved for his faith, reputation and knowledge.

When the Sisters do not have their own chaplain, they can hear Mass celebrated by any priest of good reputation and upright life. However, let them strive to procure and receive the Sacraments of Penance and the Body of the Lord from a man who is discreet, religious in life and manners, and suitable in age, except perhaps when a sister is on the point of a dangerous necessity.

12. Concerning the Visitator of this Religion the following must be carefully provided for: whoever is to be appointed as the general, or even sometimes, the special Visitator, should be such that there is full knowledge and a guarantee concerning his faith, his life and his character. When he comes to enter a monastery, let him show and manifest himself in such a way in all things, that he stimulates all from the good to the better, and always inflames and enkindles them to the love of God and to mutual love for one another.

Let [the Visitator] zealously seek the truth about their condition and about the observance of their Religion from all generally, and particularly from individuals. When he finds something that should be reformed or corrected, let him—with discretion and with zeal for charity and love for justice—reform and correct it both in the head and in the members, as seems best. But let him observe the manner of speaking as described above, so that whether he speaks with all or with many at one time, or with one privately, there may be at least two others sitting in his sight at a distance, so that the integrity of a good reputation may be preserved in all things. But if he should come upon something which he cannot suitably correct by himself, he should refer it to his superior, so that it may be corrected by his counsel and precept as it demands.

But let the Abbess beware lest the condition of her monastery in the observance of the Rule and in the unity of mutual charity be at any time hidden from the Visitator by herself or by the other ladies. This should be a wicked charge and an offense that would have to be seriously punished. In fact, we desire and decree that those things which should be established or emended according to the form of their life, should be diligently suggested or proposed to the Visitator privately and publicly as it may best be done. Whoever does otherwise, whether it is the Abbess or the others, should be punished appropriately as is proper.

In a similar way, if the chaplain is reprehensible in any thing in which he cannot conveniently and should not be supported, let him, after he has been forewarned, be modestly and reasonably punished by the Visitator. If he does not wish or spurns to amend [his ways], let him not be kept any longer as chaplain.

13. Let one of the sisters, who certainly fears God, who is mature in character, who is diligent, discreet and of fitting age, be appointed to take care of the entrance to the monastery. Let her so diligently take care of and guard the key to the door, that the door could never be opened without her or without her knowledge. Let there be another [sister] equally suitable and designated as her companion who may take her place in all things, when she is occupied and detained by some reasonable cause or necessary employment. Let them very zealously take care and beware that the door never remains open, except when it can be fittingly done for a very short time.

Let the entrance be very well secured with door panels, strong beams, and iron bars. Let it never be left without a guard, except perhaps for a moment, unless it is firmly locked with a key. Nor should it be opened immediately at every knock, unless it is undoubtedly known beforehand that it is such a person for whom the door should be opened without any hesitation according to the decree which is contained above in that *Form* about those who are about to enter religion.

But if some work has to be done sometime within the monastery, it may be entered by some seculars or other persons in order to accomplish it. But let the Abbess carefully provide that, while the work is being done, some other suitable person be appointed to guard the door. She may open it for those persons designated to do the work and not allow others to enter. For at such a time and always as far as they are reasonably able, let the ladies most zealously guard against being seen by seculars or persons from the outside.

14. We desire and decree that this *formula* for living, briefly described above, be diligently and everywhere observed in a uniform way by every sister, to the extent that unity of life and conformity of ways may unite and join in a bond of love those sisters who are separated by the distance between places. But if the far seeing discretion of the Roman Church, by reason of the nature of the place or concern for individuals, decides that

some sisters should receive a dispensation in some necessity, other sisters who do not need a similar dispensation should firmly guard and live up to their manner of life.

Therefore, let no one dare to mitigate this document of confirmation, or dare to oppose it with rash temerity. If anyone shall have presumed to attempt this, let him know that he will incur the wrath of Almighty God and His holy Apostles Peter and Paul.

Given at Rome, at St. Peter's, on the 12th of April, in the second year of our pontificate.

Letter of Cardinal Hugolino (1220)

The author of the Legend of Saint Clare writes of an exchange of letters that took place between Saint Clare and Cardinal Hugolino.[1] Unfortunately, only this document and another written by Hugolino shortly after his election as Pope remain giving us insights into their correspondence.[2]

This letter was written by Hugolino after a visit to San Damiano during which he celebrated Holy Week with the Poor Ladies. It is difficult to determine the precise year of this visit, although it may well have been when the Cardinal was visiting Saint Francis in Assisi shortly after the saint's return from the Orient, that is, 1220.[3] That was the year in which Hugolino was officially named the protector of the Order.[4]

1. Hugolino, a wretched and sinful man, the Bishop of Ostia, commends himself—all that he is and all he is capable of being—to his very dear sister in Christ and mother of his salvation, the servant of Christ, Lady Clare.

2. My very dear sister in Christ! From that very hour when the necessity of returning here separated me from your holy conversation and tore me away from that joy of heavenly treasure, such a bitterness of heart, such an abundance of tears and such an immensity of sorrow have overcome me that, unless I find at the feet of Jesus the consolation of His usual kindness, I fear that I will always encounter such trials which will cause my spirit to melt away. And this is reasonable because, just as an overwhelming sorrow ensued when the Lord was taken away from the disciples and nailed to the gallows of the Cross, so I remain desolate by your absence from me. For that glorious joy, with which I discussed the Body of Christ with you while celebrating Easter with you and the other servants of Christ, has forsaken me. And although I have always known and have considered myself to be a sinner, yet after having recognized a sure sign of your

---

[1]Cf. *Legend of Saint Clare* 27, infra p. 97.

[2]Kajetan Esser studied the authenticity of this letter in his article "Die Briefe Gregors IX an die hl. von Assisi," *Franziskanische Studien* 35 (1953), 274–295. The original Latin text of this letter can be found in the "Chronica XXIV Generalium," *Analecta Franciscana* III, 183.

[3]Concerning the dating of this letter, cf. K. Esser, *ibidem*, 281–283.

[4]See H. Fischer, *Der hl. Franziskus von Assisi während der Jähre 1219–1221* (Frieburg: Schweiz 1907) 81.

merits and having observed the rigor of your way of life, I have learned with certainty that I have been weighed down with such a burden of sin and have so offended the Lord of the whole universe, that I am not worthy of be freed from earthly concerns and be associated with the company of the elect, unless your prayers and tears obtain for me pardon for my sins.

3. Therefore, I entrust my soul and commend my spirit to you, just as Jesus on the Cross commended His spirit to the Father, so that on the day of judgement you may answer for me, if you have not been concerned for and intent on my salvation. For I have a certain belief that you will obtain from the most high Judge whatever the insistence of so great a devotion and abundance of tears implores. The Lord Pope is not coming to Assisi now, but I will seize the first opportunity in my desire to see you and your sisters. Greetings to the virgin Agnes, my sister, and to all your sisters in Christ. Amen.

Letter of Pope Gregory IX (1228)

Even after his election to the papacy on March 19, 1227, Cardinal Hugo-
lino maintained his contacts with the Poor Ladies of San Damiano for he,
no doubt, had come to see them as a powerful force of renewal in the
Church. This letter, written between January and July of 1228, sometime
before his visit to Assisi for the ceremonies of the canonization of Saint
Francis, contains a marvelous compendium of his understanding of the
contemplative life and its role in the Church. It is, moreover, a document
that reveals a Pope Gregory IX who is more a theologian than a canonist,
and more a man of the Church than a politician.

1. To my beloved daughter, the Abbess, and to the community of the
Enclosed Nuns of San Damiano in Assisi:

2. God the Father, to Whom you have offered yourselves as servants,
has mercifully adopted you as His daughters. Through the operation of the
grace of the Holy Spirit, He has espoused you, who are to be crowned in
the kingdom of heaven with your heavenly Spouse, His only begotten Son,
the Lord Jesus Christ. Therefore, since above all things you are bound to
love your Spouse, Who loves those who love Him and makes them co-
heirs, you should delight with all your affections in Him alone, so that
nothing may ever separate you from His love. For divinely inspired to this
end you have chosen to place yourselves in an enclosure, so that you may
profitably renounce the world and all that is in it and, while embracing
your Spouse with an untainted love, run after the odor of His ointments,
until He introduces you into the chamber of His mother to be refreshed
forever by the sweetness of His love (cf. Ct 1:3; 3:4).

3. We certainly hope and have confidence that, if you pay careful and
diligent attention, those things which now seem bitter will become whole-
some and sweet for you, what is hard will become soft and what is rough
will become smooth, so that you will exult, if you merit to suffer these
things for Christ Who endured for us the passion of an infamous death.

Truly, because you are our consolation among the innumerable, bitter, and endless trials by which we are constantly being afflicted, we ask
you all and we encourage you in the Lord Jesus Christ and, what is more,
we command by this Apostolic Letter that, walking and living in the Spirit

and forgetting the past *as you have learned from us* (cf. 1 Th 4:1), you be like the Apostle *always intent on what is ahead by striving after better gifts* (cf. Ph 3:13; 1 Cor 12:31), so that abounding more and more in virtue you may cause God to be glorified in you and fill up our joy, as we embrace you in intimate love as our special daughters (or ladies, if it is right to say this, because you are the spouses of the Lord).

4. Because we are confident you have been made one spirit with Christ, we ask you to remember us always in your prayers by raising your pious hands in incessant supplication to God Who knows that surrounded as we are by so many dangers we can not prevail because of human frailty. But with God strengthening us with His power, may He enable us to fulfill so worthily the ministry entrusted to us by Him, that it will bring glory to Him, joy to the angels and salvation to us and to those entrusted to our care.

Letter of Cardinal Raynaldus (1228)

Cardinal Rainaldus dei Conti di Segni, later Pope Alexander IV (December 12, 1254–May 25, 1261), was of the same illustrious family as Popes Innocent III and Gregory IX; in fact, his famous uncle, Gregory IX, seems to have discovered great promise in him since the young man appears frequently at his side. In 1221, Raynaldus accompanied the then Cardinal Hugolino throughout Tuscany and Lombardy and, after his election to the papacy in 1227, to Rieti and Perugia.[1] It must have been during one of these journeys that he encountered the Poor Ladies of San Damiano and came to admire their way of life.

Shortly after his election, Pope Gregory IX made his nephew a Cardinal Deacon and shortly thereafter made him Cardinal Protector of the Poor Ladies. As the list of monasteries at the beginning of this letter indicates, the number of followers of Saint Clare had considerably grown. Thus this letter is of considerable historical importance since it provides both a list of the existing foundations of Poor Ladies in 1228 and an insight into the role of their visitator.[2]

1. To my dear mothers, sisters and daughters, the servants of Christ the Spouse, the Son of God; to the abbesses and communities of the poor monasteries of San Damiano of Assisi: Santa Maria de ValleGloria, Perugia, Foligno, Florence, Lucca, Siena, Arezzo, Borgo, Acquaviva, Narni, Città di Castello, Todi, Santa Seraphia de Cortona, Faenza, Milan, Padua, Trent, Verona, Orvieto, Gubbio, San Paolo de Terni, San Paolo de Spoleto and de Cortona: Raynaldus by divine kindness, Cardinal Deacon of San Eustachio, Chamberlain of the Papal Household, [wishes you] health and an introduction into the royal wedding-chamber of the Spouse.

2. Let your lips return the praises due to the Creator for His gener-

---

[1]Detailed information concerning the life of Cardinal Raynaldus can be found in L. Pellegrini, *Alessandro IV e i Francescani (1254–61)* (Roma: Studi e testi francescani 34, 1966). See also Alexander IV, *Les Registres*, ed. C. Bourel de la Roncière, et al., 3 v. (Paris 1902–53); F. Tenckhoff, *Papst Alexander IV* (Paderborn, 1907).
[2]Detailed information concerning this document, as well as bibliographical information concerning the monasteries mentioned therein, can be found in *Escritos de Santa Clara y Documentos Complementarios*, ed. I. Omaechevarria (Madrid: Biblioteca de Autores Cristianos, 1983) 356–361.

osity. Let the strength of your soul be stretched in its desire for Him Whose abundance is so great in its blessings and gifts that we are completely instructed by the blessings of this life in what has been prepared for us in eternity by the everlasting grace of His kindness. Behold your father and lord! God has made him His Vicar, yet his love for you has not cooled or diminished. It increases daily in its strength. For it was appropriate and fitting that *the friend of the Bridegroom* (cf. Jn 3:29), the Vicar of Christ, the Shepherd and Bishop of the universal flock, be bound by an eternal love to these young ladies upon whom rests the Spouse's most chaste love.

We are not his successor, but since he is involved in many difficult problems, we have approached him so that he may do through his messenger what he can not do himself. For even the very King and Lord of heaven, Who has all power in and through Himself, constantly operates through the ministry of His messengers.

3. My very dear sisters, the Lord Pope has wished to entrust the care of you to me, because until this very moment we have bestowed upon you such a sincere love that with our whole heart we are zealous for your welfare, and such a way as he himself showed towards you when he was serving in a lesser position. Consequently and as a token of the paternal solicitude for our daughters, we have favored the requests of Brother Pacificus who is very devoted to God and to you. The burden [of being Visitator] seemed unbearable to him. Therefore, we have chosen our very dear friend, Brother Philip, who will be designated as your Visitator by a special mandate of the Supreme Pontiff. Brother Philip is rooted in the innermost depth of our heart and is a religious who fears God. We command you by this document in virtue of strict obedience to receive him with due reverence as a servant of God, as someone zealous for your welfare and as one who has endured very many hardships and difficulties for you. In all things listen to salutary admonitions and commands. In all things comply with his precepts and wishes as one possessing the fullest powers. Know that we will never revoke anything of those things which he has ordained for punishment or for anything else.

May final perseverance and a most happy end be given to you all, and may the blessing of Almighty God descend upon you forever.

Given at Perugia, on the fifteenth kalends of September [August 18], in the second year of the pontificate of Lord Pope Gregory the Ninth.

The Privilege of Poverty
of Pope Gregory IX, 1228

Between the promulgation of the Privilege of Poverty of Pope Innocent III in 1216 and the composition of this version twelve years later, the fame of the Poor Ladies of San Damiano grew quite rapidly. As we have seen, Cardinal Hugolino expressed his enthusiasm for them in a letter to Pope Honorius III which prompted the Pope in 1218 to extend the permission of living in such radical poverty to the new foundations springing from San Damiano and to appoint Hugolino as their protector.[1]

Upon his election to the papacy, Hugolino, now Gregory IX, renewed the Privilege of Poverty on September 17, 1228, in similar, although abbreviated terms. When studying the events of the following years, however, we might wonder if he was thoroughly aware of or committed to the implications of his decree, for he subsequently offered relaxations and dispensations to the Poor Ladies at San Damiano and elsewhere.[2] *Clare, then, petitioned that the Privilege be conceded to the other monasteries attempting to follow her form of life. Thus the text of Pope Gregory IX became widely diffused among the Poor Ladies and became a foundation block of her Rule.*

1. Gregory, Bishop, servant of the servants of God, to his beloved daughters in Christ, Clare and the other servants of Christ gathered together in the church of San Damiano of the diocese of Assisi, health and apostolic benediction.

2. As is evident, you have renounced the desire for all temporal things, desiring to dedicate yourselves to the Lord alone. 3. Because of this, *since you have sold all things and given them to the poor* (cf. Lk 18:22), you propose not to have any possessions whatsoever, clinging in all things to the footprints of Him, *the Way, the Truth, and the Life* (Jn 14:6) Who, for our sake, was made poor. 4. Nor does a lack of possessions frighten you from a proposal of this sort; 5. *for the left hand* of the heavenly Spouse *is under your head*

---

[1] Cf. supra, *Letter of Pope Honorius III to Cardinal Hugolino*, pp. 85–86. For a detailed exposition of the background of this document, see *Escritos de Santa Clara y Documentos Complementarios*, ed. I. Omaechevarria (Madrid: Biblioteca de Autores Cristianos, 1983) 229–232.

[2] For further detail, cf. I. Omaechevarria, ibidem, 230–231.

(cf. Ct 2:6) to support the weakness of your body, which you have placed under the law of your soul through an ordered charity. 6. Finally, He Who *feeds* the birds *of the heavens* (cf. Mt 6:26) and clothes *the lilies of the field* (cf. Mt 6:28) will not fail you in either food or clothing, until He ministers to you in heaven, when His *right hand* especially *will* more happily *embrace you* (cf. Ct 8:3) in the fullness of His sight. 7. Therefore, we confirm with our apostolic authority, as you requested, your proposal *of most high poverty* (cf. 2 Cor 8:2), granting you by the authority of [these] present that no one can compel you to receive possessions.

8. Therefore, let no one be permitted to tamper with this document of our concession or dare to oppose it with rash temerity. 9. If anyone shall presume to attempt this, let him know that he will incur the wrath of Almighty God and His blessed apostles, Peter and Paul.

10. Given at Perugia, the 17th of September, in the second year of our pontificate.

Letter of Saint Agnes of Assisi
to Her Sister Saint Clare (1230)

Agnes of Assisi, a younger sister of Saint Clare, was sent as abbess to the new foundation of Poor Ladies in Monticello, Florence, and remained there for a period of more than twenty years.[1] It is not difficult to imagine that there was a considerable exchange of letters between the two sisters; however this is the only one that remains.[2]

The letter can be dated at some time in 1230, that is, a year or so after her arrival in Monticello, and beautifully expresses her sorrow at being separated not only from Clare but also from the other Poor Ladies at San Damiano. Therefore it is another marvelous example of the affective literature that is found in the early documents of the followers of Saint Clare.

1. To her venerable mother and the woman beloved in Christ beyond all others, to the Lady Clare and her whole community, Agnes, the lowly and least of Christ's servants, humbly presents herself with all obedience and devotion with best wishes for her and them for whatever is sweet and precious in the eyes of the most High King.

2. The lot of all has been so established that one can never remain in the same state or condition. When someone thinks that she is doing well, it is then that she is plunged into adversity. Therefore, you should know, Mother, that my soul and body suffer great distress and immense sadness, that I am burdened and tormented beyond measure and am almost incapable of speaking, because I have been physically separated from you and my other sisters with whom I had hoped to live and die in this world. This distress has a beginning, but it knows no end. It never seems to diminish; it always gets worse. It came to me recently, but it tends to ease off very little. It is always with me and never wants to leave me. I believed that our life and death would be one, just as our manner of life in heaven would be one, and that we who have one and the same flesh and blood would be

---

[1] Further information concerning the life of Agnes of Assisi can be found in A. DeSerent, "Agnès d'Assise," *Dictionnaire d'Histoire et de Géographie Ecclésiastiques* 1 (1912), c. 976–977.

[2] The original Latin text of this letter can be found in the *Chronica XXIV Generalium, Analecta Franciscana* III, 173–182.

buried in the same grave. But I see that I have been deceived. I have been restrained; I have been abandoned; I have been afflicted on every side.

3. My dearest sisters, sympathize with me, I beg you, and mourn with me so that you may never suffer such things and *see whether there is any suffering like my suffering* (cf. Lam 1:12). This sorrow is always afflicting me, this emotional tenderness is always torturing me, this ardent desire is always consuming me. As a result, distress utterly possesses me and *I do not know what to do* (Ph 1:22), what I should say, since I do not expect to see you and my sisters again in this life.

4. Oh if only I could lay bare for you on this page the continuing sorrow that I anticipate and that is always before me. My souls burns within me, and I am tormented by the fires of innumerable tribulations. My heart groans within me, and my eyes do not cease to pour out a flood of tears. Filled with every kind of sorrow and spiritless, I am pining away entirely. *Even though I seek consolation, I do not find it* (cf. Lam 1:2). I conceive sorrow upon sorrow, when I ponder within me with fear that I will never see you and my sisters again. Under such distress I am totally disheartened.

5. On the one hand there is no one of all my dear ones to console me; but on the other hand I am very much consoled and you can congratulate me for this: I have found great harmony and no factions here, which is beyond belief. Everyone has received me with great happiness and joy, and has very devoutly promised me obedience and reverence. They all commend themselves to God, to you and to your community, and I commend myself and them to you in all things and in every way, that you may have a solicitous concern for me and for them as you have for your own sisters and daughters. Know that I and the sisters wish to observe inviolate for all the days of our lives your admonitions and precepts.

6. As far as the precepts are concerned, be assured that the Lord Pope has satisfied me, as I have said, and has satisfied you too, in all things and in every way according to your intention and mine regarding, as you know, our position on the ownership of property. I beseech you to ask Brother Elias to visit me more often to console me in the Lord.

Mandate (1238)

This little known document was published by Luke Wadding in the Annales Minorum under the year 1238, but it was Arnaldo Fortini who discovered its original in the archives of Assisi and brought it to light in this modern period of research.[1] Whereas it is of little spiritual importance, it does provide us information concerning the sisters living at San Damiano at that period and their concern for maintaining the poverty and simplicity they had originally vowed.

In the name of God. Amen.

Lady Clare, abbess of the monastery of San Damiano in Assisi, designates and establishes by this document and by the will of the ladies or sisters listed below a procurator or treasurer who will sell or hand over in her name and in that of this monastery a certain enclosure at Compiglione, together with the land adjacent to it, to the Church or Chapter of San Rufino in Assisi. The enclosure is bordered on one side by the Tescio and by roads on the other two sides. The land borders the enclosure on two sides, the fields of Maragoni's son on the third, and that of Balducino's son on the fourth side.

This procurator or treasurer shall promise and oblige himself to take charge of this enclosure and land in the name of this monastery for the purpose of transferring it to the Church or Chapter or to its delegate in the holding and possessing of this enclosure and land, and for the purpose of doing and transacting whatever this procurator or treasurer deems necessary concerning this sale.

The names of the ladies or sisters are these: Agnes, Philippa, Jacoba, Illuminata, Cecilia, Aegidia, Agnes, Anastasia, Cristiana, Iacobina, Balvina, Mansueta, Amata, Benvenuta, Bonaventura, Benvenuta, Benricevuta, Consolata, Andrea, Aurea, Leonarda, Agatha, Felicita, Angeluccia, Felicita, Massariola, Maria, Gregoria, Maria, Ioanna, Benedicta, Ionna, Bennata, Ionna, Lucia, Helia, Mathia, Clara, Stella, Lea, Beatrix, Bartholomea, Praxeda, Herminia, Daniella, Clarella, Pacifica, Vetera, Patricia.

---

[1]*Annales Minorum*, a. 1238, n. 14, ed. L. Wadding; A. Fortini, *Nova Vita di San Francesco* II (Milan, 1926), 417–424; "L'autenticità del documento del 1238," *Archivum Franciscanum Storicum* 46 (1953), 37–43.

That this present document may be confirmed for those now living, for those to come, and for posterity, Lady Clare and her sisters have placed the seal of this monastery's chapter on it on the eighth of June in the year of our Lord 1238, in indiction XVII, during the reigns of Gregory IX and Emperor Frederick.

Rule of Pope Innocent IV (1247)

After 1219, when Cardinal Hugolino provided his Rule for the Poor Ladies of San Damiano, the number of monasteries following the ideals of Saint Clare increased greatly. Many of these were not satisfied with Hugolino's Rule and its insistence on professing the Rule of Saint Benedict. Agnes of Prague, for example, explicitly asked that mention of the Benedictine Rule be omitted from the Rule granted to her monastery. At first Pope Innocent IV (1243–1254) insisted on the profession of the Benedictine Rule, as envisioned in the Rule of Hugolino, but he later promulgated his own Rule, Cum omnis vera religio, *on August 6, 1247 which adds considerably to that of his predecessor and, at the same time, omits reference to that of Saint Benedict. The Rule of Pope Innocent IV was not widely accepted. The Pope insisted upon its acceptance in a papal decree,* Quoties a nobis, *August 23, 1247.*[1]

The following document clearly shows the insistence of the gradual refining influence of St. Clare and the Poor Ladies and reveals the tensions that existed in their attempts to have their charism and ideals incorporated into the Church's official legislation.

Innocent, Bishop, servant of the servants of God, to his beloved daughters in Christ, all the abbesses and enclosed nuns of the Order of Saint Damian, health and apostolic blessing.

1. Every true Religion and approved institute of life endures by certain rules and requirements, and by certain disciplinary laws. Unless each sister has diligently striven to observe a certain correct rule and discipline for living, she will deviate from righteousness to the degree that she does not observe the guidelines of righteousness. She runs the risk of falling at the point where, in virtue of her free choice, she neglected to set for herself a sure and stable foundation for making progress. Therefore, beloved daughters in Christ, because you have chosen under the inspiration of divine grace to travel the hard and narrow path that leads to life, **we, acceding to your pious prayers, grant to you and those who come after you the ob-**

---

[1]Cf. L. Oliger, "De Origine Regularum Ordine S. Clarae, *Archivum Franciscanum Historicum* V (1912), 181–209, 413–447; I. Omaechevarria, "L'Ordine di S. Chiara sotto Diverse Regole," *Forma Sororum* 15 (1978), 141–153.

servance of the Rule of Saint Francis with respect to the three [counsels], namely obedience, the renunciation of property in particular, and perpetual chastity, as well as the Form of Life written in the present document, according to which you have particularly decided to live.[2] By doing so we establish by our apostolic authority that it be observed for all times in every monastery of your Order. This is as follows:

It is proper, therefore, and a duty that all those women who, after abandoning the vanity of the world, have resolved to embrace and hold to your Order, should observe this law of life and discipline, **living in obedience, without anything of one's own, and in chastity. And they must remain enclosed the whole time of their life professing this life.**[3] After they have entered the enclosure of this Order and have been professed, promising to observe this rule, let them never be granted any permission or faculty to leave this enclosure unless perhaps some are transferred to another place by the permission of the general minister of the Order of Friars Minor or the provincial of the province of that Order in which the monastery is situated to plant or to build up the Order, **or to reform some monastery, or by reason of discipline or correction, or to avoid a great expense of some sort. They can at times be transferred for some even pious and reasonable cause beyond those mentioned above, at least, as a general rule, with the permission of the General.**[4] Moreover, it is fitting that, when they die, both the [enclosed] as well as the serving sisters, be buried within the enclosure.

The hard and austere realities, through which, according to this Order, one is led to God and which must necessarily be observed, must be explained to all who wish to enter this Order and are received, before they actually enter and change their garb, lest ignorance be their excuse later on. One should not be received who proves to be less than sufficiently fit for the observance of this life because of age, a sickness, or a mental deficiency; **for the state and vigor of the Order is dissolved and disturbed through such persons.** Therefore, let any occasion for receiving such a person be cautiously and diligently avoided, even if at times for a reasonable cause a dispensation has to be given to someone.

All those received into the enclosure, if they are old enough to un-

---

[2]Pope Innocent thus acknowledges the Rule of St. Francis and the Form of Life as the foundation for the way of life of the Poor Sisters. The Later Rule of St. Francis was solemnly approved by Pope Honorius III in the bull *Solet annuere*, November 29, 1223; cf. K. Esser, *Die Opuscula des Hl.Franziskus von Assisi* (Grottaferrata: Collegium S. Bonaventurae, 1976): 363–372. The English translations are found in *Francis and Clare: The Complete Writings* (New York: Paulist Press, 1982), 126–145 and 44–45.

[3]Cf. RegHug 7, note 7.

[4]This is the first of several points which express a relationship with the Friars Minor. Cf. RegInn 2, 6, 8, 12.

derstand, should, according to custom, quickly put aside their secular clothes. A mistress may be appointed for them who shall mold them in the knowledge of religious life.[5] And after the completion of the space of one year, they may make their profession in this way: I, sister————, promise to God, to the ever blessed Virgin Mary, to Saint Francis, and to all the saints, to observe perpetual obedience according to the *Rule and Form of Life* given to your Order by the Apostolic See, by living all the days of my life without anything of my own, and in chastity.[6] Let this also be firmly observed for the serving [sisters] in the same way.

2. Concerning the offering of the Divine Office to the Lord both day and night: let it be observed so that those who know how to read and sing celebrate the Office according to the custom of the Order of Friars Minor, nevertheless with gravity and modesty.[7] But let those who cannot read say twenty-four *Our Father's* for Matins; five for Lauds; seven for each of the hours of Prime, Terce, Sext, and None; twelve for Vespers; seven for Compline.[8] Let this also be observed for all the hours in the *Office of the Blessed Virgin Mary.* And they shall pray for the dead.

If there are some young, or some older, ones who are humble and capable of learning, the abbess, if she sees fit, may appoint a capable and discreet mistress for them to teach them to read. But let the sisters be employed in useful and sincere work during the established hours, as it has been ordained.

3. Let a continuous silence be kept by all at all times, so that it is not permitted for them to talk either to one another or to anyone else without permission. Nonetheless, let the abbess eagerly attend to where, when, and how permission to speak is given to the sisters. But let everyone be eager to use religious as well as appropriate signs.

When some religious or secular person of whatever dignity seeks to speak to one of the sisters, let the abbess be notified first. If she gives permission, let the sister have at least two others appointed by the abbess to accompany her to the parlor. Let these be able to see the speaker and hear what is said.

Let this be firmly observed by all, so that when some sick sister within

---

[5]In contrast to the Rule of Hugolino, novices are entrusted to the care of a Mistress in agreement with *Cum secundum consilium*, November 22, 1220.

[6]This formula of profession is one of the major differences between the Rule of Innocent and that of Hugolino. Cf. C.A. Lainati, "Le formule di professione più antiche nelle Ordine di S. Chiara," *Forma Sororum* XX (1983): 199–200.

[7]In 1213 Pope Innocent III undertook the reform of the Liturgy of the Hours. Cf. Stephen J.P. Van Dijk and J.H. Walker, *The Origins of the Roman Liturgy: The Liturgy of the Papal Court and the Franciscan Order in the Thirteenth Century* (Westminster, Md.: Newman, 1960).

[8]Innocent specifies the exact form of this alternate Office. Cf. RegHug 5.

the enclosure is about to make her confession to a priest, she may not speak unless there are at least two others sitting not far away who are able to see the confessor and the penitent and to be equally seen by them.

Even the abbess herself should diligently guard this law, so that all matter for distraction may be removed except, when it seems fit to her according to God, she may speak with her sisters in appropriate times and places. But the sick sisters and those who serve them, according to the dispositions of the Abbess, may speak in the infirmary at the time of their illness.

4. Let the sisters and the servants continuously keep the fast from the feast of the Exaltation of the Holy Cross until the feast of the Resurrection of the Lord, except on Sundays and the feasts of Saint Michael, Saint Francis, All Saints, the Nativity of the Lord, and the two days following it, the Epiphany, and the Purification.[9]

But they are in no way bound to fast from the Resurrection to the Exaltation of the Holy Cross except on Fridays and those days established universally by the Church. They may legitimately use wine, fish, eggs, cheese, and other dairy products. Nevertheless, from Advent to the Lord's Nativity, the Greater Lent, Fridays and days of fast and abstinence generally established by the Church, let them not use eggs, cheese, and other dairy products.

The abbess can mercifully dispense the serving sisters from fasting except in Advent, the Greater Lent, Fridays, and other fast days established by the Church.

The adolescents less than fourteen years old, the aged or sick, are not at all bound to observe the above-mentioned law of fast and abstinence. Meat, as well as other necessities, can be mercifully provided for these, according to their weakness.

The healthy sisters are also not bound at the time of their blood-letting outside the Greater Lent and on Friday, Advent, and the fasts instituted universally by the Church.[10] Nevertheless, let the abbess be careful that she

---

[9]Nineteen years have passed since the canonization of St. Francis.

[10]It was believed that physiological imbalance would be reflected in bodily illness and in exaggerated personality traits. The notion was so influential that for many centuries physicians throughout the Western world continued the practice of bleeding people who suffered from medical and psychiatric disorders. For religious, this health measure usually adds three days' dispensation from regular observance and is provided for in detailed religious law, for example, Uldar of Cluny, *Consuetudines Cluniacenses Antiquiores* II 21 (PL 149, 709); Lanfranc, *Decreta Pro Ordine S. Benedicti* (PL 150, 494B f); Stephen Harding, *Usus Ordinis Cistertiensis* IV 91 (PL 166, 1466c); *Statuta Ecclesiae Lugdunensis* (PL 199, 1101a); and *La Regola del Primo e Secondo Ordine degli Humiliati*, XXXVIII (contained in the Bull, *Cum felicis memoriae*, June 7, 1227, of Gregory IX; cf. L. Zanoni, *Gli Humiliati nel loro rapporti con l'eresia, l'industria della lana ed i comuni nei secoli XII e XIII* [Roma: 1970], 366).

does not permit blood-letting to be celebrated commonly more than four times a year, unless manifest necessity requires that it be more. Nor may they receive blood-letting from an outsider, especially a man, when it can be conveniently avoided.

Let the greatest care and diligence be afforded the sick. Let the sick be served kindly and solicitously in a spirit of charity according to what is possible and appropriate, both in the food that their sickness requires, as well as in the other necessary things. Those who are sick may have their own place, if this is possible, where they may remain separated from the healthy, so that their well-being and quiet may not be disturbed or dissipated.

5. Each sister may have two, or even more, tunics, as it seems fitting to the abbess, besides a hair shirt and a woven one if they have it, and a mantle of suitable length and width. Let these garments be of rough cloth both in price and in color according to the various regions. But let them have a cord as a belt, except the serving sisters who may wear a belt of cloth and not a cord.

Let them also have a scapular without a hood of light, religious cloth or woven cloth, which is of appropriate length and width, as the nature of height of each one demands. Let them be clothed in these when they are working or doing something that they cannot fittingly do wearing a mantle. But if they wish to have the scapulars together with the mantles, or even wish to sleep in them, they are not forbidden to do so. They can be without them at times, if it seems fitting to the abbess, when perhaps because of excessive heat or the like, they are too heavy for the sisters to wear.

Let their heads be covered in a uniform and becoming way by a head-band or a garment that is thoroughly white, although not odd. Let the forehead, the cheeks, and the throat, as is proper, be appropriately covered. Let them not dare to appear in any other way before outsiders. Let them also have a black veil, so long and wide, that it extends over the head and hangs from each part to the scapular and from behind to a little beyond the hood of the tunic.[11]

The novices, however, should wear a white veil of the same measurement. The serving sisters, on the other hand, may wear over their head a white linen cloth like a tunic, of such length and width that it can cover their shoulders and breast, especially when they go out.

Let all the healthy sisters, the abbess as well as the others, be bound to sleep in a common dormitory. Let everyone have her own bed separate from the others. Nonetheless, the bed of the abbess may be placed in such a part

---

[11]To the prescriptions of the *Rule of Hugolino* 9 Innocent adds the cord or belt, head-band, black and white veil and reduces the comments regarding the scapular.

of the dormitory that she may see from it, if possible, the other beds of the dormitory without any interference.

Each one may be permitted to have a mat of straw or hay and a pillow covered with some linen cloth which can be made of straw or hay, wool or even feathers, as the abbess judges best. They may also have suitable woolen blankets or quilts [appropriate for] religious when wool cannot conveniently be obtained.

Let an overhead lamp always be burning at night in the middle of the dormitory.

Let their hair be cut at definite times in a uniform way in a circle as far as the ears. No sister should be tonsured, unless an evident physical infirmity demands.

6. Concerning the entrance of persons into the monastery, we firmly and strictly decree that an abbess or her sisters may never permit any religious or secular person of whatever dignity to enter the monastery. This is not allowed to anyone unless permission has been granted by the Apostolic See or by the general or provincial ministers of the Order of Friars Minor in whose province the monasteries themselves are situated.

Excused from the above law of entrance are the doctor and the blood-letter by reason of the very serious nature of the illness. Let them not be admitted without two appropriate companions of the monastic family. At the completion of this kind of business, let him quickly depart. Let them not be separated from one another inside the monastery. In a similar way, those persons may enter whom necessity demands either by reason of a fire, or the destruction of something, or some danger or loss, whether to protect the monastery itself or some persons from violence, or to perform some work that cannot be conveniently done outside the monastery.

Nevertheless, no outsider may be permitted to eat or sleep within the enclosure of the monastery.

But even if one of the Cardinals were to come at some time to a monastery of this Order and would like to enter, let him be received with reverence and devotion. But let him be asked to enter with a few upright companions. Let any other prelate, however, to whom permission is ever given to enter, be content with two or three religious and suitable companions.

If, by chance, permission is ever given to any Bishop to celebrate Mass within the enclosure for the blessing or consecration of the sisters or for some other reason, let him be content with as few and as virtuous companions and attendants as he can. Let this permission be given rarely to anyone.

No one, whether healthy or sick, should speak with anyone except in the manner mentioned above. Particular caution should be taken that those to whom permission has been given to enter the monastery be such in their words and character, in their life and manners that they edify those who see them and, thus, are incapable of generating matter for scandal.

7. When they have their own chaplain, let him be religious in life and manner and possess a good reputation. He should not be too young, but of a suitable age. When any of the sisters is gripped by a bodily illness so that she is not strong enough to come to the parlor and needs to confess or to receive the Lord's Body and the other sacraments, [the chaplain] may enter the enclosure vested in a white stole and maniple, with two suitable and religious companions, or at least one. After he has heard her confession or has given her the sacrament, let him depart with his companions, vested as he was when he entered, and not delay there any longer. Let them also beware that, while they are within the monastery, they are never separated from one another so that they are at least in the sight of one another at all times. Let him conduct himself in this way at the commendation of her soul.

He may not enter the enclosure to conduct the obsequies at the grave; let this duty be fulfilled in the chapel. Nevertheless, if it seems to the abbess that he should enter for these obsequies, let him enter vested in the manner described above and, after the burial, let him leave without delay. If, however, it is necessary for someone to enter to dig or open a grave, or certainly to close it afterwards, it is licit for him or anyone else who is upright and suitable together with one or two companions to enter for this purpose.

Otherwise let him not presume to enter the monastery. But when some sister wishes to speak to him about confession, let him listen to her through the speaking grille and through it let him then speak to her about those things that pertain to confession.

When the sisters do not have their own chaplain, they can hear Mass celebrated by any priest of good reputation and upright life. However, let them receive Penance, the Lord's Body, and the other ecclesial sacraments, only from the brothers of the Order of Minors, unless, when some sister is on the point of a dangerous necessity, it is impossible for them to have access to an above-mentioned brother.

We also desire that an iron grille of a suitable form be placed in the wall that divides the sisters from the chapel.[12] A black linen cloth should be so placed on the inside of this grille so that no sister may see anything in the chapel outside. Let them have wooden doors with iron bars and a key so

---

[12]Concerning the wall dividing the sisters from the chapel see Jacques de Vitry, *Historia Orientalis* (Ducai, 1297), 339, where the same arrangement is discussed for the Second Order of the Humiliati. Also, D. Knowles, "Gilbertini e Gilbertine," *Dizionario degli Istituti di Perfezione* IV (Rome, 1977), 1178–1182, and "Certosine," *op. cit.*, (Rome, 1975), 773–775.

that they remain closed and not opened except when celebrating the Divine Office or for the purpose of listening at times to the Word of God to be proposed in the chapel outside by a fitting and upright person.

And no one may speak to another through the grille spoken of, except when permission is at times given to someone exceptional for a reasonable cause or when necessity demands it. Because it may at times happen that some outsider approaches them or otherwise speaks to them through the grille, let them bow and cover their faces with modesty, as it is becoming for an upright religious.

But when it is necessary in order to receive Communion at certain times, let a small window be made, with a small door made of metal strips, and always kept closed with an iron bar and a key, through which the chalice can be conveniently given and the sacrament of the Lord's Body administered. And let it so extend from the ground that the priest can conveniently exercise that ministry.

8. Concerning the visitator of this Order the following must be carefully provided for: let whoever is anywhere appointed as the general visitator, or even at times the special visitator, be such that there is full knowledge and a guarantee concerning his religious life and character.

When he comes to enter a monastery, let him show and manifest himself in such a way in all things that he stimulates all from the good to the better and always inflames and enkindles them to the love of God and mutual love of one another. And when he enters the enclosure of a monastery for his visit, let him take with him two religious and appropriate companions who will stay together with him as companions; let them not be separated from one another in any way.

Let [the visitator] zealously seek the truth about the condition of the sisters and the observance of their Order from all generally and particularly from individuals. When he finds something that should be reformed or corrected, let him—with discretion and zeal for charity and love for justice—reform and correct it both in the head and in the members, as it seems best.[13]

But let him observe the manner of speaking as described above, so that whether he speaks with all or with many at one time, or with one in private, there may be at least two others sitting in his sight at a distance, so that the integrity of his good reputation may be preserved in all things, unless he wishes to speak in the parlor with one or more about things that pertain to his office.

---

[13]The expression "in the head and in the members" is typical of the reform theology of the period. For further information, see P. Strump, *Reform in Head and Members: The Reform Ideas of Constance (1414–1418)*, unpublished dissertation, University of Southern California.

But let the abbess be careful that the condition of her monastery not at any time be hidden from the visitor by herself or any other sisters. This would be a sign of evil and an offense that would have to be seriously punished. In fact, we desire and decree that those things which should be diligently established and amended according to the form of their life **and regular observance** should be zealously suggested and proposed, privately and publicly, as it may best be done, to the visitor **whom they are bound to obey in all things.** Let whoever does otherwise, whether it be the abbess or the others, be appropriately punished by the visitor, as is proper.

In a similar manner, if the chaplain is reprehensible in anything in which he cannot fittingly be supported nor should he be, let him, after he has been forewarned, be discreetly and reasonably punished by a visitor, **as is proper.** If he does not wish to amend [his ways] or spurns [the warning], **let him be removed altogether from the monastery by the same [visitator].**

Moreover, we decree that only the general or provincial minister of the above-mentioned Order, exercise among you the office of visiting, correcting, and reforming both in the head and in the members through themselves or through other qualified brothers [who have been] appointed by them in the general chapter. Nevertheless, the general and the aforesaid provincials in their provinces, for a reason, can occasionally appoint someone qualified as a special visitor from the brothers entrusted to them according to the form given by the entire gathering of ministers in the general chapter.

9. When it is possible, let there be in each monastery only one door for entering and leaving the enclosure according to the law of entering and leaving set down in this *Form.* And let the door be conveniently made in a high place as far as it can suitably be done, so that, from the outside, it may be reached by a portable ladder. Let this ladder, zealously secured by an iron chain, be taken up continually from the recitation of Compline to Prime of the following day, and at the time of *siesta* and visitation, unless some evident necessity or obvious advantage requires something else.

Let one of the sisters, who is God fearing, mature in character, and of fitting age, be appointed to take care of the aforementioned entrance. Let her so zealously care for and guard one key that the door can never be opened unknown to her or her companion. But let the abbess take care of the other key that is different from it. Let there be another [sister], equally suitable and appointed as her companion, who may take her place in all things, when she is occupied and detained by some reasonable or necessary employment.

Let them very zealously take care and beware that the door never remains open except when it may be appropriately done for a short time. Let the entrance be very well secured with wooden panels, strong beams and iron bars. Let it never be left open without a guard or even closed unless it is securely locked **by one key during the day and by two during the night.** Let it not be opened immediately at every knock, unless it is known beforehand, without a doubt, that it is such a person for whom the door should be opened without any hesitation according to the decree which is contained above in that Form concerning those who are about to enter.

But if some time some work has to be done within the monastery, it may be entered by some seculars or other persons in order to accomplish it. But let the abbess carefully provide that, while the work is being done, some other suitable person be appointed to guard the door. She may open it for those persons designated to do the work and not allow others to enter.

For at such a time and, as far as they are reasonably able, always, let **the sisters** most zealously guard against being seen by seculars or persons from the outside.

As for the rest, since we do not wish that the aforesaid door be opened for other things except for those things that cannot conveniently be delivered through the turn or some other means, we decree that in each monastery one strong turn of appropriate width and height be made in a suitable place. Necessities may be administered through it both from within and without. Let it be so used that no one may be seen either from within or without. Let the little door be strong on both sides so that it should remain closed and secure with locks and keys at night and, in the summer time, during *siesta*. Let the abbess place one sister, who is discreet, reliable, and mature in both character and age, who loves the reputation of the monastery, to guard it and procure necessities for it. She alone, or the one appointed as her companion, when she cannot conveniently be present, may speak and respond about those things that pertain to her office.

Let the common parlor, however, be placed in the chapel, or more preferably in the enclosure, when it can be done more conveniently and properly, lest, were it by chance in the chapel, it would disturb the peace of those who are praying. Let the parlor be of appropriate size, with a metal screen that is finely perforated and so secured with strong keys that it can never be opened. A black linen cloth should be so hung from the interior that those [sisters] cannot see outside nor be seen.

No one shall be given permission to speak in that parlor from Compline, which should be said at the appropriate time, until after Prime of the following day, or at the time of eating or, during the summer, during *siesta*, or when the Office is celebrated, except for such a reasonable or necessary cause that cannot be conveniently postponed.

10. Concerning the serving sisters who are not bound to remain always enclosed as the others, we wish this to be observed strictly: no one may leave the enclosure without permission and those who are sent out to

be upright and of appropriate age. Let them embark upon the highways in decent footwear, both them and those sisters whom it is necessary at times to send out, as in the cases described above. The same may also be permitted for those who remain within, if they wish.

Let a certain time for returning be given to those who go out. It may not be permitted for any of them to eat, drink, or sleep outside the monastery without special permission, or to be separated from one another, or to talk to someone in private, or to enter the dwelling-place of the chaplain of the monastery or of converts or penitents or of the brothers staying there.[14] If one of them does something contrary to this, let her be severely punished. And let them zealously be careful that they do not stop in suspicious places or become familiar with persons of a bad reputation. Upon their return let them not recount to the sisters worldly and useless things through which they can be disturbed or weakened. And while they are out, let them so conduct themselves that they are able to edify those who see them by their upright manner. Whatever is given or promised them, let them bring it and report it to the abbess or another who takes her place in this regard.

11. As far as this is concerned, you may be permitted to receive, to have in common, and to freely retain produce and possessions. A procurator—one who is prudent as well as loyal—may be had in every monastery of the Order to deal with these possessions in a becoming way.[15] Whenever it seems necessary, he should be appointed or removed by a visitator as he sees fit.

Let this procurator, established in this way, be bound to render an account to the abbess and three other sisters especially assigned for this, and to this visitator, if he wishes, concerning everything entrusted to him—what he has received as well as spent. And he may not be able to sell, exchange, obligate or alienate anything at all from the goods of the monastery, unless he has the permission of the abbess as well as the community. We decree that whatever might be attempted contrary to this be considered illicit and invalid. Nevertheless, some small bit of movable property of small worth can at times be given.

12. So that it does not happen that, through the fault of some government, you fall back at a later date from the observance of the present *For-*

---

[14]The "converts" or *conversi* were women affiliated to the monastery as workers, helpers, etc. They were not seen as professed religious, although most of them lived a life dedicated to religious pursuits.

[15]The allowance for a procurator mirrors the provisions that Innocent made for the Friars Minor at their requests in the bulls, *Ordinem vestrum*, November 14, 1245, and *Quantum studiosus*, August 19, 1247. Thus both the friars and the sisters had papal permission to have agents handle financial affairs, but it was a permission that led to further controversy.

mula briefly described above, which we wish and decree is to be followed everywhere and by everyone in a uniform way; or, that you take up different ways of living under the teaching of various [persons], we fully entrust the care of you and all the monasteries of your Order—with the authority of the present [document]—to our beloved sons, the general and provincial ministers of the Order of Friars Minor. We decree that you remain under their—or others who might be ministers for a time—obedience, government, and teaching. You are firmly bound to obey them.

And let them, having solicitude and care for your souls, strive to fulfill the office of visitator for these monasteries through themselves or their other brothers who are qualified for this [and] designated by them according to the aforesaid *Form*, as often as they deem it necessary, correcting and reforming in those places, either in the head or in the members.

Nonetheless, let them establish or abandon, change or order as, according to God, they see fit.

Let the election of the abbess, however, freely belong to the community. Its confirmation or invalidation may be done by the general minister, if he is present in the province, or, in his absence, by the provincial of that province in which the monastery is situated. Let the brothers appointed for this task hear your confessions and administer the sacraments of the Church to you. But since the brothers of the aforesaid Order may not be bound to reside continually in your monasteries, the lack of a priest can be threatening. Let them appoint other discreet and solicitous chaplains to hear your confessions at moments of need and to administer the aforesaid sacraments as well as the celebration of the Divine Office.

No monastery of your Order may be established in the future by others without the permission and consent of the general chapter of the aforementioned Order.

The chaplain and converts may promise obedience to the abbess, according to the arrangement of the visitator, promising stability of place and to live perpetually without anything of their own, and in chastity. The visitator is permitted to transfer the chaplain, the serving sisters, as well as the converts from one monastery to another for an evident need or for obvious usefulness.

They should observe the fast as the sisters do. Let the abbess, nonetheless be allowed mercifully to dispense them [from fasting] due to the heat, a journey, some work, or some other reasonable and upright reason.

They may have tunics without the hood, made of poor cloth, according to their need. Let their sleeves be short and reach only to the hands. But let the length of the tunics be such that they extend the length of four fingers from the arch of the foot. They may have a becoming strap with a knife for a belt. They may also wear a small cape above the tunics; its length may reach a little beyond the knee and its width to the elbow. The chaplain, nevertheless, may have a little cape of shorter length. He may also use a decent cape, when it is appropriate. They may have footwear and socks, as well as pants that are wide and long and which are fastened in the front.

And let the converts say the same Office as described above for the sisters who cannot read, except that they may at least be bound to the *Office of the Blessed Virgin.*

Let the chaplain and penitents be thoroughly subject to the knowledge as well as the correction of the visitator whom they are strictly bound to obey.

Therefore, let no one dare to tamper with this document of Our concession and constitution, or dare to oppose it with rash temerity. If anyone shall presume to attempt this, let him know that he will incur the wrath of Almighty God and His holy apostles Peter and Paul.

Given at Lyons, the 9th of August, in the fifth year of our pontificate.

Notification of Death (1253)

This little known text announcing the death of Saint Clare on August 11, 1253, to the sisters of one hundred and ten monasteries professing her way of life has only come to light in this century since it was discovered in the Landau Library in Florence in a collection entitled Liber epistolarum secundum, usum Curiae Romanae el aliorum Principium.[1] *It is a most difficult piece of writing that seems to have been written in distress and in haste. The style is less than polished and, at times, there seems to be no logical flow of thought. Curiously, the document ends quite abruptly and without any concluding remarks. For those reasons alone, however, it has a certain beauty and strength for it reflects the natural struggle of the sisters in their attempts to reconcile the loss of their mother, Clare, with the faith that assures them of her place in heaven.*

TO ALL THE SISTERS OF THE ORDER OF SAN DAMIANO THROUGHOUT THE WORLD, THE SISTERS LIVING IN ASSISI [WISH] SALVATION IN THE AUTHOR OF SALVATION.

Since the sting of a darkening sadness has risen, we embark upon—not without tears—the narration of a report full of sadness. We break faith—not without the sorrowful sounds of mourning—to tell [you] that the mirror of the morning star, whose image we admired as a type of the true light, has vanished from our sight. The staff of our religion has perished! The vehicle of our profession, I am sorry to say, has departed from the stadium of the human pilgrimage!

Our Lady Clare, our leader, venerable mother, teacher, was called by the separating best man of carnal bond, that is, destructive death,[2] [and] ascended not long ago to the bridal chamber of her heavenly Spouse. Her festive ascent from earth, from the shadow of darkness to brilliance, and [her] celebrated appearance in heaven—although spiritually suggesting joy

---

[1]Cf. Z. Lazzeri, "La Vita di s. Chiara," *Archivum Franciscanum Historicum* 13 (1920), 403–507. Further information can be found in I. Omaechevarria, *Escritos de Santa Clara y Documentos Conplementarios* (Madrid: Biblioteca de Autores Cristianos, 1983), 55-59.

[2]A image that is rarely found in medieval literature. It can also be found in the **Legend of Saint Clare** 6, to refer to Saint Francis. Cf. infra 164.

122

to the senses—from a temporal point of view, has, nevertheless, over-whelmed our light with an outpouring of grief. While she has taken us from the slippery path of worldly desire [and] has directed us on the path of salvation, nevertheless, she has left our sight. For by the guilt of our imperfection, perhaps deserved, the Lord was pleased to make the glorious Clare more brilliant with heavenly rays rather than have her graciously remain any longer among her sisters in their earthly places.

She certainly deserved it, however, if we reflect on the merits of her perfection because of which, from her earliest years, she flourished in vigils of divine contemplation and which were, even then, worthy of reward. Thus she poured out her devotional prayers in loving acts of worship. Thus she vowed the lily of her virginal modesty to nuptials with Christ, abhorring the princes of sensual love. Thus she pledged herself to Him in a conjugal way with a ring of love. When she attained the act of marriage, strikingly beautiful in body, rich in the resources of wealth, reared in a noble lineage, instead of a royal bridal gown she put on a poor habit, a funeral torch instead of a wedding lamp, and, instead of a wedding sash, she girded herself with a rope. Oh how solemn was this marriage! How fruitful was her virginity which was unsullied by the touches of carnal love and which resolved itself into offspring so numerous and abundant.

Pay attention! What sluggishness, O sisters! Pay attention to how the brilliant feminine sensibility shone with so many virtues, was ablaze with the vigor of such strength! She overcame the obscenities of worldly slipperiness before her steps. Wounded by the sting of a lingering sickness and delayed by the tenderness of subsequent old age, she did not break into grumbling out of weakness nor did she open the door of her mouth to complain. Moreover, the more strongly she was stung by the barbs of sickness, so much more did she devoutly offer a song of praise to the Lord. How great was the bond of seriousness with which she was bound! How great was the fire of charity with which she was inflamed so that even the attack of an angry storm was not capable of overturning the tranquility of her soul like a sail which pulls away from angry gusts when it is in modest hands.[3]

While strengthening our hearts in an embrace of the Divinity, she used to restore them socially with the medicine of continuous consolation! When it happened—as it occasionally does—that someone who was helpless needed clothing or was hungry or thirsty, she would hurry into their midst with a kind encouraging word such as "Bear it courteously . . . ", "Bear the burdens of poverty patiently . . . the weight of humility humbly. The patience of those whose vision springs from a consideration of the Di-

---

[3]A typical Augustinian theme of spiritual literature, cf. H. Rondet, "Le Symbolisme de la Mer chez Saint Augustin," *Augustinus Magister* II (Paris 1954), 691-701.

vinity produces the delights of paradise for the patient one and will purchase the riches of an eternal reward."

Why proceed any further? The depth of this blessedness does not know any explanation in human terms. But listen to that gift of the Divinity that she received towards the end of her time [on earth]. The Vicar of Christ with the venerable College of his brothers visited her when she was dying and, because he more graciously remained afterwards and did not pass up the funeral of the deceased, he honored her body at her burial.

Even though a violent pain physically wrenches our hearts at her death, let us nevertheless extend the right hand of our soul to the glory of divine praise, to the palm of cheerfulness. For as our mortal intelligence understands the dance of joy with which the heavenly army and its holy spirits go to meet her and presents the workings of her reverend body to the sight of its Creator, by the efficacious power of its Maker, shining with a variety of miracles. . . .

Acts of the Process
of Canonization (1253)

Within two months of the death of Saint Clare, Pope Innocent IV issued the papal bull, Gloriosus Deus, October 18, 1253, in which he entrusted Bishop Bartholomew of Spoleto with the responsibility of promoting the Cause of her canonization. The Bishop of Spoleto, who had previous experience in these matters, took as his associates the archdeacon, Leonardo of Spoleto, Jacobo, the archpriest of Trevi, Brothers Leo and Angelo of the Friars Minor who were close friends of Saint Francis, Brother Mark, chaplain of the monastery, and a notary. On November 24, 1253, they went to the Monastery of San Damiano in Assisi and officially interviewed under oath thirteen of the sisters who had lived with Saint Clare. Two other sisters, one of whom was in the infirmary, were questioned on November 28, 1253, and, on the same day, Sister Benedetta, the Abbess of San Damiani, spoke in the name of the entire community and declared the willingness of all the sisters to testify concerning the sanctity of Saint Clare.

That same day, November 28, 1253, the Bishop and his official party proceeded to the Monastery Church of San Paolo in the center of Assisi to officially interrogate those citizens of the city who had known the saint or experienced her intercession. Thus they examined an elderly knight, Ugolino di Pietro Giraldone, the lady Bona Guelfuccio, Ranieri di Bernardo, and Pietro di Damiano, all of whom were associated with the family of Saint Clare and had known her intimately as a child. On the following day, the officials interviewed Iovani di Ventura who testified to one of the miracles that had occurred after Saint Clare's death.

The text of the Acts of the Process of Canonization, together with the papal bull, Gloriosus Deus, comes to us in an Umbrian Italian version of the fifteenth century. Nonetheless, a critical, internal study of the text, as well as a thorough examination of the parallels that exist between it and the later Legend of Saint Clare, leaves little doubt as to its authenticity. It was only in 1920 that Zefferino Lazzeri, O.F.M., discovered and published the Acts. The text that follows provides invaluable, firsthand information concerning the life and death of Saint Clare and is, therefore, an indispensable source of our knowledge the saint.

The Following is the Process of Canonization
of Saint Clare

as Pope Innocent sent letters to the Bishop of Spoleto,[1]
entrusting him with diligence and care to look into
the life, conversion, manner of life, and miracles
of Saint Clare, as the Bull written below contains.

In the name of the Lord Jesus Christ. Amen.

I, Bartholomew, Bishop of Spoleto, have received the following letter from the most holy father, Lord Pope Innocent IV:

Innocent, Bishop, Servant of the servants of God, to our venerable brother, Bartholomew, Bishop of Spoleto, health and apostolic blessing.

In His saints, the Glorious God Who alone does and performs marvelous and great things, acknowledges His faithful after the course and passing of their lives through the wonderful declaration, in many ways, with signs that he chooses for their supreme glory and as reward of their heavenly beatitude. [He does] this so that, hearing about the signs, wonders, and witnesses of so many marvelous things, only possible through the power of God, One in Trinity and Three in Unity, the goodness of the Most High may be seen and His great and wonderful name more reverently adored on earth, He Whose kingdom remains in eternity and Whose majesty is miraculously proclaimed on high.

These desirable rewards belong to the holy memory of the blessed virgin Clare, former abbess of the Poor Ladies, enclosed nuns of San Damiano in Assisi. Heeding that saying of the prophet—*O daughter, listen, see, and incline your ear; forget your people and your father's house; because the king has desired your beauty* (Ps 44:11–12)—she turned her back on passing and fading things. Turning to things ahead and forgetting everything behind, she gave herself willingly and readily to listening to holy discourse. She did not lose time nor did she delay in fulfilling immediately what she delighted to hear, but instantly denied herself, her relatives, and all her belongings. Already a young girl of the heavenly kingdom, she chose and claimed as her spouse

---

[1] I am indebted to the work of Sister Chiara Augusta Lainati, O.S.C., in the **Fonti Francescane** (Padova: Edizioni Messagero Padova, 1977) upon which these footnotes are based, as well as to the generosity of Br. Patrick Colbourne, O.F.M. Cap., who helped in their translation.

The original manuscript of the *Acts of the Process* opens with a transcription and an Italian translation of the papal directive *Gloriosus Deus* of Innocent IV, October 18, 1253, to Bishop Bartholomew Accorombani, Bishop of Spoleto from 1236 to 1271 (cf. C. Eubel, *Hierarchia cattolica Medii Aevi* I [Münster: 1913], 458). *Gloriosus Deus* is preserved in the original Latin in the *Bullarium Franciscanum* I, ed. J.H.Sbaralea et al. (Rome, 1759–1768), 684.

the poor Jesus Christ, the King of kings. Vowing herself totally to Him, with her mind and body in a spirit of humility, she promised Him principally these two good things, almost by way of a dowry, the gift of poverty and the vow of chaste virginity.

So the modest virgin was united to the desired embraces of the virgin Spouse, and, from the bed of irreproachable virginity, a progeny came: chaste and marvelously fruitful to all, which, under the odor of her holy way of life and love of salutary profession, spread through almost every part of the world like a heavenly plant abundantly fruitful for God.

This is that spouse who, while she seemed to be dead to the world, was so pleasing to God the Most High with her desires, deeds of virtue, and studies of the holy acts. From the moment that she died joyfully, and even before she departed from this mortal life, the compassionate condescension of almighty God, rewarder of every good, in the abundance of His kindness which exceeds the merits and desires of those who pray for it, grants favors for the exaltation of His ever glorious name to those who ask for them because the clear merits of the virgin Clare were interceding. God comes down to perform on earth many different miracles through her and her prayers.[2]

It is fitting and right that she be honored in the Church Militant. For the divine mercy because of her gifts of grace and the worth of her miracles has demonstrated that she be venerated by the faithful. Therefore, we direct Your Brotherhood, through apostolic letters, to diligently and carefully research her life, conversion, and manner of life, as well as the truth of all the aforesaid miracles and all their particulars according to the questions we send you included under this Bull.[3] As for what you may find out about the aforesaid matters, be careful to send it to Us under your seal, written faithfully through a notary, so her soul, believed to be already rejoicing with happiness in heaven with the stole of immortality, may be followed in this world with fitting praise by the multitude of the just.

---

[2]The uniqueness of this document can be seen in its praise of Clare. Documents of this sort are usually quite reserved and objective; yet this one, written within two months of the death of Clare, reflects the sentiments of Innocent IV who, according to the **Legenda versificata,** considered celebrating the Liturgy of Virgins in place of that of the Dead for the funeral of Clare. His enthusiasm was shared by the participants of the entire Curia. Cf. B. Bughetti, "Legenda versificata S. Clarae Assisiensis," *Archivum Franciscanum Historicum* V (1912), 473.

[3]These questions no longer remain with the Acts of the Process. However it is clear from the procedure of the investigation of the witnesses that such questions correspond to everything in use at the time. These would have been known by Bishop Bartholomew of Spoleto who had conducted the process of Simon di Collazione a year earlier. Cf. Z. Lazzeri, "De processu canonizationis S. Clarae," *Archivum Franciscanum Historicum* V (1912), 654; "Il processo di canonizzazione di S. Chiara d'Assisi, *Archivum Franciscanum Historicum* XIII (1920), 404, 441.

Given at Saint John Lateran, the fifteenth calend of November [18 October] in the eleventh year of our pontificate.

Therefore I, the aforesaid Bartholomew, going personally to the monastery of San Damiano, received the testimonies about the life, conversion, manner of life, and miracles of the holy memory of the Lady Clare, former abbess of the monastery of San Damiano in Assisi, on the twenty-fourth day of the month of November, in the cloister of San Damiano. The names and details of those witnesses are written herein:

The first witness:	Lady Pacifica, daughter of Guelfuccio of Assisi;
the second:	Lady Benvenuta, daughter of Perugia;
the third:	Lady Filippa, daughter of Messer Leonardo di Ghislerio;
the fourth:	Lady Amata, daughter of Messer Martino of Corozano;
the fifth:	Lady Cristiana, daughter of Messer Cristiano of Parisse;[4]
the sixth:	Lady Cristiana, daughter of Bernard of Suppo;
the seventh:	Lady Benvenuta, daughter of Oportulo of Alessandro;
the eighth:	Lady Francesca, daughter of Messer Capitaneo of Col de Mezzo;
the ninth:	Lady Beatrice, daughter of Messer Favarone of Assisi, the sister of holy Clare;
the tenth:	Lady Cecilia of Spello;
the eleventh:	Lady Balvina, daughter of Messer Martino of Corozano;
the twelfth:	Lady Agnese, daughter of Messer de Oportulo;
the thirteenth:	Lady Lucia of Rome.

All are of the monastery of San Damiano and took an oath to tell the truth about the life, conversion, manner of living, and miracles of Saint Clare.[5] In the presence of these witnesses:

Leonardo, archdeacon of Spoleto;
Jacobo, archpriest of Trevi;

---

[4] This list of witnesses parallels the testimonies that follow until this point. There is no logical sequence for those remaining. Moreover, certain omissions and discrepancies in the names of the witnesses can be found: all of which have their origin in the edition of the *Acts of the Process* discovered by Lazzeri.

[5] The phrase *santa Chiara* (Saint Clare) seems presumptuous and premature. Nonetheless it underscores the reputation of sanctity enjoyed by Saint Clare even in official circles prior to the official recognition of it.

Brothers Leo, Angelo, and Marco of the Friars Minor; and the notary, Ser Martino.

In the presence of the venerable father, Lord Bartholomew, Bishop of Spoleto.

FIRST WITNESS

The Manner of Life of Saint Clare in the House of Her Father

1. Sister Pacifica de Guelfuccio of Assisi,[6] a nun of the monastery of San Damiano, said under oath she knew Saint Clare while that holy woman was in the world in her father's house; and that she was considered by all those who knew her [to be a person] of great honesty and of very good life; and that she was intent upon and occupied with works of piety.

Her Conversion

2. She said that Saint Clare began the Order that is now at San Damiano through the admonition of Saint Francis. She entered it as a virgin, and always remained such a virgin.

When she was asked how she knew these things, she responded that when she was in the world she was her neighbor and distant relative and that only the piazza was between her house and that of the virgin Clare.[7] She frequently conversed with her.

3. She said the Lady Clare loved the poor very much and all the citizens held her in great veneration because of her good manner of life. When she was asked how much time had passed since the virgin Clare had left the world, she said it was about forty-two years.[8]

---

[6]Sister Pacifica, the natural sister of Bona di Guelfuccio, the seventeenth witness, knew Clare before her conversion (cf. *Process* I:2) and was among her first companions (cf. ibid., I:3).

[7]Clare's house was located on one side of the piazza of San Rufino; cf. G. Abate, *La casa paterna di S. Chiara* (Assisi, 1946); *Nuovi studi sull'ubicazione della casa paterna di S. Chiara* (Assisi, 1954).

[8]The difficulty of the chronology of St. Clare becomes apparent at this point. The date of her death is certain, August 11, 1253. Yet that of her birth, eighteen years before her entrance into religious life, as well as that of her flight to the Portiuncula, is obscure. March 28, 1211 is suggested as the date of the Palm Sunday of Clare's flight to the Portiuncula, which would suggest her birth in 1193. Cf. Z. Lazzeri, "Il Processo di canonizzazione di santa Chiara," *Archivum Franciscanum Historicum* XIII (1920), 434–435; F. Casolini, *Vita di Santa Chiara Vergine di Tommaso da Celano* (Santa Maria degli Angeli, 1962), 34; C.A. Lainati, *Santa Chiara d'Assisi* (Assisi, 1970); *Temi Spirituali degli Scritti del Secondo Ordine* (Assisi, 1970). Others

When she was asked how she knew this, she replied she had entered the Order at the same time with her and had served her for the most part almost day and night.[9]

4. She also said Lady Clare was born of noble stock, of noble father and mother. Her father was a knight, Messer Favarone, whom she (the witness) had never seen. But she saw her mother, Ortulana. This lady, Ortulana, went beyond the sea for reasons of prayer and devotion.[10]

She likewise testified she [the witness] accompanied her beyond the sea for reasons of prayer and devotion. They also went together to Sant'Angelo and to Rome.[11]

She said she willingly visited the poor.

Asked how she knew these things, she replied: because she was her neighbor and was with her, as mentioned above.

5. She also said Lady Ortulana came to that same Order as her holy daughter, blessed Clare, and lived in it with the other sisters in great humility. There, adorned by religious and holy deeds, she passed from this life.[12]

6. The witness also said three years after Saint Clare had been in the Order, at the prayers and insistence of Saint Francis, who almost forced her, she accepted the direction and government of the sisters.[13]

Asked how she knew this, she said she was present.

---

place the date of the flight to the Portiuncula at March 18, 1212, which would place Clare's birth in 1194 (cf. M. Becker, J.F. Godet, T. Matura, *Claire d'Assise: Écrits* (Paris: Les Éditions du Cerf, 1986), 68; D. Cresi, "Cronologia di santa Chiara," *Studi Francescani* XXV (1953), 260–267; L. Hardick, Zur Chronologie im Leben der hl.Klara," in *Franziskanische Studien* XXXV (1953) 174–210; A. Terzi, *Cronologia della vita di San Francesco d'Assisi* (Roma, 1963), 56–62.

[9]It does not seem that Pacifica accompanied Clare in her flight to the Portiuncula. Her silence in this instance is significant.

[10]That is, to the Holy Land.

[11]Sant'Angelo refers to San Michele del Monte Gargano in southern Italy, a favorite place of pilgrimage for the medieval Christian.

[12]The date of Ortulana's entrance into San Damiano is not known. She seems to have died there prior to 1238 since her name does not appear on the list of sisters whose names are found on a document published by Luke Wadding concerning the sale of property, cf. *Annales Minorum* III (1238), ed. L. Wadding, 14–15 (cf. infra pp. 107–108.)

[13]The imposition of government upon San Damiano is frequently attributed to the influence of the Fourth Lateran Council (November, 1215) which prescribed in its thirteenth canon that any new religious house had to be governed according to previously existing religious Rules; cf. L. Hardick, "Zur Chronologie im Leben der hl.Klara," *Franziskanische Studien* XXXV (1953), 174–210. Nevertheless, it is plausible that both Francis and Guido, Bishop of Assisi, could have suggested a form of government when the number of Clare's companions was growing steadily.

Her Manner of Life in the Monastery

7. This witness also said the blessed mother kept vigil so much of the night in prayer, and kept so many abstinences that the sisters lamented and were alarmed. She said that because of this she herself had sometimes wept.

Asked how she knew this, she replied: because she saw when Lady Clare lay on the ground and had a rock from the river for her head, and heard her when she was in prayer.

8. She said she was so very strict in her food that the sisters marveled at how her body survived. She also said blessed Clare fasted much of the time. Three days of the week, Monday, Wednesday, and Friday, she did not eat anything. She said on other days she kept such abstinences she developed a certain illness so Saint Francis together with the bishop of Assisi commanded her to eat on those three days at least a half a roll of bread, about one and a half ounces.

9. She also said the blessed mother was assiduous and careful in her prayers, lying a long time upon the ground, remaining humbly prostrate. When she came from her prayer, she admonished and comforted her sisters always speaking the words of God Who was always in her mouth, so much so that she did not want to speak or hear of vanities.

When she returned from her prayer, the sisters rejoiced as though she had come from heaven.

Asked how she knew these things, she replied she lived with her.

10. She also said Lady Clare, when she commanded her sisters to do something, did so with great fear and humility and more often than not she wished to do what she had commanded the others.

11. She also said that when she was so sick that she could not get up from bed, she had herself raised to sit up and be supported with some cushions behind her back. She spun [thread] so from her work she made corporals and altar linens for almost all the churches of the plains and hills around Assisi.

Asked how she knew these things, she replied that she saw her spinning. When the cloth was made and the sisters had sewn it, it was hand-delivered by the brothers to those churches and given to the priests who came there.

12. She also said the blessed mother was humble, kind, and loving to her sisters, and had compassion for the sick. While she was healthy, she served them and washed their feet and gave them water with her own hands. Sometimes she washed the mattresses of the sick.

Asked how she knew these things, she replied she had seen her many times.

13. She also said she particularly loved poverty, so that she could never be persuaded to desire anything for herself, or to receive any possession for herself or the monastery.

Asked how she knew this, she replied she saw and heard the Lord Pope Gregory of happy memory wanted to give her many things and buy possessions for the monastery. But she would never consent.[14]

14. She also said Lady Clare was as careful about the [regular] observance of her Order and the government of her sisters as someone might be in safeguarding her temporal treasure.

And these things, she said, she knew because she was always with her, for about forty years and more, except for one year when, with the permission of the blessed mother, she stayed in the monastery of Valle Gloria in Spello for the formation of the sisters in that place.[15]

The Miracle of the Oil

15. This witness also said the life of blessed Clare was filled with miracles.

She learned once, when there was no oil in the monastery, the blessed mother called a certain brother of the Friars Minor, Brother Bentevenga, who used to beg alms for them. She told him to go seeking oil. He replied that they should prepare the jar for him. Then Lady Clare took a certain jar, washed it with her own hands, and placed it on a certain wall near the entrance of the house. There the brother would take it.

The jar remained there for about an hour. Then that brother, Bentevenga, went for it and found it filled with oil. After searching diligently, he did not find who had placed it there.

Asked how she knew this, she replied since she was in the house she saw when the lady had taken out the empty jar and she had brought it back filled. She said she did not know who had filled it or how it had been filled. Brother Bentevenga said the same.

Asked about the time of this event, she replied it was about the second

---

[14]Cf. *Process* II:22; III:14. The Legend portrays Pope Gregory IX as more insistent and describes the response of St. Clare to the papal pressures; cf. *Legend* 14. Clare conscientiously defended the Form of Life, together with poverty, that Saint Francis had given her. Thus she tenaciously maintained her desire to live the poor and simple life proposed by St. Francis rather than capitulate to the relaxations offered by the Pope.

[15]Leaving San Damiano to establish or participate in the formation of other monasteries occurs rather frequently in the sources. It was the only legitimate reason for leaving the enclosure according to the norms of Cardinal Hugolino given to the Ladies of San Damiano; cf. *Rule of Hugolino*, infra, For information on the monastery of ValleGloria, cf. M. Sensi, "Il patrimonio monastico di S. Maria di Vallegloria a Spello," *Bolletino della Dep. di Storia Patria per l'Umbria* 81 (1984), 77–149.

year after they had come to live in the monastery of San Damiano. Asked about what month and what day, she replied she did not remember. Asked if it were in the summer or winter, she replied, summer.

Asked which sisters were present at that time, she said Sister Agnes, Saint Clare's sister, who just a little while ago had passed from this life, was present, as well as Sister Balvina, abbess of the monastery of Valle Gloria, who had also died, and Sister Benvenuta of Perugia, still living.[16]

And she swore about these things, and the witness also said she could not explain with her own tongue the miracles and virtues which the Lord had shown through blessed Clare.

How Saint Clare Cured Five Sick Sisters with the Sign of the Cross

16. This witness also said one time when five sisters were sick in the monastery, Saint Clare made the sign of the cross with her own hand over them and all of them were immediately cured.

Frequently when one of the sisters had some pain in either the head or another part of the body, the blessed mother cured her with the sign of the cross. Asked how she knew the things mentioned, she replied she was present. Asked who the five sisters were, she replied that she, the witness, was one, some of the others had died, others were living, but she did not remember whom. Asked the length of time she, the witness, was sick, she replied it was a long time.

Asked what the sickness was, she replied it was one that made her shriek, have a great fever and shake.

Asked about the others who had been cured, the length of time they had been sick, she replied she did not remember about the others as about herself. Asked when those sisters were cured, she replied: before the Lady was sick.

17. Asked about the time Saint Clare began that long illness, she replied she believed it was twenty-nine years.[17]

18. She also said the medicine of that witness and of the other sisters

---

[16]Tradition places the death of Agnes, Clare's sister, at November 16, 1253, that is, eight days before the investigation of the witnesses. This date, however, is not supported by other sources, e.g. the Legend 48, that claim her death occurred "a few days after the death of Saint Clare." Cf. C.A. Lainati, *Cenni biografici di sant'Agnese d'Assisi* (Assisi, 1969), 101–102.

[17]While Sister Pacifica claims that St. Clare was sick for twenty-nine years, the Legend 39 maintains twenty-eight years. For a thorough treatment of the illness of Saint Clare, see O. Schumucki, "Infermità," *Dizionario Francescano* (Padova: Edizioni Messagero Padova, 1983), 725–770. Most recent material can be found in the report of E. Fulcheri, *Ricognizioni effetualte sui resti di S. Chiara d'Assisi*, upon completion of a thorough examination of the body of the saint in October 1987.

when they were sick was that their mother made the sign of the cross over them.

Asked what words Lady Clare used to speak when she made the sign of the cross, she replied they did not understand her because she spoke very softly.

19. Asked about the month and the day she, the witness, and the other sisters were cured, she replied she did not remember. Asked who was present when they were cured, she replied more sisters were present, but she did not remember how many nor who.

SECOND WITNESS

1. Sister Benvenuta of Perugia,[18] nun of the monastery of San Damiano, said under oath Lady Clare, former abbess of the monastery of San Damiano, had marvelous humility and so looked down upon herself and that those tasks which she knew were more degrading she herself performed.

She even cleaned the matresses of the sick sisters with her own hands.

Asked how she knew these things, she replied she entered religion in that same year as she did; she knew she had entered on Holy Monday, and, she, the witness, entered afterwards in the month of September.

2. Asked about the time of Saint Clare's entrance into religion, she replied that she was eighteen years old or so, according to what was said. She was a virgin in spirit and in body and held in great veneration by all who knew her even before she entered religion. This was because of her great honesty, kindness, and humility.

Asked how she knew the things mentioned, she replied she, the witness, had known her before she entered religion and had stayed with her in [the same] house. From the time she entered religion, she stayed with her until her death, for almost forty-two years, except for the aforesaid time, that is, from Holy Monday until the end of September.

The Manner of Life of Saint Clare in the Monastery

3. The witness said from the time the mother Saint Clare entered religion, she was so humble she washed the feet of the sisters. One time, while washing the feet of one of the serving sisters, she bent over, wishing

---

[18]Sister Benvenuta was the third companion of St. Clare to enter San Damiano. She knew St. Clare as a young girl when the family of Favarone had to flee to and reside in Perugia; cf. A. Fortini, "Nuove notizie intorno a santa Chiara di Assisi," *Archivum Franciscanum Historicum* XLVI (1983), 17–19.

to kiss the feet. That serving sister, pulling her foot away, accidentally hit the mouth of the blessed mother with her foot.[19]

More than this, the blessed Clare used to hand water to the sisters and, at night, covered them from the cold.

4. She was also so severe toward her body that she was content with only one tunic of "lazzo" and one mantle.[20] If she ever saw that the tunic of another of the sisters was worse than what she was wearing, she took it from her for herself and gave the better one to that sister.

5. The witness also said that the blessed Clare at one time had a certain shirt made of boar's hide. She wore it secretly under her woolen tunic with the skin and its bristles close to her skin.[21]

Likewise, another time, she had another shirt made of horsehair, knotted with certain cords. She tied it around her body, and thus afflicted her virgin flesh. She said there was still one of these shirts in the monastery.[22]

6. She also said she used such rough haircloths and shirts for herself but was very merciful to the sisters who could not endure such harshness and willingly gave them consolation.

7. Asked how she knew of these shirts, she replied she had seen them, but one time they had been borrowed by certain sisters; but she could not remember having seen the haircloth of the boar, but she heard of it from her natural sister who told her she had seen it. She knew [blessed Clare] wore it, as she had said, very secretly, so that it was not seen by the sisters. But from the time the Lady was ill, the sisters took the shirt, rough as it was, away from her.

8. She also said the mother, blessed Clare, before she was sick, practiced great abstinence: the greater Lent,[23] of Saint Martin,[24] she always fasted on bread and water, except on Sundays when she drank a little wine when there was some. Three days a week, Monday, Wednesday and Friday, she did not eat anything until that time when Saint Francis commanded her, in some way, to eat a little bit every day. Then, in order to practice obedience, she took a little bread and water.

---

[19]"Serving sisters," as they are called in the Acts of the Process, are distinguished in the Legend 12 from the "ladies" (*dominae*) by the word "servant" (*famulae*). In her Rule (II:12; III:10), St. Clare always refers to them as "the sisters serving outside the monastery," hence not bound to the law of enclosure and enjoying certain mitigations.

[20]*Lazzo*, a word of Umbrian dialect, signifies a type of home-spun cloth made of inferior wool and used by country folk.

[21]When the bristles are cut but not burnt the hairshirt is more irritating.

[22]This hairshirt was brought from San Damiano by the Poor Ladies when they moved to San Giorgio, later the Protomonastery of Saint Clare. It is still kept among the relics of St. Clare.

[23]That which precedes Easter.

[24]From the Feast of All Saints until Christmas.

Asked how she knew this, she said she had seen her and she was present when Saint Francis made that command.

9. The witness also said mother Saint Clare was very assiduous, day and night, in prayer. At about midnight she woke the sisters with certain signs in silence to praise God. She lit the lamps in the church and frequently rang the bell for Matins. Those sisters who did not rise at the sound of the bell she called with her signs.[25]

10. She also said her speech was always about the things of God. She did not wish to talk about worldly things or for the sisters to remember these things. If it happened at times that some worldly person did something contrary to God, astonishingly she wept, reproached such a person, and exhorted that one anxiously to turn to penance.

Asked how she knew the things mentioned, she replied she was with her and saw the things spoken of.

11. She said the Lady Clare frequently confessed, and, with great devotion and fear, frequently received the holy sacrament of the Body of our Lord Jesus Christ, trembling all over as she did so.

12. Concerning the corporals made from her spinning: she said the same as Sister Pacifica, the witness above. But she added she had paper boxes lined with silk made to hold them and had them blessed by the Bishop.

How She Cured a Sister Who Had Lost Her Voice

13. She also said that after she, the witness, had lost her voice so that she was barely able to speak even softly, she had a vision on the night of the Assumption of the Virgin Mary in which Lady Clare, while making the sign of the cross with her hand over her, cured her. It was done in such a way that on that same day she was cured since she did make the sign of the cross over her.

She said this sickness had persisted almost two years.

Asked how long it was the sister spoken of had been cured, she replied she did not remember. Asked who had been present, she said Sister Pacifica, who had given her testimony above, and other sisters who had died.

14. Concerning the jar of oil: she also said the same as Sister Pacifica, except that she did not remember if Saint Clare had washed the jar herself or if she had it washed by others.

---

[25]The custom of celebrating Matins or the Office of Readings at midnight is not prescribed in the Rule of St. Clare. Hence this piece of information is invaluable in confirming a practice that still exists in many communities of the Sisters of St. Clare.

How She Cured a Brother from His Insanity

15. The said witness also said that a certain brother of the Order of Friars Minor, Stephen by name, was mentally ill. Saint Francis sent him to the monastery of San Damiano, so Saint Clare would make the sign of the cross over him. After she had done this, the brother went to sleep a little bit in the place where the holy mother usually prayed. Upon waking, he ate a little and then departed cured.[26]

Asked who was present at this event, she replied the sisters of the monastery were, some [still] living, others dead.

Asked if she had known that brother beforehand, how many days she had seen him ill, and how much time well, she replied she did not know all these things, because she was enclosed. Brother Stephen, once cured, went on his way.

The Cure of the Infections of Fistulas

16. The witness also said a sister of the said monastery, Sister Benvenuta of Lady Diambra, was seriously ill and suffering great pain from a serious infection under her arm. Learning about this the compassionate mother, Saint Clare, filled with great compassion, was moved to pray for her. After making the sign of the cross over her, she was immediately cured.[27]

Asked how she knew this, she said she had first seen the infection and then seen the cure. Asked if she had been present when she made the sign of the cross, she replied she had not, but knew it had been so and done in that way. Asked when this was, she said she did not remember the day or month, nor how many days before or afterwards. But she saw her healthy and cured immediately after that day when Saint Clare made the sign of the cross over her.

17. The witness also said in that place where the Lady Clare usually

---

[26]This incident is revealing with regard to the relationship between St. Francis and St. Clare, the First and Second Orders, and their mutual assistance which went beyond sharing a common spirit to solving the problems that occasionally arose.

It is also interesting to note "the place where the holy mother usually prayed." In terms of the plan of the enclosure, the expression sounds ambiguous. However it need present no problem when we consider the place for prayer according to the Rule (V:10) is a place partly inside and partly outside the enclosure, with an iron grille in between. Cf. C.A. Lainati, "The Enclosure of St. Clare and of the First Poor Clares in Canonical Legislation and in Practice," *The Cord* 28 (1978), 4–15, 47–60.

[27]Cf. testimony of the eleventh witness, (XI 1) infra p. 163.

went to pray, she saw above it a great brilliance so she believed it was the flame of an actual fire.

Asked if anyone other than she had seen it, she replied, at that time, she was the only one who saw it. Asked how long ago this had been, she replied it was before the Lady was sick.

How a Young Boy Was Cured of a Pebble

18. She also said a young boy of the city of Spoleto, Mattiolo, three or four years old, had put a small pebble up one of the nostrils of his nose, so it could in no way be extricated. The young boy seemed to be in danger. After he was brought to Saint Clare and she made the sign of the cross over him, that pebble immediately fell from his nose. The young boy was cured.

Asked who was present, she replied some of the sisters now dead. Asked how long ago, she replied she did not remember; she was not present when the holy mother made the sign of the cross. But she affirmed she learned of it by hearing the other sisters. She had seen the young boy healthy on that day or on the day after the cure.

19. She also said she did not believe she or any other sisters could fully speak of the holiness or greatness of the life of Lady Clare of holy memory were it not that the Holy Spirit made them tell of it. Even when she was seriously ill, she never wished to leave her customary prayers.

How the Monastery Was Freed from the Saracens by the prayers of Saint Clare

20. She also said once, at the time of the war of Assisi, when certain Saracens scaled the wall and climbed down into the part within the cloister of San Damiano, holy mother Saint Clare, then seriously ill, got up from her bed and called her sisters, comforting them not to be afraid. After she prayed, the Lord delivered the monastery and the sisters from the enemy. Those Saracens, who had already entered, departed.[28]

21. She also said that, through the virtues and grace that God had placed in her, all who knew her considered her a saint.

---

[28]The episode concerning the attack upon San Damiano by the "Saracens", a band of Moslem soldiers of fortune or mercenaries in the pay of Frederick II (1210/15–1250), appears frequently in the *Acts of the Process* (III:18; IV:14; VI:10; VII:6; IX:2; X:9; XII:8; XIII:9; XIV:3). It is one of the few incidents that can be dated with certainty: a Friday in September, 1230, at about the hour of Terce. What is curious, however, is that no historical record of this episode can be found. Cf. E. Franceschini, "S. Chiara e i Saraceni", *Chiara d'Assisi, Rassegna del Protomonastero*, I (1953), 147–157; "I due asalti dei Saraceni a San Damiano e ad Assisi", *Aevum* XXVII (1953), 289–306.

22. She also said she especially had a great love of poverty. Neither Pope Gregory nor the Bishop of Ostia[29] could ever make her consent to receive any possessions.

Moreover, blessed Clare sold her inheritance and gave it to the poor. Asked how she knew these things, she replied she was present and heard the Lord Pope tell her that he wanted her to receive possessions. This Pope personally came to the monastery of San Damiano.

23. She also said mother Saint Clare knew through the Spirit that one of the sisters, Sister Andrea, was suffering from some boils in her throat. One night [Sister Andrea] squeezed her throat with her own hands so that she could not speak. [Mother Clare] immediately sent one of the sisters to her to give her support and help.[30]

THIRD WITNESS

1. Sister Filippa, daughter of Lord Leonardo di Ghislerio, nun of the monastery of San Damiano,[31] said under oath that four years after Saint Clare entered Religion through the preaching of Saint Francis, the witness entered in that same Religion, and the saint described how our Lord Jesus Christ suffered passion and death on the cross for the salvation of the human race.

The witness, moved by this, consented to be in the same Religion and to do penance together with her.

She stayed with Lady Clare from that time until the day of her death, almost thirty-eight years.

2. She said the holiness and righteousness of the ways of the blessed mother was such neither she nor any of the other sisters could fully explain them. She learned that Lady Clare, as she was a virgin from her childhood, remained such a chosen virgin of the Lord. Neither the witness nor any of the other sisters ever doubted her sanctity.

Moreover, before Saint Clare entered Religion, she was considered a saint by all those who knew her. And this was due to the righteousness of her life, the many virtues and graces which the Lord had placed in her.

---

[29]This is Rainaldo Segni, Cardinal of Ostia, Protector of the First and Second Order, subsequently Pope Alexander IV.

[30]Cf. Testimony of following witness, Sister Filippa.

[31]Similar to St. Clare, Filippa di Leonardo di Gislerio belonged to the feudal nobility of Assisi, and, like Sister Benvenuta, the second witness, knew St. Clare in Perugia "since childhood" (III:8). She was the daughter of Leonardo di Gislerio d'Alberico, the lord of Castle of Sassorosso, which was among the first destroyed by the fury of the mob as the Commune of Assisi asserted itself at the end of 1100; cf. A. Fortini, *Francis of Assisi*, trans. H. Moak (New York: Crossroad, 1981), 124–126.

The Manner of Life of Saint Clare in the Monastery

3. This witness also said from the time Saint Clare entered Religion, the Spirit increased her virtues and graces. She knew Saint Clare was very humble and devout, kind and very enamored of poverty, with compassion for the afflicted. She was assiduous in prayer. Her manner of life and speech was always concerned with the things of God so she never gave her tongue or ears to worldly things.

4. She chastised her body with coarse clothing, sometimes having her shirts made from knots of hair from the mane or tail of a horse. She had a tunic and a mantle of cheap "lazzo." Her bed was vine-branches, and she was content with these things for some time.

5. She also afflicted her body by not eating anything three days a week, on the second, fourth, and sixth days. On the other days, she fasted on bread and water.

6. Nevertheless she was always rejoicing in the Lord, was never seen disturbed. Her life was totally angelic. The Lord had given her so much grace that many times, when the sisters were sick, the blessed woman cured them by making the sign of the cross over them.

7. She also said the blessed mother had especially the gift of many tears, having great compassion for the sisters and the afflicted. She especially poured out many tears when she received the Body of our Lord Jesus Christ.

8. Asked how she knew all these things, she replied: because the witness was the third sister of Lady Clare.[32] She had known her from her childhood. From the aforesaid time she was always with her and saw the events.

9. She also said the humility of the blessed mother was so great that she consistently looked down upon herself and abased herself before the other sisters, making herself less than the other persons by serving them, giving them water by hand, washing the mattresses of the sick sisters with her own hand, and even washing the feet of the serving sisters.

One time, while she was washing the feet of one of the serving sisters of the monastery, she turned to kiss her feet. That sister clumsily withdrew her foot and thus, while pulling it away, she hit the holy mother in the mouth with her foot. Nevertheless, because of her humility, Clare did not desist, but kissed the sole of the foot of the servant.

Asked how she knew the things spoken of, she replied she saw them because she was also present.

---

[32]Sister Filippa was not a natural sister of St. Clare, but the third to join Clare, i.e., the fourth community member.

A Sister Who Was Cured of a Fistula

10. When this witness was asked what sisters were cured by the blessed Clare with the sign of the cross, she said Sister Benvenuta di Lady Diambra was one. After twelve years of having a serious infection, called a fistula, under her arm, the sign of the cross was made by the Lady with the Lord's Prayer, and she was cured of her infection.

11. She also said Sister Amata, a nun of the monastery, was seriously ill with dropsy and fever and had a very swollen stomach.[33] She had received the sign of the cross from the holy mother and had been touched with her hand. On the following morning she was cured so that her little body was restored to good health.

Asked how she knew it, she replied she saw when the holy mother made the sign of the cross and touched her, had seen that she had been sick for a long period of time; on the following day and thereafter, she saw her healthy.

12. She said the same about the cure of Brother Stephen as Sister Benvenuta, the previous witness, had.[34]

13. She also said that she was such a lover of poverty that when the begging [brothers] of the monastery brought back whole loaves of bread as alms, she reproachingly asked: "Who has given you these loaves of bread?"[35] She said this because she preferred to receive broken loaves of bread as alms rather than whole ones.

14. She could never be persuaded by the Pope or the Bishop of Ostia to receive any possessions. The Privilege of Poverty granted to her was honored with great reverence and kept well and with great diligence since she feared she might lose it.

How Saint Clare Cured a Young Boy of a Fever

15. The aforesaid witness also said a young boy, the son of Lord Giovanni di Maestro Giovanni, procurator of the sisters, was seriously ill with a fever.[36] This was mentioned to mother Saint Clare. When he received the sign of the cross from her, he was cured.

Asked how she knew this, she replied: because she was present when

---

[33]Cf. Testimony of fourth witness, Sister Amata (IV:7).

[34]Cf. supra *Process* II:15.

[35]The Friars Minor went questing for the Poor Ladies of San Damiano according to the expressed wish of the Rule of Saint Clare XII:5, 6, 7. Brother Bentevenga, mentioned by Sister Pacificia (Process I:15), was one of these questors.

[36]The "procurator" or "syndic" was a trustworthy person who took charge of carrying on the business of the monastery. He is expressly mentioned in the document of 1238 in which the sisters disposed of a piece of property; cf. supra.

the boy came and when the blessed mother touched him and made the sign of the cross over him. Asked if that boy had the fever then and if she saw him healed from that time, she replied it appeared he did have a fever then. She did not see him afterwards because the boy left the monastery, but his father told them he was immediately healed.

How She Cured Sister Andrea of Her Scrofula

16. The witness also said that when one of the sisters, Sister Andrea da Ferrara, was suffering from a scrofula in her throat, Lady Clare knew by inspiration she was very tempted by her desires for a cure. One night while Sister Andrea was below in the dormitory, she squeezed her throat with her own hands so strongly she lost her voice. The holy mother knew this through inspiration. Then she immediately called the witness, who slept near her and told her: "Go down immediately to the dormitory because Sister Andrea is seriously ill; boil an egg and give it to her to swallow. After she has recovered her speech, bring her to me." And so it was done.

When the Lady asked Sister Andrea what had been the matter, Sister Andrea did not want to tell her. Then the attentive Lady told her everything in detail as it had happened. And this spread about among the sisters.

How She Cured a Sister of Her Deafness
and Freed the Monastery of the Saracens

17. The witness also said that the Lady Clare cured a sister, Sister Cristiana, of a long-term deafness in one ear.[37]

18. She also said at the time of the war of Assisi the sisters were very much afraid of the arrival of those Tartars, Saracens and other enemies of God and the Church. The blessed mother began to comfort them, saying, "My sisters and daughters, do not be afraid because, if the Lord is with us, the enemy cannot harm us. Have confidence in our Lord Jesus Christ because He will free us. I want to be your hostage so that you do not do anything bad. If they come, place me before them."

One day, when the enemy had advanced to destroy Assisi, certain Saracens scaled the walls of the monastery and went down into the enclosure. The sisters were greatly afraid. But the most holy mother comforted all of them, looked down on the troops, and said, "Do not be afraid, because they will not be able to hurt us." After saying this, she turned to the help of her usual prayer. The strength of the prayer was such that the hostile Saracens departed as if driven away without doing any harm nor touching anyone in the house.

---

[37]Cf. Testimony of the fifth witness (V:1).

Asked how she knew the things mentioned, she replied she had been present. Asked what month and day, she did not remember.

19. She also said the greatly feared Vitalis d'Aversa had been sent by the emperor with a great army to assault Assisi. Since he had asserted he would not leave Assisi until he had taken it, Lady Clare was told in order to prevent this danger. After she had heard this, the Lady, confident of God's power, called all the sisters, had them bring some ashes and covered her unveiled head with them. Then the Lady placed the ashes on the heads of all the sisters and commanded them to go to prayer so the Lord God would free the city.

She learned the next day that Vitalis had left by night with all his army.[38]

20. The witness also said that when the Lady and holy mother was near death, one Friday night she began to speak:[39] "Go calmly in peace, for you will have a good escort, because He Who created you has sent you the Holy Spirit and has always guarded you as a mother does her child who loves her." She added: "O Lord, may You Who have created me, be blessed."

She said many things about the Trinity, so softly the sisters were not able to understand her well.

21. And the witness said to one of the sisters present: "You have a good memory; remember well what the Lady says." The Lady heard these words and told the sisters: "You will only remember these things I now say as long as He Who made me say them permits you."

22. Sister Anastasia also asked the Lady with whom or to whom she was speaking those words mentioned above. She replied, "I am speaking to my soul."

23. The witness added the whole night of that day during which she passed from this life, she admonished her sisters by preaching to them. At the end she made such a beautiful and good confession that the witness had never heard anything like it. She made this confession because she doubted that she had not offended in some way the faith promised at her baptism.

---

[38]The siege of Assisi by the troops of the Emperor Frederick II under the command of Vitale d'Aversa dates back to the summer of 1241. It is part of that war during which the Poor Ladies of San Damiano had already suffered threats (cf. supra, p. 138, n. 28). Assisi commemorates this event each year with the *festa del voto* (the feast of the vow) on June 22. Cf. U. Cosmo, "Con Madonna Povertà" (Bari, Studi Francescani, 1940), 267; G. Golubovich, "Relazione del duplice assdedio del monastero di S. Damiano (1240) e della città d'Assisi (1241) secondo il codice assisiano 341: testo latino inedito," *In Ricordo* 1212–1219, Assisi 1911, 33–35; E. Franceschini, "I due assalti dei Saraceni a San Damiano e ad Assisi," *Aevum* XXVII (1935), 289–306.

[39]The night between Friday and Saturday prior to St. Clare's death, that is, the night of August 8.

24. Lord Pope Innocent came to visit her since she was seriously ill.[40] She then told the sisters: "My daughters, praise God, because heaven and earth are not enough for such a benefit I have received from God. Today I have received Him in the Blessed Sacrament and I have also seen His Vicar."

Asked how she knew the things mentioned, she replied because she had seen them and was present. Asked how much time this was before the death of the Lady Clare, she replied a few days.

25. The said witness also said the Lady Clare was so caught up in her contemplation that during the day of Good Friday, while thinking about the Passion of the Lord, she was almost insensible throughout that entire day and a large part of the following day.

26. She said as those witnesses before had said under oath about the jar of oil.[41]

27. Asked again about the sisters who were cured, she said there were more who had been healed who had since died.

28. The witness also said Lady Clare told the sisters how her mother, when she was carrying her, went into the church. While standing before the cross and actually praying for God to help and protect her during the danger of childbirth, she heard a voice telling her: "You will give birth to a light that will shine brilliantly in the world."

29. Lady Clare also related how once, in a vision, it seemed to her she brought a bowl of hot water to Saint Francis along with a towel for drying his hands. She was climbing a very high stairway, but was going very quickly, almost as though she were going on level ground. When she reached Saint Francis, the saint bared his breast and said to the Lady Clare: "Come, take and drink." After she had sucked from it, the saint admonished her to imbibe once again. After she did so what she had tasted was so sweet and delightful she in no way could describe it.

After she had imbibed, that nipple or opening of the breast from which the milk came remained between the lips of blessed Clare. After she took what remained in her mouth in her hands, it seemed to her it was gold so clear and bright that everything was seen in it as in a mirror.[42]

---

[40]Innocent IV was in Assisi in April, May, and from June to October 6, 1253. Niccolò da Clavi's *Vita Innocentii IV* (F. Pagnotti, "Niccolò da Clavi e la sua vita di Innocenzo IV," *Archivo della Società Romana di storia patria*, XXI [1898], 4–120) records two visits of the Pope to the saint.

[41]Cf. supra *Process* I:15; II:14.

[42]An excellent treatment of this event can be found in M. Bartoli, "Analisi storica e interpretazione psicoanalitica di una visione di sant Chiara d'Assisi," *Archivum Franciscanum Historicum* 73 (1980) 449–472.

The Marvelous Hearing of Saint Clare

30. The Lady Clare also narrated how on the most recent night of the Lord's Nativity because of her serious illness she could not get up from her bed to go to the chapel.[43] All the sisters went as usual to Matins and left her alone. The Lady then said with a sigh: "Lord God, look, I have been left here alone with you."

She immediately began to hear the organ, responsories and the entire Office of the brothers in the Church of Saint Francis, as if she were present there.

31. This witness narrated these and many other miracles of speech and hearing of Lady Clare, the first Mother and Abbess of the monastery of San Damiano and the first member of the Order.

Noble by her birth and upbringing and rich in worldly goods, she so loved poverty that she sold her entire inheritance and distributed it to the poor. She so loved the Order she never wanted to neglect the slightest detail of the Order's observance even when she was ill.

32. At the end of her life, after calling together all her sisters, she entrusted the Privilege of Poverty to them. Her great desire was to have the Rule of the Order confirmed with a papal bull, to be able one day to place her lips upon the papal seal, and, then, on the following day, to die. It occurred just as she desired. She learned a brother had come with letters bearing the papal bull. She reverently took it even though she was very close to death and pressed that seal to her mouth in order to kiss it.[44]

On the following day, Lady Clare, truly clear without stain, with no darkness of sin, passed from this life to the Lord, to the clarity of eternal light.[45] This witness, all the sisters and all who knew her holiness maintain this without a doubt.

---

[43]That is, Christmas 1252.

[44]The papal bull which was brought to St. Clare as she was dying was *Solet annuere* of Innocent IV, August 9, 1253. It contained confirmation of her Rule. In the upper margin of the manuscript there is this annotation: "Let it be known. S. For reasons known to me and the Procurator of the monastery, let it be known." The initial "S" stands for Sinibaldus Fieschi, that is, Innocent IV. The original manuscript was lost until 1893 when the Abbess of the Protomonastery of St. Clare, Sister Maltilde Rossi, found it in a sealed box containing clothing of the saint. Cf. P. Robinson, "Inventarium omnium documentorum quae in Archivo Protomonasterii S. Clarae Assisiensis nunc asservantur," *Archivum Franciscanum Historicum*, I (1908), 417.

[45]This is one of those passages in which we see the contemporaries of Saint Clare play with the meaning of her name, Chiara (in Italian) or Clara (in Latin), both of which translate as the English "clear," the root of *"clarity."*

FOURTH WITNESS

1. Sister Amata, daughter of Messer Martino of Coccorano, a nun of the monastery of San Damiano, said under oath she had been about twenty-five years in that Order and had known Saint Clare.[46] The witness entered Religion because of the admonition and exhortation of the holy woman. [Saint Clare] told her she had asked the Lord for a special grace for her so she would not be allowed to be deceived by the world nor remain in it.

The witness was the natural niece of the saint she considered her mother.

2. She knew her manner of life and had heard how she had been converted: through the exhortation and preaching of Saint Francis, she had assumed religious life, even though before she entered it she was considered holy by all who knew her because of the many graces and virtues the Lord had given her, as it was known about her through her reputation.

3. From the time the witness entered Religion, she was always with her so she knew the virtues and the holiness of the conduct of her life, both of which God had given her. Though it could not be explained, the highest virginity, kindness, meekness, compassion toward her sisters and all others were present in her at the same time.

4. She was assiduous in prayer and contemplation. When she returned from prayer, her face appeared clearer and more beautiful than the sun. Her prayers sent forth an indescribable sweetness so her life seemed totally heavenly.

5. The portions of food she consumed were so small it seemed she was fed by angels. She certainly afflicted her body: three days of the week, Monday, Wednesday and Friday, she did not eat anything. On the other days, she fasted on bread and water, until Saint Francis commanded her to eat something on those days when she had not been eating at all. Then, to practice obedience, she ate a little bread and drank a little water.

6. She said the same as the witness, Sister Filippa, had said before about the coarseness of her clothes and bed.

---

[46]Sister Amata di Martino, like her sister Balvina, the seventh witness, was a *nepote carnale*, a niece of St. Clare, according to her own testimony. Z. Lazzeri corrected the early manuscript of the *Process* so that both sisters came not from *Corozano* but from *Coccorano*, a small castle located between Gubbio and Assisi (cf. Z. Lazzeri, "Il processo di canonizzazione di S. Chiara," *Archivum Franciscanum Historicum* XIII [1920], 433, n. 2). A. Fortini, however, denied this and corrected the document to *Corezano*, a short distance from Assisi. While Lazzeri maintains their status as nieces of St. Clare, Fortini claims that they were daughters of Lord Martino da *Corano*, a cousin of St. Clare (cf. A. Fortini, "Nuove notizie intorno a santa Chiara d'Assisi," *Archivum Franciscanum Historicum* XLVI [1953], 11–15).

How She Was Cured of a Fever, Cough, and Dropsy

7. The witness also said when she was seriously ill with dropsy, fever, a cough, and a pain in her side, Saint Clare made the sign of the cross over her and immediately cured her.

Asked what the saint had said, she replied that after placing her hand over her, she asked God, if it were best for her soul, to cure her from these illnesses. She was instantly cured.

Asked how long she had been ill, she said for thirteen months, but from then on, she no longer had those illnesses. She had, at that time, a greatly swollen stomach so she could hardly bend over.[47] Thus, through the merits of the saint, the Lord cured her completely.

How She Cured a Sister of a Fistula

8. In a similar way, Lady Clare cured certain sisters of their illnesses by making the sign of the cross over them.

Asked who those sisters were, she replied: Sister Benvenuta of Lady Diambra, who had certain serious infections under her arm in which five fingers could be placed. She had had that illness about eleven years. When the Lady made the sign of the cross over her, she was cured.[48]

Asked how she knew this, she replied there were growths coming out of it and she never again had that illness. Asked what that illness was, she replied they were called fistulas.

How She Cured a Sister with a Cough

9. She also said that another sister, Sister Cecilia, had a serious cough which overcame her as soon as she began to eat so it seemed she might suffocate.[49]

Therefore the holy mother gave her, on a certain Friday, a little cake to eat which she took with great fear. Nevertheless she ate it because of the command of the holy mother. From that moment, she never felt that illness.

Asked how long she had had that illness, she replied she did not remember but believed it had been for a long time.

---

[47]This is a typical symptom of dropsy.
[48]Sister Benvenuta, the eleventh witness, confirms this (cf. infra, *Process* XI 1).
[49]Cf. Testimony of the sixth witness (infra, *Process* VI 8).

How She Cured a Sister of Deafness in One Ear

10. She also said another, Sister Cristiana, had been deaf in one ear for a long time, even before entering the monastery.[50] Nevertheless, Lady Clare cured her by touching her deaf ear and making the sign of the cross over it. She said she did not remember the other sisters, although some others had been cured.

How She Cured a Young Boy With a Film Over His Eye

11. She said that a young boy from Perugia had a certain film over his eye which covered all of it. Then he was brought to Saint Clare who touched the eyes of the boy and then made the sign of the cross over him. Then she said: "Bring him to my mother, Sister Ortulana (who was in the monastery of San Damiano) and let her make the sign of the cross over him." After this had been done, the young boy was cured, so that Saint Clare said her mother had cured him. On the contrary, though, her mother said Lady Clare, her daughter, had cured him. Thus each one attributed this grace to the other.

Asked how long before that the young boy had been seen with this film, she replied she had seen him with that film when he was brought to the monastery to Lady Clare. She did not see him before or after the time he was cured since he immediately left the monastery and the witness always stayed enclosed in the monastery.

12. Asked about the humility of the saint, she said what Sister Filippa, the previous witness, had said under oath.[51]

13. She also said the same as Sister Filippa concerning the saint's love of poverty and prayer.

14. The witness also said when the sisters feared the arrival of the Saracens, Tartars, and other infidels, they asked the holy mother to do much with the Lord so the monastery would be protected from them. The holy mother responded: "My sisters and daughters, do not fear because the Lord will defend you. I wish to be your ransom; if it should happen that the enemies come down to the monastery, place me before them." Through the prayers of such a holy mother, the monastery, the sisters, and everything remained without a scratch.[52]

15. She said the same as Sister Filippa about the assault and liberation of the city of Assisi.[53]

---

[50]Cf. Testimony of the fifth witness (infra, *Process* V 1).
[51]Cf. Testimony of the third witness (Supra, *Process* III 3).
[52]Cf. Testimony of the third witness (Supra, *Process* III 18).
[53]Cf. Testimony of the third witness (Supra, *Process* III 19).

16. She said the same as Sister Filippa concerning all these things: the miracle of Saint Clare's mother, her vision and the breast of Saint Francis, the miracle of the night of the Lord's Nativity.[54] But she added she had heard from Lady Clare that, on the night of the Lord's Nativity, she also saw the manger of our Lord Jesus Christ.

17. The witness also said the Lord saw to it that the first in that Order would be so holy that no defect would be found in her. Instead all virtues and graces were seen in her, so, while she was still living, she was considered to be holy by all who knew her. She was also noble by her ancestry according to the flesh, but more so in her observance of the holy Religion and of her Order. Even during the time of her illness she never wanted to depart from anything of the Order. In her holiness, she governed herself and her sisters almost forty-three years.

18. She loved the sisters as herself. The sisters held her in reverence as a saint and the mother of the entire Order both during her life and after her death. She also said her holiness and goodness, her goods and virtues, were more than she knew or could say.

19. She also said when Lady Clare was close to the end, passing from this life, on the Friday before her death, she told the witness, who remained alone with her, "Did you see the King of Glory whom I saw?" She said this a few more times to her; some days afterwards she died.

20. The witness also said she heard from a lady of Pisa that the Lord had freed her of five demons through the merits of Saint Clare. The demons had confessed the prayers of the Lady Clare were burning them. Because of this the lady had come to the monastery, where one speaks to the sisters, so she would first thank God and then the Lady.

Asked how long ago this had been, she replied about four years.

FIFTH WITNESS

1. Sister Cristiana de Messer Cristiano de Parisse, nun of the monastery of San Damiano,[55] said under oath: since she, the witness, had been deaf in one ear for a long time, she had used many medicines which did not help at all. At last Saint Clare made the sign of the cross on her head and touched her ear. Thus her ear was opened so that she heard very well.

Asked how long ago this had been, she replied, about a year ago. Asked about the month and the day, she replied, either June or July. She did not remember the day.

2. The witness also said she did not in any way know how to explain

---

[54]Cf. Testimony of the third witness (Supra, *Process* III 28, 29, 30).
[55]Sister Cristiana de Messer Cristiano de Parisse entered San Damiano in 1246 or 1247. She was the daughter of one of the consuls of the Commune of Assisi.

the holiness of the life of Lady Clare as well as her uprightness of habits. But it might be, as she firmly believed, she was full of grace, virtue, and their holy operations. She believed all that could be said about the holiness of another woman besides the Virgin Mary, she would say truly about her. But it was impossible for her to speak of her virtues and graces.

3. She said the same as Sister Amata, the previous witness, concerning the cure of Sister Benvenuta and her infections.[56]

4. She also said seven years had not yet come to an end since she had entered the monastery.

5. She also said when a very heavy door had fallen from the monastery upon Lady Clare, a sister, Sister Angeluccia of Spoleto, shouted loudly, fearing she had been killed and knowing that she could not single-handedly lift that door which totally lay upon that Lady. Then the witness and the other sisters ran and the witness saw the door was still lying on her. It was so heavy that three brothers could hardly lift it and replace it. Nonetheless, the Lady said no harm had been done to her, but it were as if a mantle had been placed over her.

Asked how long ago this had been, she replied about seven years or so, in the month of July, during the Octave of Saint Peter.

SIXTH WITNESS

1. Sister Cecilia, daughter of Messer Gualtieri Cacciaguerra of Spoleto, nun of the monastery of San Damiano, said under oath she knew of Lady Clare of holy memory, former abbess of the monastery.[57] It could have been forty-three years or so that the Lady had been governing the Sisters. She herself entered Religion three years after the Lady had because of the preaching of Saint Francis.

The witness entered because of the exhortation of Lady Clare and Brother Philip of happy memory.[58] From that time, forty years ago, she

---

[56]Cf. Testimony of the fourth witness (Supra, *Process* IV 8).

[57]Sister Cecilia di Gaultieri Cacciaguerra of Spoleto was one of the first companions of St. Clare in San Damiano. She testifies to being in the monastery for almost forty years (cf. infra, *Process* VI 1, 5).

[58]Brother Philip the Long is one of the leading characters in the history of San Damiano. Born in Atri and, according to Celano (I Cel 25), endowed with "heavenly eloquence," he accompanied St. Francis during the secret meetings between St. Francis and St. Clare (cf. testimony of seventeenth witness, XVII 3). He was the one who, together with Francis and Bernard of Quintavalle, accompanied St. Clare from the Benedictine monastery of San Paolo near Bastia, to Sant'Angelo di Panzo on the slope of Monte Subasio (cf. testimony of twelfth witness, XII 5). While St. Francis was in the Middle East, Cardinal Hugolino appointed him General Visitator of the Poor Ladies. However, he was removed upon St. Francis' return and replaced by Brother Pacificus (cf. L. Oliger, "De origine Regularum Ordinis S. Clarae," *Ar-*

was under the government of Lady Clare, whose life, so praiseworthy and wonderful, and holy manner of life, the witness was not equal to describing completely.

2. But God chose her as mother of the virgins, as the first and principal abbess of the Order, so that she guarded the flock and strengthened the other sisters of the Order with her example in the goal of the holy Order. She was certainly most diligent about encouraging and protecting the sisters, showing compassion toward the sick sisters. She was solicitous about serving them, humbly submitting herself to even the least of the serving sisters, always looking down upon herself.

3. She was vigilant in prayer and sublime contemplation. At times, when she returned from prayer, her face appeared clearer than usual and a certain sweetness came from her mouth.

4. She had an abundance of tears in her prayers and showed spiritual joy with her sisters. She was never upset, but treated the sisters with great meekness and kindness and at times, when there was need, she diligently corrected them.

5. She never wished to excuse her body. Very early in her religious life, she was very harsh in her sleeping and in her clothing and was very strict in what she ate and drank. She seemed to have the life of an angel in that her holiness was obvious to all those who knew and heard her.

Asked how she knew these things, she replied she had been with her almost forty years and saw her holy life and manner of living. This could not in any way have been [possible] had not the Lord provided her with a superabundance of graces and many other things she could not name but with which she was adorned.

6. She also said Lady Clare had such a fervent spirit she willingly wanted to endure martyrdom for love of the Lord. She showed this when, after she had heard certain brothers had been martyred in Morocco, she said she wanted to go there. Then, because of this, the witnesses wept.[59] This was before she was so sick.

Asked who was present at this, she replied that those who were present had died.

---

chivum Franciscanum Historicum V [1912], 419–420). According to the tenth witness, Philip was one of the preachers of San Damiano (*Process* X 8). Cardinal Raynaldo da Segni in his circular letter of August 18, 1228, mentions him as Visitator and, according to a document published by Z. Lazzeri, he held that position again in 1244 (cf. Z. Lazzeri, *Archivum Franciscanum Historicum* XIII [1920], 286–289).

[59]This refers to the martyrdom of the first brothers in Morocco, Berard, Peter, Accursion, Adiuto and Ottone, on January 16, 1220. Cf. B. Capezzali, "Le Clarisse in terra di missione," *Santa Chiara d'Assisi: Studi e cronica del VII centenaio, 1253–1953* (Assisi 1953), 495–499; I. Omaechevarria, *Clarisas entre Musulmanes y otros infideles* (Bilbao, 1954); and *Las Clarisas a traves de los siglos* (Madrid, 1972).

7. She said the same as Sister Filippa concerning the humility of the saint, the harshness of her bed and clothing, her abstinences and fasting. She also added she washed with her own hands the mattresses of the sick sisters in which, at times, there were vermin. As the same Lady said, she did not smell any odor from them but very quickly smelled a good fragrance.

8. She also said the Lord had given her the grace that, when she made the sign of the cross with her hand, she cured many sisters of their illnesses. Sisters Anna, Benvenuta, Cristiana, and Andrea, like Sister Filippa, who gave her testimony before, had also said this. As Sister Amata had said, she cured the same Sister Cecilia.

9. She saw others who had been brought to the monastery to be cured by the holy mother. She made the sign of the cross over them and they were cured.

Nonetheless, she did not know their names, had not seen them at that time, and had never seen them before. But the witness had always been enclosed in the monastery.

10. She said the same as Sister Filippa concerning Lady Clare's love of poverty, the virtue of prayer, and the liberation of the city and monastery.

11. She also said when some danger was imminent, all the sisters had recourse to the help of prayer because of the holy mother's command.

12. The witness also said she heard from Saint Clare's mother when she was carrying this child and was standing before the cross praying that the Lord would help her in the danger of childbirth, she heard a voice that told her she would give birth to a great light which would greatly illumine the world. Asked how long ago she had heard it, she replied, about that time Saint Francis passed from this life.[60]

13. She also told about the vision of the breast of Saint Francis, as Sister Filippa had, except she did not remember what she had said concerning the nipple of the breast which Saint Clare held in her mouth.

14. She also said Lady Clare, never wanting to be idle at any time, even during the time of her last illness, made herself rise, sit up in bed and spin. The soft cloth made by her spinning she used to make many corporals and the cases to hold them, covered with silk or precious cloth. She sent them to the Bishop of Assisi, who blessed them, and, then, she sent them to the churches of the Assisi diocese. She believed they had been given to every church.

---

[60]This does not prove that Ortulana had already entered San Damiano before 1226, which would be three years before her daughter Beatrice who entered in 1229 (cf. *Process* XII 7). The witness may have heard this "in the place where one speaks to the sisters" (cf. *Process* IV 20).

15. She also said Lady Clare had the spirit of prophecy. Once when, one day, Saint Francis had sent five women to be received in the monastery, Saint Clare lifted herself up and [said she] would receive four of them. But she said that she did not want to receive the fifth because she would not persevere in the monastery, even if she stayed there for three years. After she did receive her because of great pressure, the woman stayed hardly a half year.

Asked who this woman was, she replied, Lady Gasdia, daughter of Taccolo. This was while Saint Francis was still living.

Asked if she had been present when Saint Clare said these words, she replied Sister Agnes, her sister, who only a little while ago had passed from this life, was there. She did not remember about the other sisters.

The Wonderful Meal

16. She also said one day, when the sisters had only a half loaf of bread, since the other half had been sent to the brothers who were staying outside,[61] the Lady directed the witness to make fifty slices out of the half loaf of bread, and to bring them to the sisters who had gone to the table. The witness then said to Lady Clare: "The Lord's miracle of the five loaves and two fishes would be needed to make fifty slices out of that!"

But the Lady told her: "Go and do as I have told you." And so the Lord multiplied that bread in such a way that she made fifty large and good slices as Saint Clare had directed her.

17. She also said the same as Sister Christiana about the door that had fallen upon the Lady, how she did not suffer any harm, saying she had seen her while she was under it.

SEVENTH WITNESS

1. Sister Balvina, daughter of Messer Martino of Coccorano,[62] nun of the monastery of San Damiano, said under oath she, the witness, was in the monastery of San Damiano for more than thirty-six years under the direction of Lady Clare of holy memory, at that time abbess of the monastery, whose life and conduct the Lord God had adorned with many innumerable gifts and virtues.

2. She knew the Lady was a virgin from her birth, was the most noble among all the sisters and had such a fervent spirit that she would have will-

---

[61] These are the brothers of whom St. Clare speaks in her *Rule* XII 5–11, who are suitable for spiritual assistance and for questing for the Poor Ladies. They lived beside the monasteries of the Clares during the first years of the Order. Cf. I. Omaechevarria, "Le 'Regla' y las Reglas de la Orden de Santa Clara," *Collectanea Franciscana* XLVI (1976), 112.

[62] Sister Blavina is the sister of the fourth witness, Sister Amata (cf. note 24).

ingly endured martyrdom for the defense of the faith and her Order for the love of God. Before she was sick, she desired to go to those parts of Morocco where it was said the brothers had suffered martyrdom.

Asked how she knew these things, she replied she, the witness, had been with her for all the time, and saw and heard of the love of the faith and the Order the Lady had.

3. She told how very diligent and solicitous she was in prayer, contemplation, and the exhortation of her sisters. She had committed herself to this.

4. She said all Sister Filippa had said about her humility, the virtue of her prayers, the harshness of her clothing and bed, and her abstinence and fasting, except that she had not seen the bed of vinebranches, but had heard she had had one for some time.[63] Nonetheless, she saw she had a bed of a somewhat crude table.

5. She also said the same as Sister Cecilia about the washing of the mattresses of the sick sisters.[64]

6. She said the same as Sister Filippa about the liberation of the city of Assisi when Vitalis d'Aversa besieged it, and the liberation of the monastery from the Saracens and other enemies by her prayers.[65]

7. She also said the same as Sister Filippa concerning the miracles done for her sisters after she made the sign of the cross over them.[66] She added Sister Benvenuta of Perugia had similarly been cured from that illness through which she had lost her voice when the sign of the cross was made by the Lady. Asked how she knew of it, she replied she had heard the same from her.

8. She said the same as Sister Filippa about her love of the Privilege of Poverty.[67]

9. The witness also said she heard from Lady Clare that during the most recent night of the Lord's Nativity she heard Matins and the other Divine Office celebrated in the Church of Saint Francis as if she were present there. Then she said to her sisters: "You left me here alone after going to the chapel to hear Matins, but the Lord has taken good care of me because I was not able to get up from my bed."

10. She also said she heard from the Lady of the vision of the breast of Saint Francis, as Sister Filippa said.[68]

11. The witness also said, because of her simplicity, she would not

---

[63]Cf. supra, *Process* III 3–5.
[64]Cf. supra, *Process* VI 7.
[65]Cf. supra, *Process* III 18–19.
[66]Cf. supra, *Process* III 10, 11.
[67]Cf. supra, *Process* III 14.
[68]Cf. supra, *Process* III 29.

know in any way how to speak about the good and the virtues in her, that is, her humility, kindness, patience, and the other virtues which she had in such abundance that she firmly believed, except for the Virgin Mary, no other woman was greater than the Lady.

Asked how she knew this, she replied she had heard about the sanctity of many other women saints through their legends, but she had seen the sanctity of the life of this Lady Clare during all this time, except for one year and five months when, because of the command of Lady Clare, she stayed in the monastery of Arezzo along with a lady who had been sent there.

The witness, because she was the actual niece of Saint Clare, paid careful attention to her life and habits which, when considered, seemed very wonderful to her.

Asked why it seemed wonderful, she replied because of the great abstinence that seemed impossible for a person to perform, and because of the other almost infinitely marvelous things that God worked for and in her, as said before.

How She Cured a Sister of a Fever and an Abscess

12. The witness added she herself, when sick, was very troubled one night by a serious pain in her thigh. She began to suffer and complain. The Lady asked her what was the matter. The witness told her about the pain. The mother threw herself directly on the place of the pain, then placed the veil she had on her head over it and immediately the pain completely left her.

Asked how long ago, she replied more than twelve years ago.

Asked who was present, she replied she, the witness, was alone with her in a room where she usually stayed in prayer. She did not remember the month or day or night.

13. Another time, before this incident, the witness was cured by Saint Clare of a continuous fever and of an abscess she had on the breast of her right side, from which the sisters believed she would die. This occurred twenty years ago.

Asked how long she had had it, she replied three days.

14. She also said she, the witness, heard from another lady the Lord had freed her of five demons through the intercession of the saint.

Asked where this lady was from, she replied from Pisa, according to what that woman said who came to the monastery to thank God and the saint when she spoke to the sisters.

Asked how long ago, she replied about four years ago. The woman said the demons told her: "The prayers of that saint are burning us!"

EIGHTH WITNESS

1. Sister Lucia of Rome, nun of the monastery of San Damiano,[69] said under oath that the holiness and goodness of Lady Clare, former abbess of the monastery of San Damiano, were such that, in no way, could she fully tell of them.

Asked what this holiness and goodness consisted of, she replied in her very great humility, kindness, uprightness, and patience.

2. Asked how long she had been in the monastery, she replied, as far as her good deeds were concerned, it seemed it had been very brief; but according to time, she had been there so long she did not remember. She knew Lady Clare had received her into the monastery because of the love of God when she was very little.

She said that she always saw Lady Clare acting in great holiness.

3. Asked in what sort of holiness, she replied in great punishment of her flesh and in great harshness of her life. In so far as she could, she tried to please God and to teach her sisters in the love of God. She had great compassion for the sisters, both for their body and soul. The witness added that since she did not possess the saint's wisdom, she should not express the goodness and holiness she saw in Lady Clare.

4. She said she heard the Lord had cured some sisters through her merits, but she was not present because she was sick.

NINTH WITNESS

1. Sister Francesca, daughter of Messer Capitaneo of Col de Mezzo,[70] nun of the monastery of San Damiano, said under oath she, the witness, had been in the monastery more than twenty-one years or so this May during which time Lady Clare had been abbess. She said if she had as much wisdom as Solomon and as much eloquence as Saint Paul, she did not believe she could tell fully of the goodness and holiness that she saw in Lady Clare throughout all the said time.

2. Asked what she saw in her, she replied one time, when the Saracens entered the cloister of the said monastery, the Lady made them bring her to the entrance of the refectory and bring a small box where

---

[69]Little is known of Sister Lucia.

[70]Massariola di Capitano di Coldimezzo, Sister Francesca, came from a castle situated on the border between Assisi and Todi. She was the aunt of Vanna di Coldimezzo, Jacapone da Todi's wife, who, wearing a hairshirt beneath her secular dress, had a profound influence on her husband (cf. A. Fortini, *Francis of Assisi*, trans. H. Moak [New York: Crossroad, 1981], 351; and "Il cilicio di Vanna da Caldimezzo," *Chiara d'Assisi: Rassegna del Protomonastero* IV [1956] 113–126). Her brother, Pietro, was an influential citizen of Assisi, as witnessed by his role on the donation of the property for the Basilica of Saint Francis (cf. ibid).

there was the Blessed Sacrament of the Body of our Lord Jesus Christ. Throwing herself prostrate on the ground in prayer, she begged with tears, saying among other things: "Lord, look upon these servants of yours, because I cannot protect them." Then the witness heard a voice of wonderful sweetness: "I will always defend you!" The Lady then prayed for the city, saying: "Lord, please defend the city as well!" The same voice resounded and said: "The city will endure many dangers, but it will be defended." Then the Lady turned to the sisters and told them: "Do not be afraid, because I am a hostage for you so that you will not suffer any harm now nor any other time as long as you wish to obey God's commandments." Then the Saracens left in such a way that they did not do any harm or damage.[71]

Asked how long ago this was, she replied it was September and, it seemed to her, Friday at nine o'clock. Asked who was present, she replied the sisters who were at prayer. Asked which other sisters heard that voice, she replied that she, the witness, heard it and another sister who had died, because they were holding up the Lady. Asked how she knew the other sister heard that voice, she replied the sister had told her. Saint Clare called both of them that evening and directed them not to tell anyone about it while she was living. Asked the name of that sister, she replied she was called Sister Illuminata da Pisa, who, she said, had died.

3. She also said that once, after Lady Clare had been told by someone that the city of Assisi must be handed over, the Lady called her sisters and said to them: "We have received many benefits from this city and I know we should pray that God will protect it." She therefore said they should come in the morning for some time with her. The sisters came, as directed, in the morning for some time with her. When they had come, the Lady made them bring her some ashes. She took all the coverings from her head and made all the sisters do the same. Then, taking the ashes, she placed a large amount on her head, as if she had been newly tonsured; after this she placed them on the heads of the sisters. Next, she directed all of them to go pray in the chapel. So it happened; being broken and defeated, the army left the following morning. From then on the city of Assisi did not have another army over it. And on that day the sisters abstained and fasted on bread and water; some of them did not eat anything on that day.

---

[71]In comparison with the preceding testimonies (II 20; III 18; IV 14; VI 10; VII 6), this more detailed testimony of Sister Francesca highlights the inaccuracy of certain traditions which survive even to this day. St. Clare did not carry the Blessed Sacrament by herself, but had the pyx containing It brought to her while hymns were sung. She prostrated herself in prayer before the Blessed Sacrament near the door to the refectory of San Damiano. This is a very different account from the usual representations of St. Clare carrying the monstrance to the dormitory door and striking the troops below with the brilliance of the Eucharist.

Asked how long ago this was, she replied it was in the time of Vitalis d'Aversa.

4. She also said once, on Calendemaggio,[72] she, the witness, saw in the lap of Saint Clare, before her breast, a young boy who was so beautiful that he could not be described. The same witness, because she saw that young boy, felt an indescribable sweetness and believed without a doubt he was the Son of God. She also said she then saw about Lady Clare's head two wings, brilliant as the sun, which at times were raised on high and at other times covered the head of the Lady.

Asked who else had seen this, she replied she alone saw it and had never revealed it to another and would not have revealed it then except to praise so holy a mother.

5. The witness also told how Saint Clare cured, with the sign of the cross and her prayers, Sister Benvenuta of Lady Diambra of the infection she had under her arm and Sister Cristiana of her deafness, just as Sister Filippa said before and Sister Cristiana had told about herself.[73]

6. She also said once she saw the son of Lord Giovanni di Maestro Giovanni of Assisi carried to the monastery of Saint Clare [because] he had a fever and a scrofula. The saint made the sign of the cross over him, touched him, and so cured him.

Asked how she knew this, she replied she later heard his father say in the parlor that he was instantly cured. But the witness had not seen him before he was brought to Saint Clare, but a little while later she did see him return to the monastery cured.

Asked how old the boy was, she replied five years old. Asked his name, she said she did not know.

7. She also said when she, the witness, was suffering from a very serious illness that struck her in the head, made her cry a great deal and took away her memory, she made a vow to the holy mother when she was near the end and was about to pass from this life. She was instantly cured. Afterwards she never again felt that illness.

Asked for how long she had that sickness, she replied more than six years.

8. The witness also said one time Lady Clare was not able to get out of bed because of her illness. When she wanted a certain towel to be brought to her and there was no one to do so, a little cat in the monastery began to pull and drag that towel to bring it to her as best it could. Then

---

[72]Calendimaggio is one of the most ancient celebrations in Assisi even to this day. Its origins come from the early custom welcoming of the month of May. Cf. G. Fortini, "Calendimaggio in Assisi," *San Francesco Patrono d'Italia* 50:236–240.

[73]Cf. supra, *Process* III 10, 17.

the Lady said to the cat: "You wicked thing! You do not know how to bring it. Why are you dragging it on the ground?" Then the cat, as if it had heard that remark, began to roll that towel so that it did not touch the ground.

Asked how she knew these things, she replied Lady Clare herself told her.

9. Concerning the corporals made by her spinning, the witness also said she herself had counted fifty sets distributed to the churches, as the other sister-witnesses have said before.

10. She also said once, when the sisters believed the blessed mother was at the moment of death and the priest had given her the Holy Communion of the Body of our Lord Jesus Christ, she, the witness, saw a very great splendor about the head of mother, Saint Clare. It seemed to her the Lord's Body was a very small and beautiful young boy. After the holy Mother had received with great devotion and tears, as was her custom, she said these words: "God has given me such a gift today, that heaven and earth could not equal it."

Asked if any other sisters had seen this, she replied she did not know, but knew well about herself. Asked when this was, she replied about the feast of St. Martin three years ago. Asked at what hour, she replied in the morning after Mass.

TENTH WITNESS

1. Sister Agnes, the daughter of Messer Oportulo de Bernardo of Assisi,[74] nun of the monastery of San Damiano, said under oath that since the time in which she, the witness, entered the monastery, as a very young girl, Lady Clare, former abbess of the monastery, used sackcloth made of horsehair. She said the Lady once loaned it to the witness for three days. During that time, however, while she was wearing it, it seemed very rough to her, so she could in no way stand it.

2. The witness also said she could in no way express the humility, kindness, patience, and the greatness of the holy life and virtues of the Lady Clare, as she saw them during the entire time that she stayed in the monastery. She said it seemed that every good was in her and nothing reprehensible, so that she could be considered a saint.

Asked how she knew this, she replied it was because she was in the monastery under her care about thirty-three years.

3. She said Lady Clare, with an abundance of tears, stayed at prayer

---

[74]Agnes was the daughter of the Podesta or Mayor of Assisi, Oportulo de Bernardo, for whom St. Francis composed the verse of pardon and peace in his *Canticle of the Creatures*. She entered the monastery in about 1220 when "just a little thing." Cf. A. Fortini, *Francis of Assisi*, trans. H. Moak (New York: Crossroad, 1981), 350, 569n., 574–580.

for a long time after Compline. At about midnight she likewise arose to pray, while she was still well, and she woke the sisters by touching them in silence. She particularly prayed the hours of Sext because she said the Lord was placed on the cross at that hour.

4. She also said the saint greatly afflicted herself by fasting. Asked how she knew these things, she replied as she had before: she was present.

5. She also said if Lady Clare ever saw any of the sisters suffering some temptation or trial, she called her secretly and consoled her with tears, and sometimes threw herself at her feet.

Asked how she knew these things, she replied she had seen some of those she had called to console. One of them had told her the Lady had thrown herself at her feet. Asked the name of that sister, she replied she was called Sister Illuminata of Pisa, who had died.

6. She also said that the humility of the Lady was such that she washed the feet of the sisters and the serving sisters. One time, while washing the feet of one of the serving sisters and wanting to kiss them as she usually did, that sister involuntarily hit [Lady Clare's] mouth with her foot. The Lady rejoiced at this and kissed the sole of that foot.

Asked how she knew this, she replied she had seen it. Asked what time, she replied it was during Lent. Asked what day, she replied a Thursday.

7. She also said during most of the time she, the witness, was in the monastery, the Lady had a mat for her bed and a little bit of straw under her head and that she was content with this bed. She knew this because she had seen it. She also said she heard before she, the witness, had entered the monastery, Lady Clare had a bed made of twigs, but after she was ill, she had a sack of straw because of a command of Saint Francis.

8. The witness also said Lady Clare delighted in hearing the Word of God. Although she had never studied letters, she nevertheless listened willingly to learned sermons. One day when Brother Filippo d'Atri of the Order of Friars Minor was preaching,[75] the witness saw a very handsome young boy, who seemed to be about three years old, appear to Saint Clare. While she, the witness, was praying in her heart that God would not let her be deceived, He answered her in her heart in these words: "I am in their midst" (cf. Mt 18:20), signifying through these words the young boy Jesus Christ Who stood in the midst of the preachers and listeners when they were preaching and listening as they should.

Asked how long ago this was, she replied: about twenty-one years ago. Asked what time, she replied it was during the week after Easter when the

---

[75]Cf. note 55.

"I am the Good Shepherd" is sung.[76] Asked who was present, she replied: the sisters. Asked if some of them saw the young boy, she replied one sister told the witness: "I know you have seen something." Asked about the length of time the young boy stood there, she replied: for a great part of the sermon. She said it seemed, then, as if there was a great brilliance around holy mother Clare, not like anything material, but like the brilliance of the stars. She also said she, the witness, smelled an indescribable sweetness because of the apparition.

After this, she saw another brilliance, not the color of the first, but all red in a way that seemed to emit certain sparks of fire. It thoroughly surrounded the holy Lady and covered her entire head. The witness, doubting this, received a reply, not with a voice but in her mind, "The Holy Spirit will come upon you" (cf. Lk 1:35).

9. She also said that, because of the power of Saint Clare's prayers, she believed the monastery had been protected from the Saracens and the city of Assisi from the assault of its enemies, as the same witness had seen the holy mother Clare pray very humbly for this with her tears, her hands joined, and her eyes raised to heaven.

10. She also said while Saint Clare was passing away, she admonished the witness and the other sisters to remain in prayer and she, the witness, said the prayer of the Five Wounds of the Lord.[77] As if [Lady Clare] were able to understand, but speaking very softly, she continually kept the Passion of the Lord on her lips and so the name of the Lord Jesus Christ.

Concerning the last words the holy mother spoke to the witness, it was: "Precious in the sight of the Lord is the death of his holy ones" (cf. Ps 115:15).

11. She also said one time, while her feet were being washed by holy mother Clare, the witness, because of her insistence, drank some of what had washed her feet. It seemed to her so sweet and delicious she could hardly drink it.

Asked if any other sister had tasted any of that water, she replied no, since holy mother Clare immediately threw it away so there was no more to taste.

---

[76]It was the Second Sunday after Easter.

[77]Z. Lazzeri offers a Latin version of these prayers which he found in a manuscript of the *Vita mirabile della Serafica Madre santa Chiara* by Brother Marianus of Florence in the Volterra Library. Cf. Z. Lazzeri, "L'orazione delle cinque piaghe recitata da santa Chiara," *Archivum Franciscanum Historicum*, XVI (1923), 246–249. No source asserts that St. Clare wrote these prayers, but only recited them and certainly in an edition that was simpler than Lazzeri discovered.

ELEVENTH WITNESS

1. Sister Benvenuta of Lady Diambre of Assisi,[78] nun of the monastery of San Damiano, said under oath she, the witness, had suffered certain infections under her arm and her breast called fistulas, in which five fingers could be placed, but they had five heads. She had borne this illness for twelve years. One night she went to the holy mother Clare asking her with tears for her help. The kind mother, moved by her usual compassion, then got out of bed and, on her knees, prayed to the Lord. After she had finished her prayer, she turned toward the witness, made the sign of the cross first upon herself and then over the witness, said the *Our Father*, and touched her wounds with her bare hand. Thus she was healed of those infections which had seemed to be incurable.

Asked how long ago this had been, she replied it seemed to her it would have been two years last September. She had not felt that sickness ever again.

2. She also said it had been more than twenty-nine years since she, the witness, had come to the monastery. Since then, she had always been under the direction of most holy mother, Lady Clare. The Lady had taught her to love God above all else; secondly, taught her to totally and frequently confess her sins; thirdly, instructed her to always have the Lord's passion in her memory.

The Wonderful Event of the Heavenly Choir
at the Joyful Passing of Saint Clare

3. The witness also said from Friday evening until the following day, Saturday, the third day before the death of the saint, Lady Clare of holy memory,[79] she, the witness, sat near the bed of the Lady with other sisters, crying over the passing of such a mother as theirs. The Lady, not speaking to any one person, began to commend her soul by saying: "Go in peace, because you will have a good escort. The One Who created you has already provided that you will be made holy. The One Who created you has infused the Holy Spirit in you and then guarded you as a mother does her littlest child."

One sister, Anastasia, when she asked the Lady to whom she was speaking and saying these words, was told by the Lady: "I am speaking to my blessed soul."

4. Then the witness began to think joyfully about the great and won-

---

[78]Little is known concerning Sister Benvenuta other than the identity of her mother and what she tells of herself in this testimony.

[79]That is, the night of August 8, 1253.

derful holiness of the Lady Clare. It seemed in that thought the heavenly court was moving and preparing to honor this holy woman. Our most glorious lady, the Blessed Virgin Mary, was especially preparing some of her garments for clothing this new saint. While the witness was lost in this thought and image, she suddenly saw with her own eyes a great multitude of virgins, all dressed in white with crowns on their heads, coming and entering through the door of that room where the holy mother Clare was lying. Among these virgins there was one greater, above and beyond what could be described, far more beautiful than all the others, and wearing a crown upon her head larger than all the others. Above her crown she had a golden cluster in the form of a thurible from which such a brilliance came forth it seemed to illumine the entire house.

These virgins approached the bed of holy Lady Clare. That virgin who seemed greater at first covered her bed with the most delicate cloth so fine that, even though she was covered with it, Lady Clare nonetheless saw through its great delicacy.

Then the virgin of virgins, who was greater, inclined her face above the virgin Saint Clare, or above her breast, so that the witness could not discern one from the other. After this was done, they all disappeared.

Asked if she, the witness, was awake at this time or asleep, she replied she was awake and well. It was the evening of that night, as had been said.

Asked who was present, she replied there were more sisters, some of whom were sleeping, some awake; but she did not know if they saw the things she did, since the witness had never revealed them to anyone until now.

Asked when and what day this was, she replied: Friday evening; the most holy Lady Clare died on the following Monday.

5. The witness also said that all that was said about the holiness of Lady Clare's life was true. She did not know how to speak of a holiness that could have been greater in her. She did not believe there had ever been another woman of greater holiness than the Lady, Saint Clare, other than our Lady, the Blessed Virgin Mary. She knew she was a virgin, humble, burning with love of God, continuously in prayer and contemplation, delighting in the harshness of her food and clothing, and wonderful in her fasting and vigils, so that many sisters marveled that she was able to live on such little food.

She had great compassion for the afflicted; was kind and generous toward all the sisters. Her entire conversation was about God, and she did not want to speak or hear about worldly things. She was thoughtful and discreet in her direction of the monastery and the sisters, far more than she was able to say.

Asked how she knew all the things mentioned, she replied she had been with her in the monastery for the entire time of twenty-nine years; she had seen all these things and, if it were necessary, she could tell all these things in detail.

TWELFTH WITNESS

1. Sister Beatrice, daughter of Messer Favarone of Assisi,[80] nun of the monastery of San Damiano, said under oath that she, the witness, was the natural sister of Lady Clare of holy memory whose life was, from her childhood, almost angelic; that she was a virgin and remained always so. She was careful about good deeds of holiness so her good reputation was spread about among all who knew her.

The Conversion of Saint Clare

2. She also said, after Saint Francis heard of the fame of her holiness, he went many times to preach to her, so that the virgin Clare acquiesced to his preaching, renounced the world and all earthly things, and went to serve God as soon as she was able.

3. After that she sold her entire inheritance and part of that of the witness and gave it to the poor.

4. Then Saint Francis gave her the tonsure before the altar in the church of the Virgin Mary, called the Portiuncula, and then sent her to the church of San Paolo de Abbadesse.[81] When her relatives wanted to drag her out, Lady Clare grabbed the altar cloths and uncovered her head, showing them she was tonsured. In no way did she acquiesce, neither letting them take her from that place nor remaining with them.

5. Then Saint Francis, Brother Filippo and Brother Bernard took her to the church of Sant'Angelo di Panzo,[82] where she stayed for a little time,

---

[80]Sister Beatrice was the third and youngest daughter of Clare's family. She entered the monastery of San Damiano in 1229.

[81]The monastery and church of San Paolo delle Abbadesse, where St. Clare was brought after her consecration at the Portiuncula, was located near Bastia, about 4km. from Assisi. A papal bull of Innocent III in 1201 granted numerous privileges to the Benedictine nuns including broad rights of asylum and forbidding the use of violence under the pain of excommunication. Therefore, in San Paolo, St. Clare was safe from any violent reaction on the part of her family. Cf. A. Fortini, "Nuove notizie intorno a santa Chiara d'Assisi," *Archivum Franciscanum Historicum* XLVI (1953), 29–33.

[82]Sant'Angelo di Panzo was a dwelling of women "*incarcerate*" (confined to one place) or "*penitenti*" (penitents) that would have been closer to the Beguine expression of women religious rather than the Benedictine or Cistercian expressions; cf. M. Sensi, "Incarcerate e penitenti a Foligno nella prima metà del Trecento," *I frati penitenti di San Francesco nella società del Due e Trecento* (Rome: Istituto Storico dei Cappuccini, 1977) 291–308. For the significance of this in the daily life of St. Clare and the Poor Ladies, cf. C. A. Lainati, "La Clausura: Non

and then to the church of San Damiano where the Lord gave her more sisters for her direction.

Asked how she knew all these things, she replied since she was her sister, she saw some things and heard some from Lady Clare and others. Asked how long ago this was, she replied: about forty-two years ago.

Saint Clare's manner of life in the monastery

6. The witness also said since Lady Clare was abbess in the monastery, she conducted herself in its direction in such a holy and prudent way. God manifested many miracles through her, that all the sisters and all who knew her revered her as a saint.

Asked in what Lady Clare's holiness consisted, she replied: in her virginity, humility, patience, and kindness; in the necessary correction and sweet admonition of her sisters; in the continuous application to her prayer and contemplation, abstinence and fasting; in the roughness of her bed and clothing; in the disregard of herself, the fervor of her love of God, her desire for martyrdom, and, most especially, in her love of the Privilege of Poverty.

7. Asked how she knew these things, she replied: because she saw these things done by her, was her actual sister, and had been with her in the monastery for twenty-four years or so. In addition, she acted and talked with her as with her own sister. She said her tongue could not tell of the Lady Clare's goodness since there was so much in her.

8. Asked also about the miracles the Lord God had done through her, she replied: after she had made the sign of the cross over them, God had cured some of the sisters through her. And many other miracles: since God, through her prayers, had protected the monastery from the Saracens and the city of Assisi from the assault of the enemy, as it was openly believed.

Asked how she knew this, she replied: because she saw when she made her prayer and when the Saracens departed without harming anyone or the monastery. And then, after her prayer, the army, at the city of Assisi, departed on the following day.

9. Asked about the cure of the sisters of their illnesses, she replied some had been cured by Lady Clare: Sister Benventua, Sister Cristiana,

---

'Mezzo di Contemplazione', Ma Modo Tipico delle Clarisse di Esprimere il Misterò Pasquale," *Forma Sororum* XX (1983), 201–203. Concerning Sant'Angelo di Panzo, cf. A. Fortini, "Un monastero sacro al ricordo di Santa Chiara," *Vie d'Italia* (September, 1954); M. Bartoli, "Francescanesimo e mondo femminile nel XIII secolo," *Francesco, Il Francescanesimo e La Cultura della Nuova Europa*, ed. I. Baldelli and A. M. Romanini (Roma: Istituto della Enciclopedia Italiana, 1986), 167–180.

and other sisters. Asked how she knew this, she replied she first had seen them sick and remaining somewhat ill until the holy mother, after making the sign of the cross, cured them with her prayer. Then she saw them well.

THIRTEENTH WITNESS

1. Sister Cristiana, daughter of Messer Bernardo da Suppo of Assisi,[83] nun of the monastery of San Damiano, said under oath the same as Sister Beatrice about her manner of living. She added that the virgin of God, Clare, left the worldly house of her father in a wonderful way.

Because she did not want to leave through the usual exit, fearing her way would be blocked, she went out by the house's other exit which had been barricaded with heavy wooden beams and an iron bar so it could not be opened even by a large number of men. She alone, with the help of Jesus Christ, removed them and opened the door. On the following morning, when many people saw that door opened, they were somewhat astonished at how a young girl could have done it.

Asked how she knew these things, she replied that she, the witness, was in that house at that time because she lived in Assisi and, before this, had been with her and had knowledge of her. Asked how long ago this was, she replied it was forty-two years or a little more. Asked what age Saint Clare was at that time, she replied, according to what was said, she was eighteen years old.

2. She also said then, in the house of her father, she was considered by everyone to be upright and holy, and that thirty-four years ago, in the month of May, she, the witness, entered the monastery. She was under the discipline and guidance of Lady Saint Clare whose holiness of life enlightened the entire monastery and infused it with all the virtues and customs required of holy ladies.

3. The witness said she could reply completely and truthfully concerning those virtues, if she were asked particulars about her virtues. Most especially, the Lady Clare was thoroughly inflamed with charity and loved her sisters as herself. If she at times heard something that was not pleasing to God, she would try to correct it with great compassion and without delay. Because she was like this and so holy and adorned with virtue, God wanted her to be the first mother and teacher of the Order. She protected the monastery, the Order, and herself from every infection of sin so her memory will be eternally held in reverence. The sisters believed the holy

---

[83]This witness seems to have entered San Damiano in 1220. Her family and that of St. Clare's were friends as a document of 1165 indicates since it contains the joint signatures of Bernardo da Suppo, Cristiana's father, and of Offreduccio de Bernardino, Clare's grandfather. Cf. A. Fortini, *Nuova Vita di San Francesco* II (Assisi, 1959), 402.

mother, who so prudently, kindly, and vigilantly protected them, the religion, and their promise of poverty on earth, was in heaven praying to God for them.

Asked how she knew these things, she replied she had seen them and was present in the monastery for the space of time mentioned and, before that, had lived with her and had known her, as said previously.

4. Concerning the roughness of her clothing and her abstinence and prayer, she said she had never heard of anyone in the world like her or of anyone who surpassed her in those things. She said this: she knew them because she saw them.

5. She said everything Sister Benvenuta said about her being cured of the fistulas because she was present.[84]

6. She also said what Sister Amata said about her being cured of the dropsy because she was present.[85]

7. She said the same as Sister Cristiana about her cure.[86]

8. She also said the same as Sister Filippa about the prayer made for the defense and liberation of the monastery from the Saracens, and that made for the liberation of the city of Assisi being besieged by the enemy. She added she, the same witness, was the one who, because of the holy mother Clare's command, called the sisters to stay at prayer.[87]

9. She also said Lady Clare, during the sickness from which she passed from this life, never stopped praising God, reminding the sisters of the perfect observance of the Order and, most especially, of the love of poverty.

Asked how she knew this, she replied many times she was present.

10. The witness also said, in selling her inheritance, Lady Clare's relatives wanted her to give them a better price. She did not want to sell it to them, but sold it to others so the poor would not be defrauded. All she received from the sale of the inheritance, she distributed to the poor. Asked how she knew this, she replied: because she saw and heard it.[88]

FOURTEENTH WITNESS

1. Sister Angeluccia, daughter of Messer Angelico of Spoleto, nun of the monastery of San Damiano, said under oath that it had been twenty-

---

[84]Cf. supra, *Process* XI 1.
[85]Cf. supra, *Process* IV 7.
[86]Cf. supra, *Process* V 1.
[87]Cf. supra, *Process* III 18, 19.
[88]This seems to have occurred before St. Clare's flight to the Portiuncula, at least according to the testimony of the twelfth witness (cf. supra XII 2, 3, 4).

eight years that she, the witness, had been in the monastery of San Damiano and, for all this time in the monastery under the direction of Lady
Clare of holy memory, she saw so many and such great good things in her
she could truthfully say of her what could be said about any saint in
heaven.

2. Asked what the good things were, she replied at that time when
she, the witness, entered the monastery, the Lady Clare was sick, yet she
nevertheless got out of bed during the night and kept a vigil in prayer with
many tears. She did the same thing in the morning at about the hours of
Terce.

3. She firmly believed her prayers once liberated the monastery from
the attack of the Saracens who had just entered the enclosure of the monastery. Another thing, she liberated the city of Assisi from the assault of
enemies.

4. She also said that her humility and kindness toward the sisters, her
patience and constancy in trial, her austerity of life, strictness in eating and
clothing, her charity toward all, her prudence and care in exhorting the
sisters subject to her, her gracious and sweet way of reminding the sisters,
and other good and holy things were so great in Lady Clare that her tongue
could not describe nor comprehend them. There was, however, much
more holiness in her than she could ever tell. Asked how she knew these
things, she replied: because she was with her all this time and saw the holiness of her life, as it has been described.

5. None of the sisters doubted that God had performed many miracles
through her, even during her life, as said before. Asked how she knew this,
she replied: because she saw when Sister Benvenuta was suddenly cured
of her infections through the sign of the cross made over her by the hand
of Lady Clare. She heard that other sisters and outsiders had been cured
in the same way.

6. The witness also saw when the door of the piazza, that is, of the
monastery fell upon Lady Clare. The sisters believed that door had killed
her and, thereupon, raised a great moan. But the Lady remained unharmed
and said that she had not felt in any way the weight of that door which was
so heavy three brothers could barely return it to its place.

Asked how she knew this, she replied: because she saw it and was
present. Asked how long ago this was, she replied: almost seven years ago.
Asked about the day, she said during the octave of Saint Peter, a Sunday
evening.

At that time, at the cry of the witness, the sisters immediately came
and found the door still lying upon her since she, the witness, could not
lift it by herself.

7. The witness also said the death of Lady Clare was wonderful and

glorious, but one evening a few days before her death, she began to speak to the Trinity and to say very softly other words to God many educated people would hardly understand. Asked what other words she said, she replied as Sister Filippa had previously.

8. The witness also said once, when holy mother Lady Clare heard the *Vidi Aquam* being sung after Easter, she was so overjoyed and kept it in her mind.[89] After eating and after Compline she had the blessed water given to her and her sisters and would say to the sisters: "My sisters and daughters, you must always remember and recall this blessed water that came from the right side of our Lord Jesus Christ as He hung upon the cross."

9. She also said when the most holy mother used to send the serving sisters outside the monastery, she reminded them to praise God when they saw beautiful trees, flowers and bushes; and, likewise, always to praise Him for and in all things when they saw all peoples and creatures.

FIFTEENTH WITNESS

1. On the twenty-eighth of November, in the infirmary of the monastery, before Brother Mark, Sister Filippa, and the other sisters, Sister Balvina of Porzano, nun of the monastery of San Damiano, told under oath, somewhat fully, of Lady Clare's holiness of life and great goodness.[90]

2. She also said she, the witness herself, saw that door upon mother Saint Clare, that it had fallen upon her, that it had not yet been lifted. She said that door had not done her any harm, but it was like a mantle over her.

The witness also said that door was very heavy, and that she, with other sisters, ran at the cry of Sister Angeluccia, since they feared that door might have killed her. Asked about the time, she said about seven years ago.

*   *   *

1. Also on the same day, the twenty-eighth of November, in the house of the cloister of San Damiano, in the presence of Lord Leonardo, archdeacon of Spoleto, Don Jacobo, parish priest of Trevi who accompanied Lord Bartholomeo, Bishop of Spoleto, and Brother Marco of the Order of

---

[89]The *Asperges* Antiphon sung during the Easter Season.

[90]On November 28, four days after the initiation of the Process of Canonization, the tribunal moved into the infirmary of San Damiano to listen to the testimony of the fifteenth witness, Sister Blavina of Porzano.

Friars Minor, chaplain of the monastery, the entire convent of the enclosed nuns of the monastery of San Damiano assembled:

After certain nuns had told the truth under oath and given testimony to the life, conversion, and manner of life of Lady Saint Clare of holy memory, to the miracles they said had been done through her merits, Lady Sister Benedetta,[91] then abbess, together with the other nuns of the monastery of San Damiano, said with one accord, in the presence of the venerable Father, the Lord Bishop of Spoleto, that all that was found in the holiness of any other holy woman, except the Virgin Mary, could be truly said of and witnessed in Lady Clare of holy memory, their former abbess and most holy mother.

* * *

SIXTEENTH WITNESS

1. On the same day, in the church of San Paolo in Assisi,[92] before the venerable Father, the Lord Bishop of Spoleto, as well as in the presence of Andreolo de Bartolo, Vianello del Benvenuto Lucchese, and some others, Lord Ugolino de Pietro Girardone, knight of Assisi, under oath, spoke of the life, conversion, manner of living, and miracles of Lady Clare of holy memory.[93] He said Saint Clare was of a very noble family of Assisi since Lord Offreduccio de Bernardino was her grandfather and Lord Favarone, the father of Saint Clare, was his son.

2. This Saint Clare was a virgin, of a very upright manner of life in her father's house, and was kind and gracious to everyone. As Saint Francis was the first in the Order of Friars Minor which, with the help of God, he founded and governed, so this holy virgin Clare, as God willed, was the first in the Order of the Enclosed Ladies. And she governed that Order in all knowledge and goodness, as was seen and testified through public knowledge.

---

[91]Sister Benedetta, known before her entrance into San Damiano as Ginevra di Giorgio di Ugone di Tebalduccio, the Abbess who succeeded St. Clare, belonged to one of the more powerful families of Assisi. Her name can be found among the list of sisters in San Damiano in 1238; cf. supra, p. 107.

[92]The tribunal left San Damiano on November 28, 1253, for the church of San Paolo in Assisi to hear the testimonies of the townspeople who knew St. Clare. San Paolo was built in 1071 by Aginaldo, abbot of the Benedictine monastery of San Benedetto on the slope of Monte Subasio. It was rebuilt in the thirteenth century and rededicated by Innocent IV in 1253.

[93]There is much documented evidence concerning Ugolino di Pietro Girardone who was an important citizen of Assisi and lived in the area of San Rufino as did St. Clare and her family. Cf. A. Fortini, *Nova vita di San Francesco* (Assisi, 1959), 322–323.

3. He also said, as is public [knowledge], the virgin, Saint Clare, entered Religion at the preaching of Saint Francis and his admonition.

4. He also said he, the witness, had left his wife, Lady Guiduzia, sent her back to the house of her father and mother, had been without her for a period of more than twenty-two years, and had never been able to be persuaded by anyone to want to send for her and receive her back, even though he had been admonished many times even by religious persons.

Finally he was told, on the part of Lady Saint Clare, that she had learned in a vision that he, Lord Ugolino, had to receive her back immediately and, by her, produce a son from whom he would have great joy and consolation. When the witness heard this, he was somewhat distressed.

But after a few days, he was impelled by great desire, so he sent for and received the woman, who for such a long time before had left him. Then, as it had been seen in a vision of Lady Saint Clare, he begot by her a son still living and from whom he is very much overjoyed and has great consolation.

5. Asked if he saw Lady Clare in the house of her father and mother, as said before, he replied: yes, he had seen her conversing in a holy and becoming way, as he had said.

6. Asked how he knew the virgin of God, Clare, had entered Religion through the preaching of Saint Francis, he replied this was public knowledge and known by everyone. He had heard Saint Francis gave her the tonsure in the church of Saint Mary of the Portiuncula. After she had entered the monastery of San Damiano, he had heard and noticed—it was obvious—that she was of such holiness and goodness in her Order she might be like any other saint in heaven.

In the same hour and place, in the presence of the witnesses, Lord Angelo de Pelcio and Bonamanzia Barbieri, and before the Lord Bishop of Spoleto, Lady Bona de Guelfuccio, Ranieri de Bernardo, and Pietro de Damiano spoke under oath about the life, conversion, manner of living and miracles of Saint Clare.

SEVENTEENTH WITNESS

1. Lady Bona, daughter of Guelfuccio of Assisi,[94] said under oath she knew Saint Clare from the time she was in her father's house and had conversed and stayed with her in the house. She firmly believed, because of the great holiness of her life which she had before and after she entered Religion, that she had been sanctified in her mother's womb. Moreover,

---

[94]Lady Bona de Guelfuccio is the sister of Sister Pacifica, the first witness of the Acts of the Process; cf. infra p. 129 n. 6.

she used to send to the poor the food she was supposed to have eaten and she, the witness, testified that many times she had brought it to them.[95]

2. Lady Clare was always considered by everyone a most pure virgin and had such fervor of spirit she could serve God and please Him.

3. Because of this, the witness many times accompanied her to speak to Saint Francis. She went secretly so as not to be seen by her parents.

Asked what Saint Francis said to her, she replied he always preached to her about converting to Jesus Christ. Brother Filippo did the same. She listening willingly to him and consented to all the good things said to her.

4. She said at the time she entered Religion, she was a prudent young girl of eighteen years. She had always stayed in the house, hidden, not wanting to be seen by those who passed in front of her house.

She was also very kind and took care of all other good deeds. Asked how she knew the things spoken of, she replied: because she used to converse with her.

5. Asked how Lady Clare was converted, she replied Saint Francis had cut off her hair in the church of Saint Mary of the Portiuncula, as she had heard, because she, the witness, was not present since had already gone to Rome to observe Lent.

6. She also said Lady Clare, before her hair had been cut, had sent her to visit the church of Saint James because Lady Clare was full of grace and wanted others to be full.[96]

7. Lady Clare, while she was still in the world, also gave the witness a certain amount of money as a votive offering and directed her to carry it to those who were working on Saint Mary of the Portiuncula so that they would sustain the flesh.

8. She said the holiness of Saint Clare was so great that she had infinite things in her heart [which] she did not know how to describe because speaking of holy mother Clare was always a thorough lesson for others.

EIGHTEENTH WITNESS

1. Lord Ranieri de Bernardo of Assisi said under oath that he did not doubt the holiness of Saint Clare of holy memory; nor that she is a saint in heaven.[97] If it were doubted by anyone, then it should not be believed

---

[95] The text is unclear as to whether Clare herself or Lady Bona de Guelfuccio brought the food to the poor.

[96] This is a reference to the Shrine of Saint James of Compostella in Spain, a famous place of pilgrimage in the Middle Ages. Cf. V. Hell, H. Hell, *The Great Pilgrimage of the Middle Ages: The Road to St. James of Compostella* (New York: Clarkson N. Potter, Inc., 1966); M. Stokstad, *Santiago De Compostella* (Norman: University of Oklahoma, 1978).

[97] A. Fortini attempts to supply some details concerning these last witnesses, Lord Ran-

about anyone else. Moreover, it seemed to him more likely that our faith should be valueless [than to doubt her sanctity].

Because the witness knew Lady Clare when she was a young girl in her father's house, [he said] she was a virgin, and, from the very beginning of her life, had begun to pay attention to deeds of holiness as if she had been made holy in her mother's womb.

2. Because she had a beautiful face, a husband was considered for her. Many of her relatives begged her to accept them as a husband. But she never wanted to consent. Since the witness himself had many times asked her to be willing to consent to this, she did not even want to hear him; moreover, she preached to him of despising the world.

Asked how he knew the things mentioned, he replied: because his wife was a relative of Lady Clare and since the witness conversed confidentially with her in her house and saw her good deeds.

3. Asked what good deeds she did, he replied she fasted, prayed, and willingly gave as many alms as she could. When she was sitting with those in the house, she always spoke of the things of God. As quickly as possible, she had her hair cut by Saint Francis. When her relatives wanted to take her from San Paolo and bring her back to Assisi, they could in no way persuade her, because she did not want to go. She showed them her tonsured head and so they let her stay.

4. Lady Clare was of the most noble [families] of the city of Assisi, on both her father's and mother's side. Asked how he knew these things, he replied it was public knowledge throughout the area.

5. The witness also said, when Lady Clare went to stay in San Damiano, since she was holy, she thus taught her daughters to serve God in holiness as is seen today in her daughters.

6. It was firmly believed by all the citizens the monastery was protected and the city liberated from the enemy through the prayers and merits of Lady Clare.

7. Asked how long ago it was that Saint Clare entered Religion, he replied that it was more than forty years ago.

NINETEENTH WITNESS

1. Pietro de Damiano of the city of Assisi said under oath he, the witness, that he lived near—he and his father—Saint Clare's house and that of her father and other members of her family. He knew Lady Clare when

---

ieri di Bernardo, Pietro di Damiano, and Giovanni di Ventura; cf. A. Fortini, *Nova Vita di San Francesco* II (Assisi, 1959) 315–348. Their testimony does not seem to add any further insights beyond what they mention about Clare herself.

she was in the world and knew her father, Lord Favarone, who was noble, great and powerful in the city—he and the others of his household.

Lady Clare was noble, of a noble family and of an upright manner of life. There were seven knights of her household, all of whom were noble and powerful. Asked how he knew these things, he replied that he had seen her because he was her neighbor.

2. At the time Lady Clare, a very young girl at that time, lived in a spiritual way, as was believed. He saw her father, mother, and relatives who wanted her to marry magnificently, according to her nobility, to someone great and powerful. But the young girl, at that time about seventeen or so, could not be in any way convinced because she wanted to remain in her virginity and live in poverty, as she demonstrated since she sold all her inheritance and gave it to the poor. She was considered by all to have a good manner of life.

Asked how he knew this, he replied: because he was her neighbor and knew that no one could ever convince her to bend her spirit to worldly things.

TWENTIETH WITNESS

1. On the twenty-ninth day of November, in the church of San Paolo, in the presence of Leonardo, Archdeacon of Spoleto, and Don Jacobo, parish priest of Trevi, and that of the Lord Bishop of Spoleto, Ioanni de Ventura of Assisi spoke under oath about these matters and said he, the witness, used to converse in Saint Clare's house while she was still a young girl and a virgin in her father's house because he was a house watchman.[98]

2. Lady Clare could then have been eighteen or so and of the most noble stock of all Assisi, on both her father's and mother's side. Her father was called Favarone and her grandfather Offreduccio de Bernardino. The young girl at that time was of such an upright life and dress, as if in the monastery for a long time.

3. Asked what sort of life she led, he replied: although their household was one of the largest in the city and great sums were spent there, she nevertheless saved the food they were given to eat, put it aside, and then sent it to the poor.

Asked how he knew the things spoken of, he replied, since he stayed in the house, he saw them and firmly believed them because they had been told to him in this way.

4. While she was still in her father's house, she wore a rough garment under her other clothes.

---

[98]It is interesting to note that Ioanni de Ventura is said to be a "*fameglio di casa*," which in old Umbrian dialect means a "man of arms" or a "watchman."

5. He also said she fasted, prayed, and did other pious deeds, as he had seen; and that it was believed she had been inspired by the Holy Spirit from the beginning.

6. He also said Lady Clare, hearing Saint Francis had chosen the way of poverty, proposed in her heart to do the same thing. So she was tonsured by Saint Francis in the church of St. Mary of the Portiuncula or in the church of San Paolo.

When her relatives wished to drag her away from the church of San Paolo and bring her back to Assisi, she showed them her tonsured head. Asked how he knew this, he replied he had heard it said and it was public knowledge.

7. Then she went to the place of San Damiano where she became mother and teacher of the Order of San Damiano, and she begot there many sons and daughters in the Lord Jesus Christ, as is seen today.

8. He also said no one, in any way, should doubt her holiness, because the Lord performs many miracles through her as is obvious.

9. He also said that year, after the death of Lady Saint Clare, he saw someone from beyond the Alps, who was mad or possessed, bound with ropes, brought to the tomb of Lady Saint Clare, and cured there.

Asked how he knew this, he replied he saw the man sick with the illness and saw him there, at the tomb of the said Lady Clare, immediately cured. Asked the name of that sick man, he replied he did not know because he wasn't from these parts.

Asked at the invocation of which saint he was cured, he replied at the tomb of Lady Saint Clare. This was public and well known. Asked about the month and day this occurred, he replied he believed it was September just passed. He said he couldn't remember the day. Asked who was present, he replied all on the piazza saw him and ran with him to the tomb of Lady Saint Clare.

Bull of Canonization (1255)

Perhaps no papal document of this period is as poetically elegant as the document proclaiming to the world the sainthood of Clare of Assisi. The author, unfortunately unknown to us, was a magnificent poet who skillfully plays with the word Clara in ways that no translation can adequately capture. In fact, nineteen different words are used to express the image of light, clara, thus stretching our imaginations in the attempt to capture the wonder of the newly proclaimed saint.

Clare was canonized on August 15, 1255, just two years after her death, by Pope Alexander IV, a close friend of the Poor Ladies and, like Cardinal Raynaldus, their Protector. This papal bull of canonization, however, was promulgated sometime between September 26 and October 19 of the same year, a date that is difficult to determine due to the confusing manuscript tradition surrounding the document.

After a very poetic, uplifting introduction, the document relies heavily on the testimony presented in the Process of Canonization. It accentuates quite strongly the miraculous aspects of Clare's life, something quite typical of the canonization procedures of the thirteenth century when there was an attempt to be more demanding in this regard. Nonetheless, the obvious reference to the Exultet of the Easter Vigil, as in the Bull of the Canonization of Saint Francis twenty-seven years earlier, subtly underscores the author's understanding of Clare's role in the Paschal Mysteries.

1. Alexander, Bishop, servant of the servants of God, to all our venerable brothers, the archbishops and bishops established throughout the kingdom of France: health and apostolic blessing.

2. Clare,
shines brilliantly:
brilliant by her bright merits,
by the brightness of her great glory in heaven,
and by the brilliance of her sublime miracles on earth.

Clare,
her strict and lofty way of religious life radiates here on earth,

176

while the magnitude of her eternal rewards glows from above
and her virtue begins to dawn upon all mortal beings with magnificent
signs.

3. Clare:
she was endowed here below with the privilege of the most exalted
poverty,
repaid on high by an inestimable source of treasure
[and] shown full devotion and immense honor by all.

Clare:
her brilliant deeds distinguished her here below.
Clare:
while on high the fullness of the divine light shines on her.
Clare:
her amazing deeds of wonder make her known to Christian people.

O Clare,
endowed with so many brilliant titles!
Bright even before your conversion,
brighter in your manner of living,
even brighter in your enclosed life,
and brilliant in splendor after the course of your mortal life!

In this Clare,
a clear mirror of example has been given to this world;
by this Clare
the sweet lily of virginity is offered among the heavenly delights;
through this Clare
obvious remedies are felt here on earth.

O the ineffable brilliance of blessed Clare!
The more eagerly she is sought after for something
the more brilliant she is found in everything!
This woman, I say, was resplendent in the world,
shone brilliantly in her religious life;
enlightened as a radiant beam in her home,
dazzled as lightning in the enclosure.

She shone forth in life;
she is radiant after death.

Enlightening on earth,
she dazzles in heaven!

O how great is the power of this light
and how intense is the brilliance of its illumination!

While this light remained certainly in a hidden enclosure,
it emitted sparkling rays outside.

Placed in the confined area of the monastery,
yet it was spread throughout the whole world.

Hidden within,
she extended herself abroad.

In fact,
Clare was hidden,
yet her life was visible.

Clare was silent,
yet her reputation became widespread.

She was kept hidden in a cell,
but was known throughout the world.

4. It should not be surprising that a light so enkindled,
so illuminating could not be kept from shining brilliantly
and giving clear light *in the house of the Lord;*[1]
nor could a vessel filled with perfume be so hidden
that it would not emit its fragrance
and suffuse the Lord's house with a sweet aroma.

Moreover,
since in the austerity of her cloistered solitude,
she broke the alabaster jar of her body
with her severity,
the whole Church *was thoroughly imbued*
with the aroma of her sanctity.[2]

---

[1] Cf. Mt 5:14, 15.
[2] Cf. Jn 12:3; Mt 26:7.

5. While still a young girl in the world, she was striving to pass rapidly along a clean path, past the fragile and unclean world. Keeping the precious treasure of her virginity with an undiminished modesty, she carefully dedicated herself to works of kindness and brilliance, so that her reputation spread freely to those near and far. After hearing this praise, blessed Francis immediately began to encourage her and to lead her to the perfect service of Christ. Quickly adhering to this man's sacred admonitions and desiring to reject entirely the world with everything mundane and to serve the Lord alone in voluntary poverty, she fulfilled this as quickly as possible because she finally *sold all her goods* and *distributed them as alms* to the poor (cf. Lk 12:33), so that, one with him, whatever she had she too would consider for the service of Christ.

6. Then, fleeing from the clamor of the world, she went down to the church in the field and, after receiving the sacred tonsure from blessed Francis himself, she went to another [church]. When her relations endeavored to bring her back, she immediately took hold of the altar and its cloths, uncovered her shorn head and strongly and resolutely resisted her relatives in this way. She could not permit herself to be separated from God's service because she was already joined to Him with her whole mind.

7. When she was finally led by the same blessed Francis to the church of San Damiano outside of Assisi, from which she took her origin, the Lord brought many companions to her for the love and assiduous adoration of His name. The distinguished and sacred Order of Saint Damian, now widely diffused throughout the world, came and had its salutary beginning, then, from this woman. It was this woman, encouraged by blessed Francis, who gave the beginning to this new and holy observance; this woman who was the first and solid foundation of this great religious way of life; this woman who stood as the cornerstone of this lofty work.

8. This woman, noble by birth, but nobler still by manner of life, preserved under this rule of holiness the virginity she had already protected from the first. Her mother, named Ortulana, intent upon pious deeds, followed her daughter's footprints and afterwards accepted this religious way of life. In this excellent garden which had produced such a plant for the Lord, she happily ended her days. But after a few years, that blessed Clare, very much urged by the insistence of the same Saint Francis, accepted the government of the monastery and the sisters.

9. This woman was undoubtedly *an eminent and most celebrated tree with far reaching branches that brought forth the sweet fruit* of a religious way of life in the field of the Church (cf. Dt 4:8). So many students of the faith ran and still run from everywhere to *its refreshing shade* and, in *its delight, taste its fruit* (cf. Ct 2:3).

This clear spring of the Spoleto Valley furnished a new *fountain of* living *water* (cf. Est 3:13) *for the refreshment and comfort of souls* (cf. Wis 3:13), which, already coming together in many streams in the territory of the Church, *has irrigated the nursery-gardens* of the regions (cf. Est 11:10). This was *a lofty candelabra* of sanctity (cf. Est 15:31; 26:1), strongly burning *in the tabernacle of the Lord* (cf. Heb 9:2), to whose remarkable splendor many have and are still hastening, *lighting their lamps* (cf. Mt 25:7) by its light.

Truly in a field of faith, this woman planted and cultivated a vineyard of poverty, from which abundant and rich fruits of salvation have been gathered. This woman set up a garden of humility in the domain of the Church, bound by immense needs. Here she produced a great abundance in the area of religion, where a wide refreshment of spiritual nourishment was served.

10. This woman, the first of the poor, the leader of the humble, the teacher of the continent, the abbess of the penitents, governed her monastery and the family entrusted to her within it with solicitude and prudence, in the fear and service of the Lord, with full observance of the Order: vigilant in care, eager in ministering, intent on exhortation, diligent in reminding, constant in compassion, discreet in silence, mature in speech, and skillful in all things concerning perfect government, wanting to serve rather than to command, to honor than to be extolled.

Her life was an instruction and a lesson to others who learned the rule of living in *this book of life* (Rev 21:27). The remainder learned to behold the path of life in this mirror of life.

Although in the body on earth, nevertheless she was dwelling in spirit in heaven. [She was] a vessel of humility, a fortress of chastity, a fire of charity, the sweetness of kindness, the strength of patience, the bond of peace, and the communion of familiarity: meek in word, gentle in deed, and lovable and tolerant in everything.

11. Because each one is stronger after overcoming an enemy, she had only the bare ground and sometimes twigs for her bed, and [a piece of] hard wood as pillow for her head in order to grow stronger in spirit after her body was supressed. Content with one tunic and a mantle [made of] poor, disgarded, and coarse material, she used these lowly clothes to cover her body. Near her flesh she wore a rough shirt made out of horsehair.

Abstemious also in food and disciplined in drink, she restrained herself so much by abstinence from these things that for a long time she did not taste any food three days a week, on Monday, Wednesday, and Friday, while, on the other days when she limited herself to a meager bit of food. Others marveled that she was able to survive on so rigorous a diet.

12. Moreover, she especially spent day and night giving herself assiduously *to vigils* (cf. 2 Cor 11:27) and prayers. When she was finally laid up with a long-term illness so she could not raise herself by physical exertion,

she was lifted up with the help of the sisters. With supports for her back, *she worked with her own hands* (cf. 1 Cor 4:12), not to be idle even in her sickness. Then, out of the linen made by her skill and labor, she had many corporals made for the sacrifice of the altar and had them distributed throughout the plains and mountains of Assisi.

13. She was, above all, a lover and firm supporter of poverty. She so rooted it in her spirit, so fixed it in her desires that, firmer in love of it and more ardent in its embrace, she never departed from her stronger and more eager union with it for any necessity. She could not be induced by any persuasion to consent to have any possessions in her monastery, even though Pope Gregory of happy memory, our predecessor, thinking about the great indigence of her monastery, generously wanted to endow sufficient and appropriate possessions for the sustenance of her sisters.

14. In truth, because a great and splendid light cannot be restrained from displaying the brilliance of its rays, the power of holiness shone in her life through many and various miracles.

Thus she restored the voice of one of the sisters of the monastery [after] it had been almost totally lost for a long time. She restored the ability of speaking to another who had long lost the use of her tongue. She opened the deaf ear of another. She cured one struggling with a fever, one swollen with dropsy, one infected with a fistula, and others oppressed with various ailments by making the sign of the Cross over them. She healed a certain brother of the Order of Minors from insanity.

15. When once, by accident, the oil in the monastery was totally depleted, she called for the brother assigned to gather alms for that monastery. She took a jar, washed it, and placed it empty by the door of the monastery so that the same brother would take it for acquiring oil. When he went to pick it up, he found it filled with oil, a gift of divine generosity.

16. Again, one day when only a half a loaf of bread was available for feeding the sisters in that monastery, she directed that half [of it] be distributed in pieces among the sisters. He Who is *"the living bread"* (Jn 6:41) and *"gives food to the hungry"* (Ps 145:7) multiplied it in the hands of the one who broke it so that there were then fifty sufficient portions made and *distributed* to the sisters *seated at table* (cf. Lk 9:14).

17. The pre-eminence of her merits was made known through these and other signs when still living. When she was about to die, a white-robed choir of blessed virgins crowned with glittering crowns, among which one seemed to be more eminent and brilliant, was seen to enter the house where that servant of Christ lay ill. She was seen to approach Clare's bed and on her behalf to show, as it were, the duty of visitation and comforting the sick with a certain human zeal.

18. After her death, however, a certain man suffering from epilepsy,

and unable to walk because of a withered leg, was brought to the tomb. There he was cured from both infirmities; his leg made a noise as if it were breaking. The hunchbacked and the paralyzed, the mad and demented received perfect health in that same place.

Someone who had lost the use of his right hand by a violent blow so that it was totally useless had it completely restored to its original state through the merits of the saint. Another who had long lost the light of his eyes in blindness came to her tomb under the guidance of another. After he recovered his sight there, he returned home without a guide.

The venerable virgin shines with these and so many other glorious deeds and miracles. What her mother heard when she was pregnant with her and was praying appears to be clearly fulfilled: that she would give birth to a light that would illuminate the entire world.

19. Therefore
let Mother Church rejoice
because she had begotten and reared such a daughter
who,
as a parent fruitful with virtues,
has produced many daughters
for religious life by her example
and has trained them
for the perfect service of Christ by her thorough teaching.

Let the devout multitude of the faithful be glad
because the King and Lord of heaven
has chosen their sister and companion as His spouse
and has introduced her with glory
to His lofty and brilliant palace.

Finally,
let the multitude of saints *rejoice*
because *the nuptials of a* new *royal bride*
are being celebrated in their heavenly midst.[3]

20. Therefore, it is fitting that the universal Church venerate on earth her whom the Lord exalted in heaven; because her sanctity of life and miracles are very evident from a thorough and careful investigation, a distinct examination and a solemn discussion—even though, both near and far, her deeds were widely known before this.

---

[3]Cf. Mt 22:2; 25:10.

By the common advice and assent of our brothers and all the prelates who were then at the Holy See, and relying firmly upon the divine omnipotence, We, by the authority of the blessed Apostles, Peter and Paul, and our own, have directed she be inscribed in the catalogue of the holy virgins.

21. Therefore We admonish and earnestly exhort all of you, commanding through the apostolic letters addressed to you, that you devoutly and solemnly celebrate the feast of this same virgin on the twelfth of August and that you have it venerably celebrated by your subjects, so you may merit to have a pious and diligent helper before God.

And so a multitude of people may come together more eagerly and in greater numbers to venerate her tomb, and so her feast day may be honored with greater numbers, We, relying on the mercy of the All-Powerful God and on the authority of His Apostles, Peter and Paul, grant an indulgence of one year and forty days from the punishment due to their sins to all who are truly contrite and have confessed their sins, and who humbly seeking her aid go each year with reverence to this tomb on the feast of this same virgin or during its octave.

Given at Anagni, the twenty-sixth day of September, in the first year of our pontificate.

The Legend
of Saint Clare

The composition of an official biography was part of the entire process of canonizing a saint in the Middle Ages. For the most part, it was a work undertaken by a writer familiar with the data gathered to establish someone's sanctity either through personally interviewing eye-witnesses or reviewing the transcripts of official ecclesiastical investigations. This is very much the case in the writing of the Legend of Saint Clare. It obviously is based on interviews with those who personally knew Clare or the Poor Ladies of San Damiano and the Acts of the Process of Canonization.

It is worthwhile reviewing the opinions of the prominent Franciscan or hagiographical experts of this century who have treated the question of the authorship of the Legend of Saint Clare. The starting point is undoubtedly the work of Professor Francesco Pennacchi who presented the text of the Legend based upon the Assisi Codex 338.[1] Since Pennacchi attributes the authorship of the Legend to Thomas of Celano, it is understandable that Thomas' name is most frequently associated with the work, at least in the English-speaking world. But it is not surprising that this 1910 edition paved the way for a variety of other publications of the Legend based on a wide variety of manuscripts to which Pennacchi paid no heed.

Of these, that of Zefferino Lazzeri in 1912 is most worthy of our attention since it proposes Saint Bonaventure as its author, although the author never went to great lengths to prove his reasons for such a claim.[2] Later, however, Lazzeri changed his opinion and, in 1920, suggested that the author may well have been Brother Mark the Chaplain of the Poor Ladies, who was present with Brs. Leo and Angelo and the others at the canonical investigation of Clare's sanctity in 1253. No doubt there is some grounds for speculation here since Salimbene wrote of Brother Mark, a companion of the ministers general Crescentius, John of Parma and Bon-

---

[1] Francesco Pennacchi, *Legenda Sanctae Clare Virginis* (Assisi, 1910). For those of us from the English speaking world, it is useful to note that the translations to which we have become accustomed, those of Paschal Robinson in 1910 and Ignatius Brady in 1953, are based on the Pennacchi text, introduction and notes.

[2] Z. Lazzeri, "De Processu canonizationis S. Clarae," *Archivum Franciscanum Historicum* 1912, pp. 644–651.

aventure, as "bonus dictator et velox et intelligibilis, *a good, swift and understanding dictator.*" *He was, therefore, a good secretary who could easily have been called upon to rework the accounts of the* Acts of the Process of Canonization, *at which he was present, into a readable hagiography. Nonetheless, while he builds a good case, Lazzeri does not produce convincing evidence and forces us to leave the question open.*

In the same year of Lazzeri's first publication, 1912, Benvenuto Bughetti also published a study of the Legend of Saint Clare in which he suggested yet another candidate: Brother Buon-Giovanni of Mantova or Cavriana, the author of a poetic exposition of a moralistic type of spiritual literature, the Anticerberus.

After the 1920 publication of Lazzeri, there was little significant work done on the Legend of St. Clare until Fausta Casolini produced a translation and study of the work in 1953 during the celebration of the sixth centenary celebration of Saint Clare's death.[3] *Seven years later, she published a second edition and sixteen years later yet another. Throughout all these years, Casolini maintained her original position, following the judgment of Pennacchi, that Thomas of Celano is the author of the Legend. To support her position, Casolini reviews the opinions of a number of scholars such as Lazzeri, the friars of the Collegio San Bonaventura of Quarracchi, Franceschini, Bughetti, and Battelli. She even offers the judgment of George Mailleux who placed the Pennacchi text into the computer analysis of the* Corpus des Sources Franciscaines, *although Mailleux himself indicates that the work is only attributed to Thomas and suggests that a variety of authors had a role in its composition.*[4] *Unfortunately Casolini does not give much attention to differing opinions except to note that of Lorenzo Di Fonzo in his article in* L'Osservatore Romano, *October 6, 1960, which suggests that the Legend has been attributed wrongly to Thomas.*[5] *The opinions of Casolini are most important since she has published a considerable number of articles on Saint Clare and is widely respected in Italian circles.*

Equally as important, however, is the work of Sister Chiara Augusta Lainati whose contributions to the field of research concerning Saint Clare and the Poor Ladies is vast. In a thorough article in Forma Sororum, *Lainati completely sidesteps the question of the authorship of the Legend by simply stating that it was commissioned by Pope Alexander IV between*

---

[3]F. Casolini, *La Leggenda di S. Chiara Vergine*, Assisi, 1953.

[4]G. Mailleux, *Corpus des Sources Franciscaines I: Thesaurus Celanensis* (Louvain: Centre de Traittement Électronique des Documents de l'Université Catholique de Louvain), p. XI, n. 11.

[5]L. DiFonzo, "Fra Tommaso da Celano nel VII centenario della morte, *L'Osservatore Romano*, 6 Ottobre 1960.

1255 and 1256.[6] *Elsewhere, however, she laments the absence of a modern critical edition of the work and, from this perspective, maintains that such a lack makes a definite statement on its authorship impossible.*[7]

Beyond the Italian peninsula, however, there are a wide variety of opinions concerning the Legend's authorship. In Germany, for example, Englebert Grau, following the opinions of Pennacchi and Casolini, favors the Thomas of Celano position, as does Maria Fassbinder.[8] In France, the Bollandists maintain the anonymity of the author since he does not in any way claim to be an eyewitness or to have personally seen the Lady Clare.[9] Damien Vorreux, on the other hand, also accepts the Thomas authorship although he presents the positions of Lazzeri and Bughetti.[10] The Spanish author, Ignacio Omaechevarria, in both his 1970 and 1982 edition of Escritos de Santa Clara y Documentos Complementarios reviews all the arguments pro and con the Thomas authorship and proceeds to leave the question open by not giving the name of any author. In another section, however, he specifically publishes the "Testimony of Br. Thomas of Celano (1228 and 1246)," that is, the texts of the First and Second Lives of St. Francis of Assisi which may well suggest his belief in a different author for the Legend of Saint Clare. The English-speaking world, meanwhile, following the opinions of Paschal Robinson and Ignatius Brady, accepted, as we have noted, the Pennacchi position favoring Thomas.[11] In 1978 Rosalind B. Brooke and C.N.L. Brooke provided an overview of the question which simply states that Thomas' authorship has been "generally accepted in modern studies, though it is far from certain."[12]

Perhaps one of the more thorough introductions to the Legend of Saint Clare is that contained in the Dutch edition, Clara Van Assisi: Geschriften, leven, documenten.[13] The author offers his views on the date of its composition (between 1256, the canonization of St. Clare, and 1261, the death of

---

    [6]C.A. Lainati, "Le Fonti Riguardanti il Secondo Ordine Francescano dlle Sorelle Povere di Santa Chiara," *Forma Sororum*, 131–145.

    [7]C.A. Lainati-F. Olgiati, "Scritti e Fonti Biografiche di Chiara d'Assisi," *Fonti Francescane*, sez. IV (Assisi, Movimento Francescano: 1977), p. 2391.

    [8]E. Grau, *Leben und Schriften der heiligen Klara*, (Werl/Westf., 1960), pp. 13–16. M. Fassbinder, "Untersuchungen über du Quellen zum Leben der hl. Kara von Assisi," *Franziskanische Studien* 23 (1936), pp. 298–335.

    [9]*De Sancta Clarae Virginis, Acta Sanctorum* Augusti II, 11: 739–768.

    [10]*Sainte Claire d'Assise*, transl. and ed. Damien Vorreux (Paris: Éditions Franciscaines, 1983), pp. 23–25.

    [11]Cf. supra. p. 1, no. 2.

    [12]Cf. Rosalind B. Brooke and Christopher N.L. Brooke, "St. Clare," *Medieval Women: Studies in Church History, Subsidia I*, ed. Derek Baker (Oxford: Blackwell, 1978), P. 276, n.1.

    [13]*Clara van Assisi: Geschriften, leven, documenten*, ed. A. Hollenboom, P. Van Leeuwen, S. Verheij (Haarlem: Gottmer, 1984).

Pope Alexander IV), the hagiographical style it employs (that traditionally employed in "official" lives of the saints), and its author. Although no conclusion is reached, the author relies heavily on a study done by P. Hoonhout, Het Latijn van Thomas van Celano, which attributes the Legend to Thomas for internal and external reasons.[14] *Arguing from internal evidence, Hoonhout perceived strong similarities between the earlier works of Thomas, specifically his* Vita Prima *and* Vita Secunda *of St. Francis, in the areas of biblical citations, ascetical terminology, and the use of the Latin cursus. While he did not present a large amount of external evidence, Hoonhout seemed content to rely upon a fifteenth century manuscript of a Tuscan author which attributes the Legend's authorship to Thomas.*[15] *Curiously, while the Dutch editors of* Clara Van Assisi: Geschriften, leven, documenten *give considerable attention to the study of Hoonhout, they prefer to leave the question open and simply state that the* Legend's *author is unknown.*

In light of this brief and certainly not exhaustive survey, we can, therefore, arrive at certain conclusions concerning the authorship of The Legend of Saint Clare. *The first of these is the obvious reliance on the Pennacchi text of 1910 and the subsequent arguments proposed by its editor suggesting that Thomas of Celano is the author of the Legend. Nonetheless, a further conclusion can now be reached that contemporary scholars prefer to consider other possibilities, although they have only suggested anonymous authors. Finally, while a definitive resolution of the question seems almost impossible, further steps cannot be taken without the publication of a critical edition of the text.*

Preface

The aging world was almost oppressed by the weight of years:[16]
the vision of faith faltering in the darkness,
the footing of morals slipping away,
the strength of virile deeds waning;
yes indeed,
the dregs of the times were following those of vice;
when God, the Lover of humanity,
raised from the treasures of His kindness
a newness of sacred Orders,
providing through them

---

[14]P. Hoonhout, *Het Latijn van Thomas van Celano* (Amsterdam, 1947).

[15]Cf. E. Grau, *Leben und Schriften der heiligen Klara* (Werl, 1980), pp. 32–35.

[16]The translator has attempted to maintain the poetic sense of many passages of the Latin text. It is clear that these were added to the author's interpretation of the **Acts of the Process of Canonization** and express the theological insights of the author of this work.

both a support of the faith
and a discipline for renewing morals.
I would certainly say that
these modern fathers and their sincere followers were
lights of the world,
leaders of the way,
teachers of life.
In them
the brightness of noonday dawned on a world at evening,
so that *one who walks in the darkness might see the light*.[17]

It was not fitting that help be lacking for the more fragile sex,[18]
caught in the maelstrom of passion,
which no less a desire drew to sin
and no greater a frailty impelled.

Therefore
God in His kindness raised up the venerable virgin Clare
and in her enkindled a brilliant light for women
whom You, most loving Father,
placing her
upon a lampstand to enlighten all in the house[19]
inscribed in the catalogue of saints
by the forceful power of her signs.[20]

We honor you as the father of these Orders,
we recognize you as their sustainer,
we embrace you as their protector,
we venerate you as their lord,
[you], upon whom rests
the entire guidance of the immense ship,
so that

---

[17]Is 9.2; Lk 1:79.

[18]Jane Tibbets Schulenberg provides a helpful examination of medieval attitudes toward female potential for a life of authentic sanctity. She sees the Mendicant beginnings as a time most favorable to the advancement of women as spiritual leaders. Cf. J.T. Schulenberg, "Sexism and the Celestial Gnaeceum from 500 to 1200," *Journal of Medieval History* 4 (1978), 117–133.

[19]Cf. Mt 5:15.

[20]Before his election to the papacy, Raynaldo dei Conti Segni, Bishop of Ostia and Velletri, was appointed Cardinal Protector of the entire Order of San Damiano by his uncle, Pope Gregory IX, and, as such, approved and presented to Pope Innocent IV Clare's Rule. As Pope Alexander IV, to whom this legend is dedicated, he canonized Clare in August, 1255.

it does not exclude
the particular care and sollicitude of even a little boat.[21]

It has obviously pleased Your Lordship to command my lowliness to mold from the recent deeds of Saint Clare a text to be read aloud.[22] I would certainly dread this task because of my ignorance of writing except that the papal authority has again and again placed it before me. Therefore, placing myself at your command, I did not consider it safe to proceed with what might be incomplete, resorted to the companions of blessed Francis[23] and to the community of Christ's virgins, [and] turned over and again in my heart that [axiom]: no one should write history except those who have seen it or received it from those who have.

When, with the fear of God, these had more fully instructed me in the complete truth, I then set it down in a simple style, accepting some things and dismissing others. [I did this] that it will delight the virgins to read about the wonders of the virgin [and my] uncultivated intelligence will not fall upon the ignorant where it might be unintelligible by reason of an excess of words.

Therefore,
let the men follow the new male disciples of the Incarnate Word
[and] the women imitate Clare, the footprint of the Mother of God,
a new leader of women.[24]

But the authority to correct, subtract, or add to these things remains more fully in you, most holy Father, so that, in all things, my will may be subject, agreeable, and malleable.

May
the Lord Jesus Christ

---

[21]"The immense ship" refers to the Church, the "little boat" to the Order of the Poor Ladies of San Damiano.

[22]This is the sense of the medieval term **legenda,** that is, an official text to be read aloud.

[23]At this time Brother Angelo (+ 1258?) was Minister Provincial of Umbria and Brother Leo (+ 1270) was still living. Both were present at the investigation at San Damiano (cf. **Process**).

[24]This comparison of Clare to the Virgin Mary comes from the statement of all the sisters of San Damiano given in the **Acts of the Process** in which they claimed that Clare was a perfect copy of the Mother of the Lord (cf. **Process**, p. v2; vii 11; ix 5; xv 1). It later passed into the First Vespers of the Liturgy of the Hours celebrated for the feast of Saint Clare. In the hymn, **Concinat plebs fidelium,** written by Pope Alexander IV, Clare is referred to as "the footprint of the Mother of Christ" (cf. supra.).

make you prosper
now and forever.
Amen.

PART ONE
THE BEGINNING OF THE LEGEND OF SAINT CLARE
VIRGIN.
FIRST: HER BIRTH

1. A woman, admirable by name,
[Clare],
—illustrious by designation and in virtue—
took her origin from a lineage already sufficiently illustrious
in the city of Assisi:
at first a fellow citizen with blessed Francis on earth,
afterwards reigning with him in heaven.

Her father was a knight, as were all her relatives on both sides of the knightly [class].[25] [Her] home was well-endowed and had abundant means following the same fashion of her native place.[26] Her mother, Ortulana, [who] would give birth to a fruitful plant in the garden of the Church, was herself overflowing in no small way with good fruits.[27] Even though she was bound by the bond of marriage and was burdened with the cares of the family, she, nonetheless, devoted herself as much as possible to divine worship and applied herself to works of piety. She, therefore, devoutly traveled with pilgrims beyond the sea and, after surveying those places which the God-Man had consecrated with His sacred footprints, she afterwards returned home filled with joy. She set out again to pray to Saint Michael the Archangel[28] and visited with even more devotion the basilicas of the Apostles.

---

[25]Cf. **Process** I:4; 19:1; 20:2. In general, all historial and biographical notes will be provided in the **Acts of the Process of Canonization** to which cross-references will be made when necessary.

[26]Cf. **Process** 1:4; 16:1; 18:4; 19:1; 20:2, 3.

[27]The symbolism of the name, Ortulana or "Gardener" provides another example of the author's desire to underscore the symbolic implications of the life of St. Clare. It is also highlighted in the **Bull of Canonization**; cf. supra p. 179.

[28]The shrine of Saint Michael in Gargano, Apulia, was a favorite site of pilgrimage in medieval Italy. Legend maintained that Michael the Archangel appeared there in the fifth century.

2. What else?[29]

A tree is known by its fruit[30]
and
the fruit is recommended by its tree.

The richness of the divine generosity
preceded in the root,
so that
an abundance of holiness
would follow in the branch.

While the pregnant woman, already near delivery, was attentively praying to the Crucified before the cross in a church to bring her safely through the danger of childbirth, *she heard a voice saying to her* (Acts 9:4): "Do not be afraid, woman, for you will give birth in safety to a light which will give light more clearly than light itself."[31] Taught by this oracle, when the child was born [and then] reborn in sacred Baptism, she ordered that she be called Clare, hoping that the brightness of the promised light would in some way be fulfilled according to the divine pleasure.

3. Hardly had she been brought into the light, than the little Clare began to shine sufficiently in the darkness of the world and to be resplendent in her tender years through the propriety of her conduct.[32] From the mouth of her mother she first received with a docile heart the fundamentals of the faith and, with the Spirit inflaming and molding her interiorly, she became known as a most pure vessel, a vessel of graces. *She* freely *stretched out her hand to the poor* (Prov 31:20) and *satisfied the needs* of many *out of the abundance of her house* (2 Cor 8:14). In order that her sacrifice would be more pleasing to God, she would deprive her own body of delicate foods and,

---

[29]This is an awkward and, at times, jarring transitional phrase that the author uses to continue his narrative. The translator would have preferred to omit it were it not another indication of the style of the author of the *Legend* and further proof that the author is not Thomas of Celano who never uses such a phrase. See also **Legend** 15.

[30]Mt 12:33.

[31]Cf. **Process** 3:28; 6:12. The religious literature of this period contains a number of accounts of this nature, e.g. the miraculous Crucifix of San Damiano that spoke to Saint Francis (cf. I Cel 10; LM II 1), that of Cortona that spoke to Saint Margaret, etc. Cf. Gabriele di S.M.Maddalena, **Visioni e rivelazioni nella vita spirituale**, Florence, 1941; K. Rahner, **Visionen und Prophezeiungen**, Freiburg i.Br., 1958.

[32]The phrase " . . . brought into the light" is, even today, a typical phrase for "to be born." In this sentence, however, the author seems also to be highlighting the symbolic or poetic sense of the phrase. Cf. **Process** 1:1, 3.

sending them secretly through intermediaries, she would *nourish the bodies of the poor* (Job 31:17).

Thus,
from her infancy,
as *mercy* was growing with her,[33]
she bore a compassionate attitude,
merciful towards the miseries of the destitute.[34]

4. She held the pursuit of holy prayer as a friend
[and]
after she was frequently sprinkled with its holy fragrance,
she gradually entered a celibate life.

When she did not have a chaplet with which to count the *Our Father's*, she would count her little prayers to the Lord with a pile of pebbles.[35] When she began to feel the first stirrings of holy love, she judged that the passing scene of worldly pride should be condemned, being taught by the unction of the Spirit to place a worthless price upon worthless things. Under her costly and soft clothes, she wore a hairshirt,[36] blossoming externally to the world, *inwardly putting on Christ* (cf. Rom 13:14; Gal 3:27). Finally, when her family desired that she be married in a noble way, she would in no way consent, but, feigning that she would marry a mortal at a later date, she entrusted her virginity to the Lord.[37]

Such were the offerings of her virtue in her paternal home,
such the beginnings of the Spirit,
such the preludes of her holiness!

As
a chest of so many perfumes,
even though closed,

---

[33]Job 31:18.

[34]Cf. **Process** 1:3; 17:1–4; 18:1, 3; 20:3, 5. In general a comparison between this work and that of the *Life of Marie d'Oignies* (+ 1213) by Jacques de Vitry is most interesting. Several points of comparison suggest themselves both for the treatment of the childhood and later years of both women. Cf. J. de Vitry, "De Maris Oigniacensi in Namurcensi Belgii Diocesi," ed., D. Papebroec, *Acta Sanctorum*, Junii 5 (Paris, 1866), 542–572; cf. **Matrologia Latina** Draft Translation Series (Saskatoon: Peregrina Publishing Co., 1986).

[35]This detail cannot be found in the **Process** and comes, no doubt, from the author's interviews with the witnesses to whom he referred in his introduction; cf. supra p. 189.

[36]Cf. **Process** 20:4.

[37]Cf. **Process** 18:2; 191:2.

reveals its content by its fragrance;[38]
so
she unknowingly began to be praised
by the mouth of her neighbors
and,
when the true recognition of her secret deeds appeared,
the account of her goodness
was spread about among the people.[39]

5. Hearing of the then celebrated name of Francis,
who,
like *a new man*,[40]
was renewing with new virtues
the way of perfection forgotten by the world,
she was moved by *the Father of the spirits*,[41]
—Whose initiatives each one had already accepted
although in different ways—
and immediately desired to see and hear him.

No less did he desire to see and speak with her,
impressed by the wide-spread fame of so gracious a young lady,
so that,
in some way,
he, who was totally longing for spoil
and [who] had come to depopulate the kingdom of the world,
would be also able *to wrest* this noble spoil *from the evil world*[42]
and win her for his Lord.

---

[38]The image of the fragrance of perfume, which will return (cf. **Legend** 10), is inspired by the **Bull of Canonization** 3; cf. supra p. 177.

[39]Cf. **Process** 1:3; 2:2; 3:2; 4:2; 12:1.

[40]Cf. Eph. 4:24; Col 3:3, 9, 10. The "newness" of Francis' vocation possibly reflects the influence of the biographies of Thomas of Celano and the inspiration of the wider "reform" literature of the period. Cf. G.B. Ladner, **The Idea of Reform: Its Impact on Christian Thought and Action in the Age of the Fathers** (New York, Evanston, and London: Harper & Row: 1967); "Two Gregorian Letters: On the Sources and Nature of Gregory VII," in **Studii Gregoriani** V (1956), 221–242; R.J. Armstrong, " 'Mira circa nos': Gregory IX's View of the Saint Francis of Assisi," in **Laurentianum** 3 (1984), 385–414. Francis himself seems to have been the first to suggest this "newness" in his vocation when he wrote in his Testament 14: " . . . no one showed me what I should do, but the Most High Himself revealed to me that I should live according to the form of the Holy Gospel."

[41]Cf. Heb 12:9. A most unusual biblical allusion that cannot be found in any other Franciscan biographical work.

[42]Gal 1:4. The imagery of "depopulating the kingdom of the world" does not appear elsewhere in the Franciscan biographical literature, nor does this biblical passage.

He visited her and she more frequently him,[43] moderating the times of their visits so that this divine pursuit could not be perceived by anyone nor objected to by gossip. For, with only one close companion accompanying her,[44] the young girl, leaving her paternal home, frequented the clandestine meetings with the man of God, whose words seemed to her to be on fire and whose deeds were seen to be beyond the human.

The Father Francis encouraged her to despise the world,
showing her by his living speech
how dry the hope of the world was
and how deceptive its beauty.

He whispered in her ears
of a sweet espousal with Christ,
persuading her to preserve the pearl of her virginal purity
for that blessed Spouse Whom Love made man.

6. Why dwell on many things?

The virgin did not withhold her consent for very long,
because of the insistent most holy father
and
his role as a skillful agent of the most faithful Groom.[45]

Immediately
an insight into the eternal joys was opened to her
at whose vision the world itself would become worthless,
with whose desire she would begin to melt, [and]
for whose love she would begin to yearn for heavenly nuptials.

Burning with a heavenly fire,
she so thoroughly condemned
the glory of earthly vanity
that

---

[43]Sister Beatrice, a sister of the saint, testified that St. Francis made the first visit (cf. **Process** 12:1).

[44]**Process** 17:3.

[45]**Process** 1:2; 3:1; 4:2; 6:1; 12:2; 16:3, 6; 20:6. A unique description of the role of Saint Francis in the calling of Clare that is not found elsewhere. It is interesting that the author does not hesitate to use the image which really does not fit. Usually the groom or his agent would discuss terms with the bride's family or their agent. It would be highly unlikely for anyone to deal directly with the bride.

nothing of the applause of the world
would ever cling to her affections.

Trembling with fear at the allurements of the flesh,
she already proposed to be ignorant
of the transgression of the marriage bed,[46]
and desired to make of her body
a temple for God alone
and
strove by her virtue to be worthy
of marriage with the great King.

Then she committed herself thoroughly to the counsel of Francis, placing him, after God, as the guide of her journey. Her soul relied on his sacred admonitions and received whatever he said of the good Jesus with a warm heart. She was already troubled by the tinsel of an ornate world and *considered as almost dung everything acclaimed by the world, in order that she might be able to gain Christ* (cf. Phil 3:8).

7. Quickly,
so that the mirror of her unblemished mind
might not be stained any further
by the dust of the world[47]
or
that mundane contamination
might not ferment in unleavened youth,
the kind father
hurried to lead Clare
from the dark world.

The Solemnity of the Day of the Palms was at hand[48] when the young girl went with a fervent heart to the man of God, asking [him] about her

---

[46]Cf. Wis 3:13. Vocational attitudes and options of medieval women are briefly summarized by A. Valerio in "Women in the 'Societas Christiana': 10th–12th Centuries," *Theology Digest* 33:1 (Spring, 1986), 155–158.

[47]Cf. Gregory the Great, **Dialogues**, Prologue (PL 77:152A). This exhortation was also used by Thomas of Celano, **First Life** of Saint Francis, n. 71 (Omnibus, p. 288): "[Francis'] greatest concern was to be free from everything of this world lest the serenity of his mind be disturbed even for an hour by the taint of anything which was mere dust." Clare herself uses it in her second letter to Agnes of Prague 12: "But with swift pace, light step, [and] unswerving feet, so that even your steps stir up no dust. . . . "

[48]Concerning the date of the flight of Clare from her home, cf. **Process**, n. 8.

conversion and how it should be carried out. The father Francis told her that on the day of the feast, she should go, dressed and adorned, together with the crowd of people, to [receive] a palm, and, on the following night, *leaving the camp (Heb 13:13) she should turn her* worldly *joy into mourning* (Ja 4:9) the Lord's passion.

Therefore, when Sunday came, the young girl, thoroughly radiant with festive splendor among the crowd of women, entered the church with the others. Then something occurred that was a fitting omen: as the others were going [to receive] the palms, while Clare remained immobile in her place out of shyness, the Bishop, coming down the steps, came to her and placed a palm in her hands. On that night, preparing to obey the command of the saint, she embarked upon her long desired flight with a virtuous companion.⁴⁹ Since she was not content to leave by way of the usual door, marveling at her strength, she broke open—with her own hands—that other door that is customarily blocked by wood and stone.⁵⁰

8. And so she ran to Saint Mary of the Portiuncula, leaving behind her home, city, and relatives. There the brothers, who were observing sacred vigils before the little altar of God, received the virgin Clare with torches. There, immediately after rejecting the filth of Babylon, she gave the world *"a bill of divorce"* (Dt 24:1).⁵¹ There, her hair shorn by the hands of the brothers, she put aside every kind of fine dress.⁵²

Was it not fitting
that an Order of flowering virginity
be awakened
in the evening
or in any other place
than in this place of her,
the first and most worthy of all,
who alone is Mother and Virgin!

---

⁴⁹The Latin text is awkward here and could suggest that Clare went to the Portiuncula on Monday night, i.e., "the following night." In the Middle Ages, however, the day did not begin at midnight but at sunset. It is clear, moreover, the night of Palm Sunday was the actual moment when Clare made her way from her home to the Portiuncula. Concerning the "virtuous companion" who escorted Clare to the Portiuncula, cf. Process, n. 9.

Only the author of the **Legend** makes notes of this detail. In addition, the entire preceding passage is missing in the **Process**.

⁵⁰**Process** 13:1.

⁵¹Deuteronomy speaks of a man issuing a bill of divorce against his wife. In this instance, however, Clare herself takes the initiative in issuing such a bill.

⁵²**Process** 12:4; 16:6; 17:5; 18:3; 20:6.

This is the place
in which
a new army of the poor,
under the leadership of Francis,
took its joyful beginnings,
so that
it might be clearly seen
that it was the Mother of mercies[53]
who brought to birth
both Orders
in her dwelling place.

After she received the insignia of holy penance before the altar of the blessed Virgin and, as if before the throne of this Virgin, the humble servant was married to Christ, Saint Francis immediately led her to the church of San Paolo to remain there until the Most High would provide another place.[54]

9. But after the news reached her relatives, they condemned with a broken heart the deed and proposal of the virgin and, banding together as one, they ran to the place, attempting to obtain what they could not. They employed violent force, poisonous advice, and flattering promises, trying to persuade her to give up such a worthless deed that was unbecoming to her class and without precedence in her family. But, taking hold of the altar cloths, she bared her tonsured head, maintaining that she would in no way be torn away from the service of Christ. With the increasing violence of her relatives, her spirit grew and her love—provoked by injuries—provided strength.[55] So, for many days, even though she endured an obstacle in the way of the Lord and her own [relatives] opposed her proposal of holiness, her spirit did not crumble and her fervor did not diminish. Instead, amid words and deeds of hatred, she molded her spirit anew in hope until her relatives, turning back, were quiet.

10. After a few days, she went to the church of San Angelo in Panzo,[56]

---

[53]Bonaventure uses the same image of the Mother of Mercy in his reference to the birth of the Order at the Portiuncula; cf. LM III 1. The origin of the title seems to be linked to the writings of St. Odone, abbot of Cluny (+942) and was used with some frequency in the Roman liturgy. It suggests both that Mary is the mother of Jesus, mercy incarnate, and that she herself is the most excellent merciful mother.

[54]Cf. **Process**, note 81. See A. Fortini, **Francis of Assisi**, trans. H. Moak (New York: Crossroad, 1981), 344–345, notes g and h for information concerning (a) the right of sanctuary and (b) the family's reaction to Clare's decision.

[55]**Process** 12:4; 18:3.

[56]**Process** 12:7. Cf. **Process** n. 92.

where her mind was not completely at peace, so that, at the advice of Saint Francis, she moved to San Damiano.[57]

There,
as if casting the anchor of her soul
in a secure site
she no longer wavered
due to further changes of place,
nor did she hesitate
because of its smallness,
nor did she fear its isolation.

This is that church
for whose repair Francis sweated with remarkable energy
and to whose priest he offered money for its restoration.[58]

This is the place where,
while Francis was praying,
the voice spoke to him from the cross:
"Francis, go repair my house,
which, as you see,
is totally destroyed."[59]

In this little house of penance
the virgin Clare enclosed herself
for love of her heavenly spouse.

Here
she imprisoned her body
for as long as it would live
hiding it from the turmoil of the world.

*In the hollow of this wall,
the silver-winged dove, building a nest,*[60]
gave birth to a gathering of virgins of Christ,
founded a holy monastery,
and began the Order of the Poor Ladies.

---

[57]**Process** 12:5; 20:7.
[58]Cf. I Cel 18.
[59]Cf. II Cel 10.
[60]Cf. Ct 2:14; Jer 48:28.

Here
on a path of penance
she trampled upon the earth of her members,
sowed the seeds of perfect justice,
and showed her footprints to her followers
by her own manner of walking.

In this confined retreat
for forty-two years
she broke open the alabaster-jar of her body
by the scourgings of her discipline
so that the house of the Church
would be filled
with the fragrance of her ointments.

How gloriously she spent her life
in this place
will ultimately be told
after it is initially told
how many and how great
were the souls
[who] came to Christ
through her.

For within a short time
the reputation of the holiness of the virgin Clare
had spread through the neighboring areas
and from all sides
women ran after *the odor of her ointments.*[61]

Virgins ran after her example to serve Christ as they were;
married women to live a chaste life more completely;
nobles and illustrious women,
spurning their ample palaces,
built strict monasteries for themselves
and considered it a great glory to live for Christ
in sackcloth and ashes.[62]

---

[61]Cf. Ct 1:3. From the **Acts of the Process of Canonization**, it appears that almost half of the community at San Damiano did not come from Assisi, but from the Spoleto Valley and further afield.

[62]Cf. Mt 11:21; Lk 10:13. This could be a reference to Bl. Agnes of Prague; cf. supra. pp. 33–34

The ardor of young men was no less moved to enter the struggle
and was provoked to spurn the allurements of the flesh
through the strong example of the more fragile flesh.

Finally,
many who were already joined in marriage
bound themselves in mutual consent to the law of continence:
the men entering the Orders,
the women the monasteries.

A mother would invite her daughter to follow Christ,
a daughter, her mother;
sister attracted sister.
an aunt, her nieces.

Everyone desired to serve Christ in a jealous fervor
and wished to become a participant in this angelic life
which so clearly shone through Clare.
Any number of virgins,
excited by the stories of Clare,
although they were not able to enter the enclosed life,
strove to live a regular life without a rule
in their own home.

So many of these seeds of salvation
did Clare bring to fruition
by her example,
that in her
that prophecy was seen fulfilled:
*Many are the children of the barren one
more than of her who has a husband.*[63]

11. Meanwhile
so that the stream of this heavenly blessing
sprung up in the Spoleto Valley
would not be confined within limited boundaries,
it was so channeled into a river

---

[63]Is 54:1. For further information on forms of religious dedication available to women
of this period, see Brenda Bolton, "Mulieres Sanctae," **Studies in Church History** 10 (1973),
77–97, and "Vitae Matrum: Further Aspects of the Frauenfrage," in **Medieval Women**, ed.
D. Baker (Oxford, 1978), 253–273.

by divine providence
that
the current of the river would gladden
the entire *city* of the Church.[64]

For the newness of such great things went far and wide in the world
and everywhere it began to gain souls
for Christ.

Remaining enclosed
Clare began to enlighten the whole world
and
her brilliance dazzled it
with the honors of her praises.
The fame of her virtues filled the chambers of noble ladies
reached the palaces of duchesses,
even the mansions of their queens.[65]

The highest of the nobility stooped to follow her footprints
and left its race of proud blood
for her holy humility.

After the invitation of Clare was made known,
not a few,
worthy of marriage to dukes and kings,
did severe penance,
and
those who were married to rulers
imitated Clare in their own way.

Innumerable cities were enriched with monasteries,
even fields and mountains were beautified with the structure of this
celestial building.

The cult of chastity intensified in the world
under the leadership of Clare
and the renewed order of virgins was recalled in its midst.

---

[64]Ps 46:5.
[65]Before the death of St. Clare, in addition to Bl. Agnes of Prague, there were also St. Elizabeth of Hungary (+ 1231) who entered the Third Order of St. Francis, and B. Salome of Krakow (+ 1268) who entered the Poor Ladies in 1245.

Today
the Church is happily adorned
with these beautiful flowers that Clare brought forth
and with them
She asks to be supported, saying:
Support me with flowers,
encompass me with apples,
because I languish with love.[66]

But let my pen return to its intention, so that the quality of her life may be made known.

HER HOLY HUMILITY

12. This woman,
the cornerstone and foundation of her Order,
from the very beginning
sought to place the building of all virtues
on the foundation of holy humility.[67]

For she promised holy obedience to blessed Francis and never deviated from her promise. Three years after her conversion, declining the name and office of Abbess, she wished in her humility to be placed under others rather than above them and, among the servants of Christ, to serve more willingly than to be served.

Compelled by blessed Francis,
however,
she accepted the government of the Ladies,
out of which
fear, not arrogance,
was brought forth from her heart,
and freedom did not increase,
as did service.[68]

---

[66]Ct 2:5.

[67]The passage reflects the tradition of monasticism which regarded humility as the guardian and foundation of the virtues. This is expressed most clearly in St. Bernard of Clairvaux's First Sermon for the Feast of the Nativity, 1: "Be attentive to humility which is the foundation and guardian of the virtues" (P.L. 183:115), a phrase used by Thomas of Celano (II Cel 140) and later echoed by St. Bonaventure (LM VI 1).

[68]Process 1:6; Bull of Canonization 9, 10.

What is more,
the higher she was perceived in [this] type of prelacy,
the more worthless she became in her own judgment,
the more ready to serve,
the more unworthy she considered herself of veneration by others.

She never shirked any familial chores, to such an extent that she very often washed the hands of the sisters, assisted those who were seated [at table], and waited on those who were eating.[69] Rarely would she give an order; instead she would do things spontaneously, preferring rather to do things herself than to order her sisters. She herself washed the mattresses of the sick; she herself, with that noble spirit of hers, cleansed them, not running away from their filth nor shrinking from their stench.[70] She frequently and reverently washed the feet of the serving [sisters] who returned from outside and, after washing them, kissed them. Once when she was washing the feet of one of these servants, while bending to kiss them, that [sister], not tolerating such humility, withdrew her foot and, with it, struck the Lady on her mouth. Yet she calmly took the foot of the sister again and, on its sole, placed a firm kiss.[71]

HER HOLY AND SINCERE POVERTY

13. Poverty in all things
was
in harmony with
poverty in spirit,
which is true humility.[72]

---

[69]Process 1:12; 2:1, 3; 3:9. Cf. M. Goodich, "Ancilla Dei: The Servant as Saint in the Late Middle Ages," *Women of the Medieval World: Essays in Honor of John H. Mundy*, ed. J. Kirshner and S.F. Wemple (Oxford: Blackwell, 1985), 119–178. In this article, the author traces the development of the motif of servanthood that appears in thirteenth century hagiography.

[70]Process 1:12; 2:1; 6:2,7. The Latin word **sedilia** (stools) appears to be an archaic term for what would be commonly "matresses" or cloth sacking filled with straw provided for the sick sisters. These would frequently be filthy and vermin-filled. An excellent treatment of the responsibilities of the abbess for the health care of the monastery can be found in M. W. Labarge, *Women in Medieval Life: A Small Sound of the Trumpet* (London: Hamish Hamilton, 1986), 169–171.

[71]Process 2:3; 3:9; 10:6; cf. Process, note 28.

[72]The author is in keeping with the Franciscan tradition that links poverty with humility. Francis himself views them as sisters (cf. **SalVirt** 2), understands the sin of the first human being in their light (**Adm II** 3), and underscores them as foundational virtues of his vision of life in the Church (cf. **RegNB XII** 4).

From the very beginning of her conversion,
she sold the paternal inheritance that would have come to her,
keeping nothing of its worth for herself,
and gave it all to the poor.[73]

Thus
after leaving the world outside
and enriching her mind within,
she ran after Christ
without being burdened with anything.[74]

The pact that she had established with holy poverty[75]
was so great and brought such love,
that she wanted to have nothing but Christ the Lord
and
would not permit her sisters to possess anything.[76]

In fact,
she considered
that *the most precious pearl* of heavenly desire,
which *she purchased by selling everything,*[77]
could not be possessed
with the gnawing concern for temporal things.

Through frequent talks
she instilled in her sisters
that their dwelling-place would be acceptable to God
only when it was rich in poverty
and
that it would continue to be secure
only if it were always fortified

---

[73]**Process** 3:3; 12:3; 13:11. The author is again in keeping with the Franciscan tradition in which Francis, inspired by the Gospel (Mt 19:21; Mk 10:21; Lk 12:33; 18:22), envisioned the embrace of material poverty—selling one's possessions and giving the proceeds to the poor—as the first prerequisite for his way of life (cf. I Cel 24).

[74]Cf. Lk 10:4; 22:35.

[75]Consideration of an agreement or pact established by poverty is continually present in the Franciscan literature of the thirteenth century. One of its earliest and most beautiful expressions is found in the **Sacrum Commercium S. Francisci cum Domina Paupertate**. It is found in both biographies of Thomas of Celano (I Cel 35; II Cel 70). Clare herself reveals the depth of her understanding of the concept in her **First Letter to Agnes of Prague** 30; cf. infra.

[76]**Process** 1:13.

[77]Mt 13:46.

by the strong watchtower of the most exalted poverty.[78]
She encouraged them in their little nest of poverty
to be conformed to the poor Christ,
Whom a poor Mother *placed* as an infant *in a* narrow *crib*.[79]

With this special reminder,
as if with a jewel of gold,
she adorned her breast,
so that no speck of the dust of earthly things would enter her.

14. She asked a privilege of poverty of Innocent III of happy memory, desiring that her Order be known by the title of poverty.[80] This magnificent man, congratulating such great fervor in the virgin, spoke of the uniqueness of her proposal since such a privilege had never been made by the Apostolic See. The Pope himself with great joy wrote with his own hand the first draft of the privilege [that was] sought after, so that an unusual favor might smile upon an unusual request.

Pope Gregory of happy memory, a man as very worthy of the papal throne as he was venerable in his deeds, loved this holy woman intensely with a fatherly affection. When he was [attempting to] persuade her that, because of the events of the times and the dangers of the world, she should consent to have some possessions which he himself willingly offered, she resisted with a very strong spirit and would in no way acquiesce.[81] To this the Pope replied: "If you fear for your vow, We absolve you from it." "Holy Father," she said, "I will never in any way wish to be absolved from the following of Christ."

She received with great joy the fragments of alms and the scraps of bread that the questors brought[82] and, as if saddened by whole [loaves of] bread, she rejoiced more in the scraps.

What else?

By most perfect poverty
she was eager to conform to the Poor Crucified,

---

[78]Cf. **Third Letter to Agnes of Prague** 15–28 in which Clare writes of the poverty of the Virgin Mary, the model of the enclosed life. While we use the symbol of a rock as a sign of strength or resistance, those of the Middle Ages used the symbol of the watchtower.

[79]Cf. Lk 2:7. Clare herself expresses these same sentiments in her **Fourth Letter to Agnes of Prague** 19–21, as well as in her Rule II 18.

[80]Cf. infra p. ; **Process** 3:14, 32; 12:6.

[81]**Process** 1:13; 2:22; 3:14; cf. note 23.

[82]**Process** 3:13; cf. note 46.

so that
nothing transitory would separate
the lover from her Beloved
or would impede her way with the Lord.

Here are two miracles [that] took place which this lover of poverty merited to perform.

THE MIRACLE OF THE MULTIPLICATION OF BREAD

15. There was only one [loaf of] bread in the monastery when both hunger and the time for eating arrived. After calling the refectorian, the saint told her to divide the bread and to send part [of it] to the brothers, keeping the rest for the sisters.[83] From this remaining part she told her to cut fifty [pieces] according to the number of ladies and to place them on the table of poverty. When the devoted daughter replied to her: "It would be necessary to have the ancient miracles of Christ occur to receive fifty pieces from such a small [piece of] bread," the mother responded by saying: "Confidently do whatever I say, [my] child." The daughter hurried to fulfill the command of her mother; the mother hurried to direct her pious aspirations for her sisters to her Christ. Through a divine gift, that little piece [of bread] increased in the hands of the one breaking it and a generous portion existed for each one in the convent.[84]

ANOTHER MIRACLE OF THE OIL GIVEN BY GOD

16. One day the oil had been so completely drained by the servants of Christ that there was not even anything of seasoning for the sick. The Lady Clare took one of the jars and this teacher of humility washed it with her own hands. She placed the empty jar aside so that the Brother Questor might take it. That brother was summoned so that he might go to acquire [some] oil. The devoted brother hurried to relieve such need and ran to get the jar. *However, it does not depend upon him who wishes or upon him who runs, but on the mercies of God* (Rm 9:19). For by the bountiful God alone that jar was replenished with oil, since the prayer of the holy Clare had anticipated the concern of the brother for the welfare of the poor daughters.[85] In truth, however, that brother grumbled to himself as if he had been sent for nothing, and he said: "These women have called me to make fun of me, since, look, the jar is full!"

---

[83]Cf. **Process**, note 75.
[84]**Process** 6:16.
[85]**Process** 1:15; 2:14; **Bull of Canonization** 19.

THE MORTIFICATION OF THE FLESH

17. Perhaps it would be better to be silent rather than to speak
of her marvelous mortification of the flesh,
since she did such things that would astonish
those who hear of them
and they would challenge the truth of these things.[86]

For it was not unusual that she covered rather than warmed her frail body with a simple tunic and a poor mantle [made] of rough material.[87] We should not marvel that she completely ignored the use of shoes. It was not out of keeping for her to fast continually or to use a bed without a mat. For in all these things, she perhaps does not merit any special praise since the other sisters of the enclosure did the same.

But what agreement could there be between the flesh of the virgin and a pigskin garment? For the most holy virgin obtained a pigskin garment which she secretly wore under her tunic with its sharp, cutting bristles next to her skin. At other times she would use a rough shirt woven from knotted horsehair which she would tie to her body with rough cords. Once she loaned this garment to one of her daughters who had asked for it; but, after three days, when that sister had worn it, immediately overwhelmed by such roughness, she not only gave it up far more quickly but also more joyfully than when she had asked for it.[88]

The bare ground and sometimes branches of vines were her bed, and a hard [piece of] wood under her head took the place of a pillow. But in the course of time, when her body became weak, she placed a mat [on the ground] and indulged her head with a little bit of straw. After a long illness began to take hold of her weakened body [and] the blessed Francis had commanded it, she used a sack filled with straw.[89]

18. Moreover, the rigor of her abstinence in her fasts was so great that she barely kept her body alive on the meager food she took were it not for some other strength that sustained her.

---

[86]It is helpful to recall that "mortification" or "to mortify" is used infrequently in the Franciscan sources. Francis uses it only twice in his writings (RegNB XVII:14; SalVirt 15), Thomas of Celano only five times (I Cel 41; 42; 43; LegCh 6), Bonaventure three times in quoting Thomas of Celano (LM I 6; V 5; XV 1), and the other authors never at all. It is curious that it appears four times in this work and receives such prominence. Among other things, this supports the theory that the concept was undergoing a change from the more positive concept of twelfth century spiritual theology. Cf. C. Morel, "Mortification," DSAM 10, Paris (1977–1980), 1791–1799.

[87]Process 2:4; 3:4.

[88]Process 2:7; 3:4; 10:1; cf. Process, note 31.

[89]Process 1:7; 3:4; 10:7.

While [she enjoyed] her health, she tasted wine, if there were any, only on Sundays since she was fasting on bread and water during the time of the greater Lent and that of St. Martin the Bishop. So that you who hear [these things] might marvel at what you cannot imitate, she took nothing in the way of food on three days of the week during those Lents, that is, on Monday, Wednesday, and Friday. Thus one after another, the days of a meager meal and those of strict mortification followed one another so that a vigil of perfect fast passed over into a quasi-feast of bread and water.

It is not surprising that such rigor, observed for a long [period of] time, subjected Clare to sicknesses, consumed her strength, and enervated the vigor of her body. Therefore, the very devoted children of the holy mother suffered with her and lamented with their tears those "deaths" which she willingly endured each day. Finally, blessed Francis and the Bishop of Assisi prohibited the holy Clare [to continue] that deadly fast of three days, directing her to let no day pass without taking at least an ounce and a half of bread.

> While serious affliction of the body
> usually generates that of the spirit,
> it shone far differently
> in Clare.
> For she maintained
> a festive and joyful appearance
> in every one of her mortifications
> so that
> she seemed either not to feel
> her corporal afflictions
> or
> to laugh [at them].

> From this
> it is clearly given
> to our understanding
> that
> the holy joy
> with which she was flooded within
> overflowed without
> because the love of the heart
> lightens
> the scourges of the body.[90]

---

[90]**Process** 1:7, 8; 2:8; 3:5, 6; 4:5; 6:4. Cf. **Process**, note 58. The author wisely describes with psychological perceptiveness the remarkable mystical joy that filled Clare despite her daily embrace of mortification.

THE EXERCISE OF HOLY PRAYER

19. Truly dead to the flesh
she was thoroughly a stranger to the world,
continually occupying her soul
with sacred prayers and divine praises.[91]

She had already focused
the most fervent attention of her entire desire
on the Light
and
she opened more generously the depths of her mind
to the torrents of grace
that bathe a world of turbulent change.

She would pray with the sisters for long periods [of time] after Compline and the torrents of tears that burst forth in her excited [them] in others.[92] But after the others went to their hard beds to rest their tired bodies, she remained in prayer, thoroughly vigilant and invincible, *so that she could then secretly receive the divine whispers* (Jb 4:12) while sleep occupied the others.[93] Very frequently while she was prostrate on her face in prayer, she flooded the ground with tears and caressed it with kisses, so that she might always seem to have her Jesus in her hands, on whose feet her tears flowed and her kisses were impressed.[94]

---

[91]The prayer life of Saint Clare—and the miracles that flowed from it—receives the longest treatment in the **Legend** (nn. 19–35). Thus, the considerations of Clare's humility, poverty, and mortification supply the background or ambient of this quintessential aspect of her life. While it is continually interspaced with the author's theological reflections, it is helpful to note that a great deal of the material is taken from the Acts of the Process of Canonization, that is, from the observations of the sisters who lived with Saint Clare.

[92]The presence of tears in the context of prayer was frequently present in the spiritual theology of this period. It stems from the tradition of ancient monasticism and is expressed clearly in the Rule of St. Benedict XX: "We shall not be heard for our speaking much, but for our purity of heart and tears of compunction." The twelfth century life of Aelred of Rievaulx by Walter Daniel contains this description of the saintly Cistercian: "He would hardly ever pray without tears; tears, he would say, are the signs of perfect prayer, the ambassadors between God and people; they reveal the whole feeling of the heart and declare the will of God." Cf. W. Daniel, **The Life of Aelred of Rievaulx**, ed. F.M. Powicke (London, 1959): 20. The presence of this expression of spirituality in central Italy at the time of Saint Clare can be seen in R. Davidson, **Firenze ai Tempi di Dante** (Florence, 1929): 599, in which the author claims that the thirteenth century was a period of "excessive tearfulness." Cf. J. Huizinga, **The Waning of the Middle Ages** (London, 1968): 184.

[93]Process 1:7; 10:3.
[94]Process 3:7; 6:4.

Once in the depth of night, while she was sleeping, an angel of darkness stood by her in the form of a black child and warned her, saying: "You should not cry so much because you will become blind."⁹⁵ But when she replied immediately: "Whoever sees God will not be blind," he departed confused. That same night, after Matins, while Clare was praying, bathed as usual in a stream [of tears], the deceitful admonisher approached. "You should not cry so much," he said; "otherwise your brain will dissolve and flow through your nose because you will have a crooked nose." To which she responded quickly: "Whoever knows the Lord suffers nothing that is twisted." Immediately he fled and vanished.⁹⁶

20. The usual signs prove
how much strength she received in her furnace of ardent prayer,
how sweet the divine goodness was to her in that enjoyment.

For when she returned with joy from holy prayer,
she brought from the altar of the Lord burning words
that also inflamed the hearts of her sisters.

In fact,
they marveled
that such sweetness came from her mouth
and
that her face shone more brilliantly than usual.

Surely,
in His sweetness,
*God has waited upon the poor,*⁹⁷
and
*the True Light*⁹⁸
which was already revealed outwardly in her body,
had filled her soul in prayer.

---

⁹⁵In keeping with the overwhelming light/darkness motif, "western" society has, until recently, regarded all black things, people and animals as representing evil, e.g. black sheep, crows and ravens, black cats, as well as the modern distinction between black witch/white witch, and even black magic.

⁹⁶Cf. J. de Vitry, *De Maria Oigniacensi in Namurcensi Belgii Diocesi*, ed. D. Papebroec, **Acta Sanctorum**, Junii 5 (Paris, 1866), 542–572, nos. 6, 18, where similar temptations are described giving us the impression that this was a frequent literary device. It seems that fear of deformity is associated with evil, e.g. II Cel 9; L3C 12.

⁹⁷Ps 67:11.

⁹⁸Jn 1:9.

Thus
in a fleeting world,
united unfleetingly to her noble spouse,
she delighted continuously in the things above.

Thus,
on the wheel of an ever changing world,
sustained by stable virtue
and *hiding a treasure of glory in a vessel of clay,*[99]
her mind remained on high
while her body lingered here below.

It was her custom to come to Matins before the younger [sisters], whom she called to the praises by silently arousing them with signs. She would frequently light the lamps while others were sleeping; and she would frequently ring the bell with her own hand.[100]

There was no place for tepidity,
no place for idleness,
where a sharp reproof prodded laziness
to prayer and service of the Lord.

THE MIRACLES OF HER PRAYER
FIRST: THE SARACENS ARE MIRACULOUSLY PUT TO FLIGHT

21. I would like to recount the great things of her prayers with as much fidelity to the truth as they merit in veneration.

The Spoleto Valley more often *drank of the chalice of wrath* (Rev 14:10) because of that scourge the Church had to endure in various parts of the world under Frederick the Emperor. In it there was a battle array of soldiers and Saracen archers swarming like bees at the imperial command to depopulate its villages and to spoil its cities. Once when the fury of the enemy pressed upon Assisi, a city dear to the Lord, and the army was already near its gates, the Saracens, the worst of people, who thirsted for the blood of Christians and attempted imprudently every outrage, rushed upon San Damiano, [entered] the confines of the place and even the enclosure of the virgins.[101] The hearts of the ladies melted with fear; their voices trembled with it, and they brought their tears to their mother. She, with

[99]Cf. 2 Cor 4:7.
[100]Process 2:9; 10:3; cf. Process, note 36.
[101]Cf. Process, note 40.

an undaunted heart, ordered that she be brought, sick as she was, to the door and placed there before the enemy, while the silver pyx enclosed in ivory in which the Body of the Holy of Holies was most devotedly reserved, preceded her.[102]

22. When she had thoroughly prostrated herself to the Lord in prayer, she said to her Christ with tears [in her eyes]: "Look, my Lord, do you wish to deliver into the hands of pagans your defenseless servants whom You have nourished with Your own love? Lord, I beg You, defend these Your servants whom I am not able to defend at this time." Suddenly a voice from the mercy-seat of new grace, as if of a little child, resounded in her ears: "I will always defend you." "My Lord," she said, "please protect this city which for Your love sustains us." And Christ said to her: "It will suffer afflictions, but will be defended by my protection."

Then the virgin, raising her tear-filled face, comforted the weeping [sisters], saying: "My dear children, I guarantee, you will not suffer any harm. Just have confidence in Christ." Without delay, the subdued boldness of those dogs began immediately to be alarmed. They were driven away by the power of the one who was praying, departing in haste over those walls which they had scaled.

Immediately Clare advised those who had heard the voice mentioned above, saying eagerly [to them]: "Dearest children, be careful not to reveal in any way that voice to anyone while I am [still] in the body."

THAT MIRACLE OF THE LIBERATION OF THE CITY

23. Another time Vitalis d'Aversa,[103] captain of an imperial army, a man craving glory and bold in battle, directed that army against Assisi. He stripped the land of trees, devastated the entire countryside, and so settled down to besiege the city. He declared with threatening words that he would in no way withdraw until he had taken possession of that city. It had already come to the point that danger to the city was feared imminent.

When Clare, the servant of Christ, heard this, she was profoundly grieved, called her sisters around her, and said: "Dearest children, every day we receive many good things from that city. It would be terrible if, at

---

[102]**Process** 2:20; 3:18; 4:14; 9:2; 10:9; 12:8; 18:6. Cf. **Process**, note 83 for an interpretation of the period surrounding these events. Iconography often depicts Clare holding a monstrance, which is not verified here. This iconography, however, may well reflect a trend that has its roots in 13th century feminine mystical experience according to the study of C.W.Bynum, **Jesus as Mother: Studies in the Spirituality of the High Middle Ages** (Los Angeles: University of California Press, 1982), especially "Women Mystics and the Clericalization of the Church," 247–262. This episode illustrates with moving beauty how deeply Clare made her own the intense Eucharistic faith of Francis.

[103]**Process** 3:19; 9:3; 13:9: 14:3. Cf. **Process**, note 52.

a proper time, we did not help it, as we now can." She commanded that some ashes be brought and that the sisters bare their heads. First she scattered a lot of ashes over her own head and then placed them on the heads of those sisters. "Go to our Lord," she said, "and with all your heart beg for the liberation of the city."

Why should I narrate the details?
Why describe again the tears of the virgins,
their *impassioned* prayers?[104]

On the following morning, the merciful God *brought about a happy ending to the trial* (1 Cor 10:13) so that, after the entire army had been dispersed, the proud man departed, contrary to his vow, and never again disturbed that land. A little while afterwards that leader of war was cut down by the sword.

THE POWER OF HER PRAYER IN THE CONVERSION OF HER SISTER

24. Certainly
that wonderful power of her prayer
should not be buried in silence,
which in the very beginning of her conversion
turned one soul to God
and [then] defended her convert.

In fact,
she had a sister, tender in age,
a sister by flesh and by purity.
In her desire for her conversion,
among the first prayers that she offered to God with all her heart,
she more ardently begged this [grace] that,
just as she had an affinity of spirit with her sister in the world,
she might also have now a unity of will in the service of God.

Therefore she prayed continuously to the Father of mercy
that the world might become insipid to Agnes,
her sister at home,
and that God might become pleasing
and so move her from the thought of a carnal marriage

---

[104]Cf. Mt 11:13.

to the union of His love
that she might together with her
be espoused in eternal virginity
to the Spouse of glory.

A marvelous mutual love
had taken hold of both of them,
a love that, to both, brought
a new division,
a sorrowful division,
although with feelings
diverse.

The divine majesty answered without delay
the exceptional [woman of] prayer
and quickly gave her that first gift
that she so eagerly sought
and that was so greatly pleasing for God to present.

Sixteen days after the conversion of Clare, Agnes, inspired by the divine spirit, ran to her sister, revealed the secret of her will, and told her that she wished to serve God completely. Embracing her with joy, [Clare] said: "I thank God, most sweet sister, that He has heard my concern for you."

25. A defense
—no less marvelous—
followed this conversion.

For while the joyous sisters were clinging to the footprints of Christ in the church of San Angelo in Panzo and she who had heard more from the Lord was teaching her novice-sister, new attacks by relatives were quickly flaring up against the young girls.

The next day, hearing that Agnes had gone off to Clare, twelve men, burning with anger and hiding outwardly their evil intent, ran to the place [and] pretended [to make] a peaceful entrance. Immediately they turned to Agnes—since they had long ago lost hope of Clare—and said: "Why have you come to this place? Get ready to return immediately with us!" When she responded that she did not want to leave her sister Clare, one of the knights in a fierce mood ran toward her and, without sparing blows and kicks, tried to drag her away by her hair, while the others pushed her and lifted her in their arms. At this, as if she had been captured by lions and been torn from the hands of the Lord, the young girl cried out: "Dear sister, help me! Do not let me be taken from Christ the Lord!" While the violent robbers were dragging the young girl along the slope of the mountain, ripping her clothes and strewing the path with the hair [they had] torn out, Clare prostrated herself in prayer with tears, begged that her sister would be given constancy of mind and that the strength of humans would be overcome by divine power.

26. Suddenly, in fact, [Agnes'] body lying on the ground seemed so heavy that the men, many [as there were], exerted all their energy and were not able to carry her beyond a certain stream. Even others, running from their fields and vineyards, attempted to give them some help, but they could in no way lift that body from the earth. When they failed, they shrugged off the miracle by mocking: "She has been eating lead all night; no wonder she is so heavy!"

Then Lord Monaldus, her enraged uncle, intended to strike her a lethal blow; [but] an awful pain suddenly struck the hand he had raised and for a long time the anguish of pain afflicted it.

But, notice how after the long struggle, Clare came to the place and asked her relatives to give up such a conflict and to entrust Agnes, half-dead on the ground, to her care. After they departed with a bitter spirit at their unfinished business, Agnes got up joyfully and, already rejoicing in the cross of Christ for which she had struggled in this first battle, gave herself perpetually to the divine service. In fact, Blessed Francis cut off her hair with his own hand and directed her together with her sister in the way of the Lord.

Because a brief word is not able to explain the magnificent perfection of [Agnes'] life, let it be directed to Clare.

ANOTHER MIRACLE: THE CASTING OUT OF DEMONS

27. It is not surprising that,
if the prayer of Clare was strong
against the wickedness of men,
it should also inflame demons.

There was, in fact, a certain devout woman of the diocese of Pisa who came to the place to thank God and Saint Clare for the fact that, through her intercession, she had been freed from five demons.[105] Indeed, at their expulsion, the demons admitted that the prayers of Saint Clare incensed them and expelled them from [this] possessed vessel.

---

[105]**Process** 4:20; 7:14.

Not without reason, Lord Pope Gregory had marvelous faith in the prayers of this holy woman whose efficacious power he had experienced. Frequently when some new difficulties arose, as is natural, both when he was Bishop of Ostia and, later, when he was elevated to the Apostolic See, he would request assistance of that virgin by means of a letter and would experience her help.[106]

Certainly
it is something to be imitated
with all eagerness,
just as
it is something to be considered
in humility:
the Vicar of Christ seeking help
from the servant of Christ
and entrusting himself to her powers!

He knew clearly
what love can do
and how free access to the throne of majesty
opens up to pure virgins.

For
if the King of heaven gives Himself to those who love Him fervently,
what is it that He would not give,
were it expedient,
to those who devoutly pray for it?

HER WONDERFUL DEVOTION TO THE SACRAMENT OF THE ALTAR

28. How great was
Saint Clare's affection and devotion
to the Sacrament of the Altar
is shown by their effect.

In that serious illness that confined her to bed, she would sit upright and would be propped up and, sitting up [in this way], she made the most

---

[106]There are, in fact, two letters of Cardinal Hugolino or Pope Gregory IX. The first one, to which the **Legend** refers, was written in 1220; cf. infra p. 97. The second was written in 1228 after his election as Pope; cf. infra, p. 99. Cf. B. Bolton's "Vitae Matrum: Further Aspects of the Frauenfrage," **Medieval Women**, ed. D. Baker (Oxford, 1978), 268–269, concerning Gregory's attentiveness to the sanctity of Marie d'Oignies as well.

delicate cloth. From these she made over fifty sets of corporals enclosed them in silk or purple covers, and sent them to various churches throughout the plains and mountains of Assisi.[107]

When receiving the Body of the Lord, however, she at first shed burning tears and, approaching with trembling, she feared [Him Who was] hidden in the Sacrament no less than [Him Who was] ruling heaven and earth.[108]

A CERTAIN WONDERFUL CONSOLATION THAT THE LORD JESUS GAVE HER IN HER SICKNESS

29. Just as the memory of her Christ
was present to her
in her sickness,
so too
Christ visited her
in her sufferings.[109]

At that hour of the Nativity when the world rejoices with the angels at the newly born child,[110] all the ladies went to the oratory for Matins and left their mother alone weighed down by her illnesses. When she began to think about the Infant Jesus and was greatly sorrowing that she could not participate in His praises, she sighed and said: "Lord God, look at how I have been left alone in this place for You!" Behold that wonderful concert that was taking place in the church of Saint Francis suddenly began to resound in her ears. She heard the jubilant psalmody of the brothers, listened to the harmonies of their songs, and even perceived the very sounds of the instruments.

The nearness of the place was in no way such that a human being could have heard this unless either that solemnity had been divinely amplified for her or her hearing had been strengthened beyond human means. But what totally surpasses this event: she was worthy to see the very crib of the Lord!

In the morning when her daughters came to her, blessed Clare said: "Blessed be the Lord Jesus Christ, Who did not leave me after you did. In

---

[107]**Process** 1:11; 2:12; 6:14; 9:9. St. Francis also wished to provide precious vessels for the reservation of the Eucharist. Cf. Thomas of Celano, **Vita secunda** 201; anonymus, **Legenda Perugina** 80.

[108]**Process** 2:11; 3:7.

[109]This is one of the few references in the biographical literature to the motivation for Clare's serene and resigned suffering. It is helpful to recall that she was sick for at least twenty-eight years, that is, from 1224/1225—1253; cf. **Legend** 39.

[110]**Process** 3:30; 4:16; 7:9.

fact, I heard, by the grace of Christ, all those solemnities that were celebrated this night in the church of Saint Francis."[111]

THE VERY FERVENT LOVE OF THE CRUCIFIED

30. Crying over the Lord's passion
was well known to her.

At times
she poured out feelings of bitter myrrh
at the sacred wounds.

At times
she imbibed sweeter joys.

The tears of the suffering Christ made her quite inebriated
and
her memory continually pictured Him
Whom love had profoundly impressed upon her heart.[112]

She taught the novices to weep over the Crucified Christ[113] and, at the same time, what she taught with her words, she expressed with her deeds. For frequently when she would encourage them in private in such matters, a flow of tears would come before the passage of her words.

During the Hours of the day, at Sext and None,
she was usually afflicted with a greater sorrow
as she was immolated with her immolated Lord.[114]

One time, in fact, while she was praying None in her little cell, the devil struck her on the cheek, filled her eye with blood and her cheek with a bruise.

---

[111]This incident prompted Pope Pius XII to proclaim St. Clare the patroness of television in his Apostolic Brief **Miranda prorsus**, 14 February 1958.

[112]Clare's letters to Agnes of Prague reveal how central is this devotion to the Crucified Christ; cf. I 13–14, 18; II 19–21; IV 23–27. It is helpful to recall the strong, ancient tradition of devotion to the Crucifix that is associated with the path to San Damiano (cf. A. Fortini, **Francis of Assisi**, trans. H. Moak, New York [1981], 213–215) and to recall the presence of the Crucifix that spoke to Saint Francis in the monastery of the Poor Ladies (cf. op. cit., p. 216, n. 1).

[113]**Process** 11:2.

[114]**Process** 10:3. The theme of these hours has traditionally been centered on the Passion and Death of Christ, for they represent the time from noon to 3:00 P.M., the hours Christ hung on the cross.

She repeated more frequently the Prayer of the Five Wounds of the Lord so that she might nourish her mind on the delights of the Crucified without any interruption.[115] She learned the Office of the Cross as Francis, a lover of the Cross, had established it and recited it with similar affection. Underneath her habit she girded her flesh with a small cord marked with thirteen knots, a secret reminder of the wounds of the Savior.

A CERTAIN MEMORIAL OF THE LORD'S PASSION

31. Once, the day of the most sacred Supper arrived, in which *the Lord loved His own until the end (Jn 13:1)*. Near evening, as the agony of the Lord was approaching, Clare, sad and afflicted, shut herself up in the privacy of her cell.

While in her own prayer she was accompanying the praying Savior
and when *saddened even to death*[116] she experienced the effect of His sadness,
she was filled at once with the memory of His capture and of the whole mockery
and she sank down on her bed.

All that night and the following day,
she was so absorbed that
she remained out of her senses.[117]

She seemed to be joined to Christ
and to be otherwise totally insensible.
always focusing the light of her eyes on one thing.

A certain sister close to her often went to see if she might want something and always found her the same way. But with Friday night coming on, the devoted daughter lit a candle and, with a sign not a word, reminded her mother of the command of Saint Francis. For the saint had commanded her that no day should pass without some food. With that [sister] standing by, Clare, as if returning from another world, offered this word: "What need is there for a candle? Isn't it daytime?" "Mother," she replied, "the night has gone and a day has passed, and another night has returned!" To which Clare said: "May that vision be blessed, most dear daughter! Be-

---

[115]**Process** 10:10. Cf. **Process**, note 88.
[116]Mk 14:34.
[117]**Process** 3:25.

cause after having desired it for so long, it has been given to me. But, be careful not to tell anyone about that vision while I am still in the flesh."

VARIOUS MIRACLES THAT SHE PERFORMED BY THE SIGN AND POWER OF THE CROSS

32. The beloved Crucified took possession
of the lover,
and she was inflamed with such love
of the mystery of the Cross
that the power of the Cross
is shown by signs and miracles.

In fact,
when she traced the sign of the life-giving Cross
on the sick,
sickness miraculously fled from them.[118]

I will touch on some of the many instances.

Because he knew of her great perfection and respected the great power in her, Blessed Francis sent to the Lady Clare a certain brother Stephen [who was] afflicted with madness in order that she might make the sign of the holy Cross over him.[119] The daughter of obedience made the sign over him at the command of her Father and permitted him to sleep for a short while in the place where she was accustomed to pray. But that [brother], after being refreshed by a little sleep, got up healed, and returned to the father, freed from his insanity.

33. A certain three year old boy from the city of Spoleto, named Mattiolo, had a pebble caught in his nose.[120] No one was able to remove it from his nose and the boy was not able to force it out. The child, endangered by great distress, was brought to the Lady Clare and while she was tracing the sign of the Cross on him, he was cured when the pebble was immediately expelled.[121]

Another boy from Perugia with a sickness that completely covered his eye was brought to the holy servant of God.[122] Touching the eye of the

---

[118]**Process** 1:18; 3:6; 6:9.

[119]**Process** 2:15. Cf. **Process**, note 38.

[120]In the **Legend**, as in the **Process**, "children" frequently experienced the miraculous power of St. Clare, either during her life or after her death. Her familiarity with the Infant Christ makes the gestures of curing children particularly significant; in fact, both the **Legend** and the **Process** indicate that the majority of St. Clare's miracles were for children.

[121]**Process** 2:18.

[122]**Process** 4:11. Cf. **Process**, note 48.

boy, she made the sign of the Cross on it and said: "Take him to my mother so that she might repeat the sign of the Cross over him."

Her mother, Lady Ortulana,
as I have said,
having followed her little plant,
had entered the Order after her daughter
and used to serve the Lord as a widow
with the virgin
in the enclosed garden.[123]

The eye of the body, after it had received the sign of the Cross from her, purified of its illness, saw clearly and distinctly. Clare, therefore, insisted that the boy had been healed by the merit of her mother; the mother [however] turned the burden of praise toward her daughter and considered herself unworthy of such an event.

34. One of the sisters, Benvenuta, had been suffering patiently for almost twelve years with an infection of a fistula under her arm which gave out pus through five lesions.[124] The virgin of God, Clare, out of compassion for her, administered that special salve of salvation. Immediately, at the sign of the Cross, she received the perfect healing of the long-standing ulcer.

Another of the number of sisters, Amata, was laid up for thirteen months, affected by dropsy and weakened moreover by a fever, coughing, and a pain in her side.[125] The Lady Clare, moved by pity for her, had recourse to that noble proof of her medicine. She signed her with the Cross in the name of her Christ and [the sister] was immediately restored to full health.

35. Another servant of Christ, born in Perugia, had so lost her voice for two years that she could barely shape outwardly any words.[126] When, on the night of the Assumption of our Lady, it was shown to her in a vision that the Lady Clare would free her, she waited longingly for daylight. When dawn had come, she ran to her mother, asked for the sign of the Cross, and soon after she had been signed, she regained her voice.

A certain sister, Cristiana, suffering for a long time from deafness in one ear, had used many medicines against that evil, but in vain. The Lady

---

[123]Cf. Ct 4:12. Once again the author uses symbolic imagery to accentuate the depth of meaning he perceives in the figure of Ortulana. Cf. super, **Legend** 1.

[124]**Process** 2:16; 3:10; 4:8; 10:1; 14:5.

[125]**Process** 3:11; 4:7.

[126]The sister is Sister Benvenuta of Perugia; **Process** 2:13; 7:9.

mercifully signed her head, touched her ear, and she received the power of hearing.[127]

There was a great number of sick (Jn 5:3) sisters in the monastery [who were] afflicted with various pains. Clare, as usual, entered the place with her customary medicine and, after making the sign of the Cross five times, immediately relieved five [sisters] of their illnesses.[128]

It should be perfectly clear from this
that the Tree of the Cross was planted
in the breast of the Virgin;
while its fruit refreshes the soul,
its leaves externally provide medicine.

THE DAILY INSTRUCTION OF THE SISTERS

36. Because she was clearly the teacher of the uneducated
and, as it were,
the directress of young women *in the palace of the King*,[129]
she taught them with such discipline
and encouraged them with such love,
that no word will describe it.[130]

First of all she taught them to drive every noise away from the dwelling place of the mind so that they might be able to cling to the depths of God alone. She taught them not to be affected by a love of their relatives and to forget the homes of their families so that they might please Christ. She encouraged them to consider the demands of the flesh as insignificant and to restrain the frivolities of the flesh with the reins of reason. She showed them how the insidious enemy lays traps for pure souls, in one way tempting the holy, in another, the wordly. Finally she wanted them to so work with their hands during certain hours that, according to the desire of the Founder, they would keep warm through the exercise of prayer and, fleeing the lukewarmness of neglect, would put aside the coldness of a lack of devotion by the fire of holy love.

Nowhere was the strict rule of silence greater;
nowhere was the brightness and the quality of every virtue more
abundant.

---

[127]Process 3:17; 4:10; 5:1.
[128]Process 1:16, 19.
[129]Ps 44:16.
[130]Process 1:9, 14; 2:10; 2:13; 6:2; 8:3; 11:2.

There was
no lax talk bespeaking a lax spirit
nor a frivolity of words producing a frivolous disposition of mind.

For the teacher herself was sparing in her words
and
she abundantly compressed in few words
the desires of her mind.

HER EAGER DESIRE TO HEAR THE WORD OF HOLY PREACHING

37. She provided for her children,
through dedicated preachers,
the nourishment of the Word of God
and from this
she did not take a poorer portion.

She was filled with such rejoicing at hearing a holy sermon;
she delighted at such a remembrance of her Jesus
that, once,
when Brother Philippo d'Altri was preaching,[131]
a very splendid child stood by the Virgin Clare
and during the greater part of the sermon
delighted her with his sighs of joy.

That sister who merited to see such a thing in her mother
experienced an indescribable sweetness
from the sight of this apparition.

Although she was not educated in the liberal arts, she nevertheless enjoyed listening to the sermons of those who were, because she believed that a nucleus lay hidden in the text that she would subtly perceive and enjoy with relish. She knew what to take out of the sermon of any preacher that might be profitable to the soul, while knowing that to pluck a flower from a wild thorn was no less prudent than to eat the fruit of a noble tree.

Once when Lord Pope Gregory forbade any brother to go to the mon-

---

[131]**Process** 10:8. Cf. **Process**, note 70.

asteries of the Ladies without permission,[132] the pious mother, sorrowing that her sisters would more rarely have the food of sacred teaching, sighed: "Let him now take away from us all the brothers since he has taken away those who provide us with the food that is vital." At once she sent back to the minister all the brothers, not wanting to have the questors who acquired corporal bread when they could not have the questors for spiritual bread. When Pope Gregory heard this, he immediately mitigated that prohibition into the hands of the general minister.

HER GREAT CHARITY TOWARD HER SISTERS

38. This venerable Abbess loved not only the souls of her sisters, she also took care of their little bodies with wonderful zeal of charity.

Frequently, in the cold of night, she covered them with her own hands while they were sleeping.[133] She wished that those whom she perceived unable to observe the common rigor be content to govern themselves with gentleness.[134] If a temptation disturbed someone, if sadness took hold of someone, as is natural, she called her in secret and consoled her with tears. Sometimes she would place herself at the feet of the depressed [sister] so that she might relieve the force of [her] sadness with her motherly caresses.[135]

Her children, not ungrateful for her favors, repaid her with the total dedication of themselves. Indeed, they cherished the depth of love in their mother, reverenced the office of superior in their teacher, followed eagerly the path of their governess, [and] marveled at the gift of holiness in the spouse of God.

HER SICKNESS AND PROLONGED ILLNESS

39. For forty years she had run the course of the highest poverty, when, preceded by a number of illnesses,

---

[132]Cf. *Quo elongati*, 28 September 1230, which interpreted strictly the **Later Rule** (*Regula bullata*) of the Friars Minor, XI 2, 3 ("I firmly command all the brothers not to have any associations or meetings with women which could arouse suspicions. Moreover, they should not enter the monasteries of nuns, except those [brothers] to whom special permission has been given by the Apostolic See"). No doubt the prohibition was strictly observed after the promulgation of the papal bull causing such a reaction on Clare's part. Cf. L. Oliger, "De origine regularum Ordinis S. Clarae," **Archivum Franciscanum Historicum**, V (1912), 421–422.

[133]**Process** 2:3.
[134]**Process** 2:6.
[135]**Process** 10:5.

she was obviously approaching the prize of her exalted calling.[136]

Since the strength of her flesh had succumbed
to the austerity of the penance [she had practiced] in the early years,
a harsh sickness took hold of her last years,
so that she who had been enriched with the merits of [good] deeds
[when] well
might be enriched with the merits of suffering when sick.
For *virtue is brought to perfection in sickness.*[137]

How her marvelous virtue had been perfected in her sickness will be hereafter told at length: because during the twenty-eight years of her prolonged sickness "she did not murmur or utter a complaint" but holy comments and thanksgiving always came from her mouth.[138]

But, although the burden of her infirmities had become heavy [and] she seemed to be coming quickly to the end, yet God was nonetheless pleased to delay the time of her death in order that she might be able to be exalted with fitting honors by the Roman Church whose product and special child she was. For while the Pope and cardinals took their time in Lyons, a sword of enormous sorrow was afflicting the mind of her children since Clare began to be afflicted more than usual by her illness.

40. Suddenly a vision of this kind was given to a certain servant of Christ, a virgin dedicated to God in the monastery of San Paolo of the Order of Saint Benedict. It seemed to her that she was together with her sisters in San Damiano assisting at the sickness of the Lady Clare, and that Clare was lying on a precious bed. However, while they were grieving at the passing of the blessed Clare, crying and eyes [filled with] tears, a certain beautiful woman appeared at the head of the bed [and] said to those who were weeping: "Do not weep, children, for her who is about to be victorious," she said. "She will not be able to die until the Lord comes with His disciples."

And, behold, in a little while the Roman Curia arrived in Perugia.[139]

---

[136]Cf. **Process**, note 17, concerning the illness of St. Clare.

[137]2 Cor 12:9. In this brief introduction to the consideration of the illness of Saint Clare, the author summarizes its role in the development of sanctity.

[138]Cf. Hymn of Vespers, Common of Several Martyrs: "non murmur resonant, non querimonia." **Process** 1:17; also XIV 2. Cf. **Process**, note 26. The author thus presents a proof of the extraordinary virtue of Saint Clare in her identification with the martyrs and the sentiments of thanksgiving.

[139]This is not our sense of the administrative organ of the Church, but the "Papal Court," that is, the Pope and his advisors.

The Lord of Ostia, after hearing about the increase of her sickness, hurried from Perugia to visit the spouse of Christ. [He had become] a father [to her] by his office, a provider by his care, always a dedicated friend by his very pure affection. He nourished the sick [woman] with the Sacrament of the Body of the Lord, and fed [those] remaining with the encouragement of his salutary word.

Then she begged so great a father with her tears to take care of her soul and those of the other Ladies for the name of Christ. But, above all, she asked him to petition to have the Privilege of Poverty confirmed by the Lord Pope and the cardinals.[140]

Because he was a faithful helper of the Order,
just as he promised by his word,
so he fulfilled in deed.

After a year had passed, the Lord Pope moved with his cardinals from Perugia so that the vision described above concerning her passing might be brought to realization.

For
the Supreme Pontiff,
standing above human beings and below God,
represents the person of the Lord.

The lord cardinals
surround him more closely as disciples
in the temple of the Church Militant.

41. Divine Providence had already hurried to fulfill its plan concerning Clare:
Christ hurried to lift up the poor pilgrim to the palace of the heavenly kingdom.

She already desired and longed with all her desire
to be freed from the body of this death[141]
and to see reigning in the heavenly mansions
Christ, the Poor One,
Whom, as a poor virgin on earth,
she followed with all her heart.

---

[140]For Cardinal Raynaldus' role in the approval of the **Rule** of St. Clare, see supra. pp. 28–29.
    [141]Rom 7:24.

Therefore,
since her sacred limbs had deteriorated with her illness,
a new weakness took hold
that indicated her impending call to the Lord
and prepared the way for her eternal health.

Lord Innocent IV of happy memory together with the cardinals hurried to visit the servant of Christ. Since he considered her life to be beyond that of the women of our time, he did not hesitate to honor her death with the papal presence.[142] Entering the monastery, he went to her bed and extended his hand so that she might kiss it. The most grateful woman accepted it and asked that she might [also] kiss the foot of the Pope with the greatest reverence. The Curial Lord appropriately offered her his foot [which he had] placed on a wooden stool and she reverently inclined her face toward it, kissing it above and below.

42. Then, with an angelic expression, she asked the forgiveness of all her sins of the Supreme Pontiff. He thereupon said: "Would that my need of pardon were such [as yours]!" He granted her the gift of perfect absolution and the grace of his fullest blessing.

When everyone had left, since she had received [earlier] that day the sacred host from the hands of the provincial minister, she raised her eyes to heaven, joined her hands toward God, and, with tears, said to her sisters: "Praise the Lord, my children, because today Christ has condescended to give me such a blessing that heaven and earth are not enough to compensate for it. Today," she said, "I have received the Most High and have been worthy to see His Vicar."

HOW SHE RESPONDED TO HER CRYING SISTER

43. Her daughters,
who would very soon be left as orphans,
stood around the bed of the mother,
a sword of sorrow piercing their souls.[143]

Sleep did not restrain them
and hunger did not tear them away,
but,
forgetting their beds and tables,
the only thing that pleased them,

---

[142]**Process** 3:24.
[143]Lk 2:35.

night and day,
was crying.

Among them was Agnes, the devoted virgin, filled with salty tears and begging her sister not to depart and leave her. Clare replied: "It is pleasing to God that I depart. But stop crying, because you will come to the Lord a short time after me. And the Lord will console you greatly after I have left you."[144]

HER FINAL PASSAGE
AND THOSE THINGS THAT WERE DONE AND SEEN IN IT

44. It was finally seen that she was laboring for many days in her last agony during which the faith of the neighboring regions and the devotion of the peoples increased. She was honored daily as a real saint by the frequent visits of prelates and even cardinals. What is truly remarkable to hear is that when she was not able to take any food for seventeen days, she was so invigorated by the strength of the Lord that she strengthened everyone who came to her in the service of Christ.

In fact, when a kind man, Brother Raynaldo, encouraged her to be patient in the long martyrdom of so many illnesses, she responded with a very unrestrained voice: "After I once came to know the grace of my Lord Jesus Christ through his servant Francis, no pain has been bothersome, no penance too severe, no weakness, dearly beloved brother, has been hard."

45. But since the Lord was very near and, as it were, already standing at the door, she wished the priests and her spiritual brothers to stand by and read the Passion of the Lord and holy words. When Brother Juniper appeared among them, that excellent jester of the Lord who uttered the Lord's words which were often warming, she was filled with a new joy and asked him if he had had anything new from the Lord. When he opened his mouth, he burst forth with words that were like burning sparks coming from the furnace of his fervent heart. The virgin of the Lord took great comfort in his parables.

Finally she turned to her weeping daughters to whom she recalled in a praising way the divine blessings while entrusting them with the poverty of the Lord.[145] She blessed her devoted brothers and sisters and called down the fullest graces of blessings upon the Ladies of the poor monasteries, those in the present and those in the future.

---

[144]Cf. Fourth Letter to Agnes of Prague, p. 48.
[145]**Process** 3:23, 32.

Who could narrate the rest without crying?

Those two blessed companions of the blessed Francis were standing there: Angelo was one of them who, while mourning himself, consoled those who were mourning; the other was Leo who kissed the bed of the dying woman.

The daughters, distraught at the departure of their kind mother, followed her departure with their tears, knowing they would not see her anymore. They grieved most bitterly since all their comfort was to depart with her and, being left *in the valley of tears* (Ps 83:7), they would no longer be consoled by their mistress.

Propriety alone hardly restrained the hand from beating the body
and that made the flame of sorrow the more bitter
for it was not allowed to be dissipated through outward grief.

The discipline of the enclosure demands silence,
[yet] the violence of sorrow wrenched cries and sobs.

Faces were swollen with tears
and the fury of the mourning heart supplied ever new waters.

46. But the most holy virgin, turning toward herself, silently addressed her soul. "Go without anxiety," she said, "for you have a good escort for your journey. Go," she said, "for He Who created you has made you holy. And, always protecting you as a mother her child, He has loved you with a tender love. May you be blessed, O Lord," she said, "You Who have created my soul!" When one of the sisters asked her to whom she was speaking, she replied: "I am speaking to my blessed soul."[146] That glorious escort was not standing afar off. So turning to another daughter she said: "Do you see, O child, the King of glory Whom I see?"

The hand of the Lord was placed upon another (Ez 1:3) and she, amid her tears, received a joyful vision with her bodily eyes. Since she had been wounded by a dart of profound sorrow, she turned her attention to the door of the house. And, behold, a multitude of virgins in white garments entered, all of whom wore gold garlands on their heads. One more splendid than the others walked among them and from her crown, which at its peak gave the appearance of a latticed thurible, such a splendor came forth that it turned the night within the house into daylight. She moved toward the bed where the spouse of the Son was reposing and, bending most lovingly

---

[146]**Process** 3:20–22; 11:3; 14:7. Cf. **Process**, note 53.

over her, gave her a most tender embrace. A mantle of the most remarkable beauty was brought by the virgins and, with all of them working zealously, the body of Clare was covered and the bridal bed was decorated.

On the day after the feast of Saint Lawrence,[147]
therefore,
that most holy soul departed
to be crowned with an eternal reward;
since the temple of the flesh was dissolved,
the spirit passed happily to heaven.

Blessed is that passing from the valley of misery
that became for her the entrance to a blessed life.

Now
in place of the farewell meal
she is rejoicing at the table of the heavenly citizens;
now
in place of the coarseness of ashes
she is decorated with a robe of eternal glory
and is blessed in the heavenly kingdom.

HOW THE ROMAN CURIA CAME WITH A LARGE CROWD OF PEOPLE FOR THE FUNERAL OF THE VIRGIN

47. Like an unexpected piece of news, the word of the untimely passing of the virgin struck the entire population of the city.

Men and women ran to the place;
people flooded the place in such great number
that the city seemed deserted.

Everyone proclaimed her a saint;
everyone proclaimed her dear to God.
Among the words of praise not a few flowed with tears.

The Podesta with a squadron of soldiers and a crowd of armed men kept careful guard that night and day so that the loss of the precious treasure that lay within might be prevented.

---

[147]**Process** 3:32; 11:4. Cf. **Process**, n. 8 (regarding date).

The next day the entire Curia came. The Vicar of Christ with the cardinals arrived at the place and the entire city directed its steps to San Damiano. It came time to celebrate the divine praises when, after the brothers had begun the Office of the Dead, the Lord Pope suddenly declared that the Office of the Virgins should be celebrated, not that of the Dead. It seemed as though he would canonize her before placing her body in the tomb. When the most eminent Lord of Ostia replied that it would be better to proceed more slowly in these matters, the Mass of the Dead was celebrated.

Then, when the Supreme Pontiff with the group of prelates and cardinals was seated, the Bishop of Ostia, taking as his theme "Vanity of vanities" (Eccl 1:2), eulogized this outstanding woman, contemptuous of vanity, in a celebrated sermon.

48. The Cardinal priests then gathered with devout respect for the holy funeral and completed the customary rites over the body of the virgin. Finally, because they did not judge it safe or fitting to leave such a precious trust so far from the citizens, they carried it with hymns and [songs of] praise, the sound of trumpets and solemn rejoicing, and brought it honorably to San Giorgio.

This is also the site
where the body of the holy Father Francis
had been buried
so that
he who had prepared
the way of life while she lived
also prepared
—as if by foreknowledge—
the place for her death.

Afterwards
a gathering of many peoples came to the tomb of the virgin
praising God and saying (Lk 2:13):

"Truly holy,
truly gloriously,
she reigns with the angels
she who has received such honor from all on earth.

First among the poor ladies
who has led untold numbers to penance

[and] untold numbers to life
intercede with Christ for us!"

After a few days,
Agnes,
called to the wedding feast of the Lamb,
followed her sister to the eternal delights
where both daughters of Sion,
sisters by nature, graces and the Kingdom,
rejoice in God without end.

And in fact,
Agnes received that consolation
which Clare had promised her
before she departed.

For
just as her sister had gone before her,
she [too] passed from the world to the Cross.
As Clare shone brilliantly with signs and wonders,
Agnes kept watch over her throughout the night
for the proper time to pass from the feeble light
to God.[148]

Through our pre-eminent Lord
Jesus Christ
Who lives and reigns
with the Father and the Holy Spirit
forever
Amen.

PART TWO
THE MIRACLES OF SAINT CLARE
AFTER SHE PASSED FROM THE WORLD

49. These are the marvelous signs of the saints,
these are the testimonies of miracles that should be honored
that rest on their foundation of holiness of character
and the perfection of their deeds.

---

[148]This could be a further reference to Luke 2:8, the shepherds keeping watch over the
flock by night.

Certainly John performed no signs;[149]
nevertheless, those who did were no holier than John.

For this reason the proclamation of her most perfect life
would be sufficient
to witness to her holiness
except that something more is required
partly [due to] the tepidity of the people,
partly [due to] their devotion.

Therefore,
while she was living,
Clare made it marvelously clear
through her merits;
and now that she is taken up in the depths of eternal brilliance
she does so
through the brilliance of her miracles
to the end of the world.

A truth, sincere and told under oath,
compels me to list many things;
their number
compels me to pass over many.

THE FREEING OF DEMONS

50. A certain boy of Perugia, Giacomino, seemed not so much to be sick as to be possessed by a very evil demon. In fact, he would at times throw himself desperately in the fire or hurl himself on the ground or bite stones until he had broken his teeth or miserably wounded his head and covered his body with blood. With his mouth distorted and sticking out his tongue, he often twisted his limbs so easily that he frequently placed his leg around his neck. Twice each day this insanity afflicted the boy and two persons were unable to restrain him from taking off his clothes. The assistance of medical experts was required, but no one could be found who knew what to advise.

His father Giudolotto, not finding among men any sort of remedy for such a misfortune, turned to the merits of Saint Clare. "O most holy virgin," he said, "O Clare, honored by the world, I entrust my pitiable son to you and, with every prayer, I beg you for his cure."

---

[149]Jn 10:4

He hurried to the tomb filled with faith, brought the boy, and placed him on her grave. While he prayed, he immediately obtained her help. For the boy was at once free from that illness and never again afflicted by an injury of this kind.

ANOTHER MIRACLE

51. Alexandrina di Fratta, of the diocese of Perugia, was afflicted by a very bad demon.[150] The demon had so brought her into his power that he would make her fly like a bird above a high rock that stuck out over the bank of the river. He also made her land upon a very thin branch hanging over the Tiber and kept her there as if for fun. Moreover, since she had completely lost [use of] her left side and had a withered hand because of her sins, she did not profit from any of the medicines she had frequently tried.

She came to the tomb of the glorious virgin Clare with a contrite heart. After calling upon her merits, she received an effective cure for that threefold danger. In fact, her withered hand was restored, her side was returned to health, and she was freed from possession of the evil demon.

At the same time, another woman of the same place received before the tomb of the saint the gift of being freed from [possession by the] devil and many illnesses.

HEALING FROM THE SICKNESS OF FRENZY

52. An illness of frenzy, which both took away the use of speech and made the body horribly disturbed, possessed a certain young Frenchman who was attached to the Curia.[151] He could at least be restrained by someone, but, while in the hands of those willing to restrain him, he all the more bruised himself. He was tied with ropes to a bier and carried against his will by compatriots to the church of Saint Clare, placed before her grave, and was immediately freed through the faith of those who had presented him there.

THE CURE OF SOMEONE WITH EPILEPSY

Valentino of Spoleto was so afflicted with epilepsy that, regardless of where he was, he was thrown into seizures six times a day. He was not able to walk freely, inflicted as he was by a paralysis of a leg. He was taken on an ass to the grave of Saint Clare where he lay for two days and three

---

[150]Fratta is presently known as Umbertide, a small village not too far from Perugia.

[151]**Process** 20:9. This young man would have been in the service of some member of the court, not necessarily, and probably not, a cleric.

nights. On the third day, without anyone touching him, his leg made a sound like a great break, and he was instantly cured of both infirmities.

GIVING SIGHT TO THE BLIND

Iacobello, said to be the son of a woman of Spoleto, had suffered for twelve years with blindness, followed a guide in his journeys, and could not walk anywhere without falling. In fact, one time when he had been left alone by a young boy, he had fallen, managed to break his arm, and wound his head.

One night while this man was sleeping near a bridge in Narni, a certain woman appeared to him in his dreams and said: "Iacobello, why don't you come to me in Assisi and be cured?"[152] On waking in the morning, trembling he recounted the vision to two other blind men. They replied: "We have heard of a certain woman who recently died in Assisi and that the hand of the Lord is said to honor her grave with gifts of healing and many miracles."

When he heard this, he eagerly hurried off in excitement and, spending the night as a guest near Spoleto, he had the same vision once more. He ran the more quickly, giving himself completely to his journey out of love of the light.

53. When he arrived in Assisi, however, he encountered such large crowds of people gathered before the burial place of the virgin that there was no way for him to enter to [go to] the tomb. He placed a stone under his head and, with great faith yet sorrowing that he wasn't able to enter, he caught some sleep before the gates. And, behold, a third time the voice said to him: "The Lord will bless you, Iacobe, if you can enter."

Waking up, therefore, he begged the crowds with tears [in his eyes], shouting and repeating his requests, for the love of God to let him through. Once a way was given to him, he threw off his shoes, took off his clothes, tied a shoe-lace around his neck, and so, humbly touched her tomb, and fell into a light sleep. "Get up!" the blessed Clare said to him. "Get up, because you have been freed!"

Getting up at once, since his blindness totally disappeared and all the emptiness of his eyes had dissipated, he clearly saw the clearness of light through Clare. He glorified Clare through his praise and invited all peoples to bless God for the wonder of such marvels.

---

[152]This is the bridge over the River Neva.

THE RESTORATION OF A LOST HAND

54. A certain man from Perugia, Bongiovanni Martini, had gone off with his countrymen against the people of Foligno.[153] A confrontation had barely begun when a heavy rock was thrown at him, and shattered his hand with its hard impact. He spent a great deal of money on doctors, hoping to have a cure, but he could not be helped by any medical advice so that he carried a hand about that was useless and completely incapable of any work. Distressed, therefore, that he had to carry the weight of his right hand as though it were not his own because he didn't have the use of it, he frequently wished that it had been amputated.

But hearing what the Lord was pleased to reveal through His servant Clare, *after making a vow* (Gen 28:20), he hurried off to the burial place of the virgin, offered a wax image of his hand, and lay down before the tomb of Saint Clare.[154] Immediately, even before leaving the church, his hand was restored to health.

THE LAME

55. A certain Petruccio of the village of Bettona, who was wasted away with sickness for three years, seemed to be totally drained by the force of such an enervating illness. He had also been crippled by the violence of sickness to his kidneys that, always bent over and turned toward the ground, he could hardly walk even with a cane.

The boy's father tried the skill of many doctors, especially those who had expertise in treating broken bones. He was prepared to spend all his wealth to recover the boy's health. When he was told that help could not be provided for that illness by their skills, he turned to the help of the new saint of whose miracles he had just heard.

The boy was carried to the place where the precious remains of the virgin were resting, remained before her grave for a while, and received the grace of perfect health.

He stood upright and healthy without delay, *walking, jumping about, and praising God* (Acts 3:8), and invited the crowd of people to the praises of Saint Clare.

56. There was a ten year old boy from Villa of San Quirico, in the diocese of Assisi, *who was crippled from his mother's womb* (Acts 3:2).[155] He

---

[153]This must have occurred in May or June, 1254, the date of a war between Perugia and Foligno; cf. A. Fortini, **Assisi nel Medioevo,** Roma 1939, 198–199.

[154]This was not an infrequent custom of the time: to present the saint with an artistic representation of the part of the body that was in need of healing or had been healed.

[155]There are only a few ruins left of this small medieval village which was located near the present day town of Bettona on the road to Cannara.

had shinbones that were weak, walked crookedly with his feet turned at angles, and was hardly capable of getting up when he had fallen. His mother had offered him many times to Saint Francis but did not receive any help for his improvement.

Hearing, however, that the blessed Clare was radiant with new miracles, she took the boy to the saint's burial place. After a few days, when the shinbones had made some noise, the limbs were restored to their correct position, and that which Saint Francis had not granted even though he had been implored with many prayers, his disciple Clare achieved through divine power.[156]

57. A citizen of Gubbio, Giacomo di Franco, having a five year old boy who had never walked or been able to use his weak feet, deplored that boy as a public spectacle of his house and as a disgrace to his flesh. He was accustomed to sleep on the ground, to crawl in the ashes, wanting at times to lift himself up with a cane but being incapable of doing so—someone to whom nature had given the desire to walk but had denied the ability.

His parents dedicated the boy to the merits of Saint Clare and, to use their own words, desired that he be "a man of Saint Clare" should he obtain a cure through her.[157] Shortly after the vow had been uttered, the virgin of Christ healed "her man," [and] restored the ability to walk to the boy who had been offered to her. The parents immediately hurried to the virgin's tomb with the boy and offered him, jumping up and rejoicing, to the Lord.

58. A certain woman from the town of Bevagna, Plenaria, suffering for a long time with a paralysis of her kidneys, was unable to walk unless she were supported by a cane. Even with a cane, however, she could not straighten her bent-over body but took whatever tottering steps [she could]. She made her way on a certain Friday to the tomb of Saint Clare where, devoutly pouring out prayers to her, she quickly obtained what she had faithfully requested. In fact, on the next day, Saturday, after receiving a complete cure, she who had been brought by others returned to her home on her own feet.

CURES OF THROAT TUMORS

For a long time a certain young girl of Perugia suffered with great pain from tumors of her throat which are commonly called swollen glands. Twenty swellings could be counted on her throat so that the throat of the

---

[156]This is one of the extraordinary incidents that suggest the author's admiration for the miraculous power of Saint Clare which was operative when that of Saint Francis was not. It is somewhat surprising that it has survived the work of editors throughout the centuries.

[157]This is a feudal allusion, similar to fealty or becoming a "knight of St. Clare."

girl seemed to be even larger than her head. Her mother frequently brought her to the memorial of Saint Clare where she devoutly implored the help of the saint. Once, while the girl was laying before her burial place for an entire night and broke into a sweat, those swellings began to soften and to move gradually from their position. With the process of time, in fact, they disappeared through the intercession of Saint Clare so that not a trace of them remained.

59. Andrea, one of the sisters, had a similar sickness in her throat while Saint Clare was still in the flesh.

It is certainly strange that,
in the midst of glowing coals,
a soul so cold could lay hidden
and, *among prudent virgins*,[158]
an imprudent one would act so foolishly.

One night, in fact, she squeezed her throat in order to force that swelling through her mouth and almost suffocated, since she wished to supersede the divine will herself.

But Clare knew of this imprudence through the Spirit. "Run," she said to one [of the sisters]. "Run quickly to the lower [part of the] house and take a warm egg to Sister Andrea da Ferrara to drink and then come back to me with her."

That [sister] hurried off, found Andrea deprived of her speech and near to suffocating because of what she had inflicted with her own hand. She comforted her as she could and brought her to her mother. The servant of God said to her: "Pitiable one, confess to the Lord your thoughts which I also know well. Look, you wanted to be cured. The Lord Jesus Christ will cure you. But change your life for the better, because you will not get up from another sickness that you will suffer."

At her words she accepted the spirit of repentance and changed her life noticeably for the better. A little while after the healing of the tumors, therefore, she passed away from another sickness.[159]

THOSE FREED FROM WOLVES

60. The savage frenzy of cruel wolves frequently disturbed the countryside; they would attack the people in those [areas] and would frequently feed on human flesh.

Therefore a certain woman, Bona di Monte Galliano, in the diocese

---

[158]Cf. Mt 25:1–13.
[159]Process 2:23; 3:16.

of Assisi, had two sons, one of whom the wolves dragged away. She had barely stopped crying when, behold, they pursued the second boy with the same ferocity. For while the mother was in the house doing some of her domestic chores, a wolf fixed his teeth into the boy who was walking outside, dragged him off by his neck, and made for the woods as quickly as possible with its prey.

Some men who were in the vineyards, however, heard the cries of the boy [and] shouted to his mother: "See if you have your son, because we have just heard some unusual shouts!"

The mother, learning that her son had been seized by the wolf, shouted to heaven, filled the air with her cries, and called upon the virgin Clare: "O holy and glorious Clare, return my poor son to me! Return," she said, "return my poor little boy to his mother, because, if you don't, I will drown myself."

The neighbors ran after the wolf [and] found the boy who had been brought into the woods by the wolf and next to him a dog that was licking his wounds. The ferocious beast had first thrust his fangs into the [boy's] neck; then, in order to carry off its prey more easily, it had filled its jaws with the boy's loins. But it had not left in either place any sign of its sudden attack.

After obtaining the answer of her prayers, the woman ran off with her neighbors to her helper and poured out abundant thanks to God and the holy Clare, showing everyone who wished to see the boy's various wounds.

61. A certain young girl from the village of Cannara was sitting in a field on a certain clear day and another woman had placed her head in her lap. Behold, a man-eating wolf suddenly made quick, furtive steps toward its prey. The young girl saw him, in fact, but she was not afraid since she thought it was a dog. While the woman directed her attention to inspecting the [other's] hair, which she had just been doing, the savage beast jumped on her, enclosed her face in his massive jaws, and carried off its prey to the woods.

The dumbfounded woman got up immediately and, recalling Saint Clare, cried out: "Help, Saint Clare, help! I now entrust that young girl to you!" At that moment—it's wonderful to state—that girl who had been carried off in the teeth of the wolf was reprimanding it and was saying: "Will you take me any further, you thief, after I have been entrusted to such a virgin?" Confused by this reproof, it immediately placed the girl gently on the ground and, as though it were a thief caught off guard, quickly departed.

THE CANONIZATION OF SAINT CLARE

62. When the throne of Saint Peter was occupied by the most gentle prince, Lord Alexander IV, a man who was a friend of all holiness, who was both a guardian of religious and a firm supporter of the Orders, the news of these wonderful things spread and the fame of the virgin's virtue resounded more widely from day to day.[160] Thus the world itself was looking forward with desire to the canonization of such a virgin. At last the Pontiff, prompted by the number of so many signs as though something singular, began to consider with his cardinals her canonization.

The miracles were submitted for examination by qualified and prudent persons and the wonders of her life were also brought into discussion.

Clare was found to have been, while she lived, most brilliant in the exercise of every virtue. She was found to be admired after her death for tried and true miracles.

Then, on the day established for this, when the College of Cardinals had been convened, a gathering of archbishops and bishops was present, and a very large number of clergy and religious, as well as the wise and powerful, was in attendance, the Supreme Pontiff proposed this salutary business in their midst and sought the judgment of the prelates. Everyone, expressing immediately a favorable reply, said that Clare, whom God had glorified in heaven, should be glorified on earth.

On a day close to the second anniversary of her passing over to the Lord, before a crowd of prelates and all the clergy, the happy Alexander, for whom this grace had been reserved by the Lord, after delivering the sermon, inscribed Clare with the greatest solemnity in the catalogue of saints and solemnly ordained that her feast be celebrated throughout the entire Church. He himself was the first to most solemnly celebrate it with the entire Curia.

These things occurred in the Cathedral of Anagni in the year 1255 of the Incarnation of the Lord, in the first year of the pontificate of Lord Alexander,

To the praise of our Lord Jesus Christ
Who lives and reigns
with the Father and the Holy Spirit
forever and ever.
Amen.

---

[160]Alexander IV, the former Cardinal Raynaldus dei Conti di Segni, Bishop of Ostia and Velletri, and Cardinal Protector of the Order of Friars Minor and the Poor Ladies of San Damiano, was elected Pope on 12 December 1254. Cf. supra, p. 101.

Part III

WRITINGS
CONCERNING SAINT CLARE,
THE POOR LADIES
AND THEIR RELATIONSHIP
WITH
SAINT FRANCIS
AND HIS BROTHERS

The Form of Life
Given by Saint Francis
to Saint Clare and
Her Sisters (1212/1213)

Saint Clare herself is the source of this brief text which she placed in what we now consider chapter six of her Rule.[1] *"When the Blessed Father [Francis] saw that we had no fear of poverty, hard work, suffering, shame or the contempt of the world, but that, instead, we regarded such things as great delights, moved by compassion he wrote a form of life for us."*[2] *What follows is clearly not the entire pattern of religious life given to the Poor Ladies by Saint Francis, but it does provide the Trinitarian foundations upon which their daily life would be built.*

When the form of life is examined in the context of the entire Rule of Saint Clare, it is striking that it introduces the very heart of her vision. The previous sections, what we consider chapters one to five inclusive, and the final paragraphs, chapters eleven and twelve in our view, form the framework in which the monastic directives of the earlier legislation of Hugolino and Innocent IV are preserved. Saint Clare places the Franciscan elements very clearly at the center of the document and does not tire of presenting the inspiration of Saint Francis or his Rule.[3]

1. Because by divine inspiration[4] you have made yourselves daughters and servants of the most high King, the heavenly Father, and have taken

---

[1] The original manuscript of the Rule of Saint Clare does not contain chapter headings or divisions, although the tradition of dividing the Rule into twelve chapters after the example of the Rule of the Friars Minor, is quite ancient. Cf. supra, p. 62, n. 5.

[2] Cf. *Rule of St. Clare* VI 1, supra, p. 69.

[3] For a provocative study on the Rule of St. Clare that presents this approach, see J.F. Godet, "Progetto evangelico di Chiara oggi," *Vita Minorum* LVI (1985): 198–301.

[4] Saint Francis uses the term *divina inspiratio*, divine inspiration, to express the dynamic principle of the call of Saint Clare and the Poor Ladies to live the perfection of the Holy Gospel. In the Earlier Rule, he describes the calling to the life of the Friars Minor in the same way (cf. RegNB II 1), and does so again in both the Earlier (RegNB XVI 1) and Later (RegB XII 1) Rule to explain the special call to the missions among non-believers. Cf. O. Van Asseldonk, "Lo Spirito del Signore e la sua santa operazione," *Laurentianum* (1983), 133–195.

the Holy Spirit as your spouse, choosing to live according to the perfection of the holy Gospel,[5] 2. I resolve and promise for myself and for my brothers to have that same loving care and special solicitude for you as [I have] for them.[6]

---

[5]It is helpful to see the Trinitarian pattern of Gospel life Saint Francis envisions as a result of the working of the Holy Spirit in the soul; cf. I EpFid 8–10; II EpFid48–53; RegNB XVII 9–16. This consciousness appears most especially in the Rule of Saint Clare and her call to a life of "the mutual unity of love and peace" (RegCl IV 16; X 5).

[6]The special bond established between Saint Francis and the Poor Ladies of San Damiano can best be seen in the early biographies of both saints, e.g. Thomas of Celano, *Second Life of Saint Francis*, 204–207.

Testimony of Jacques de Vitry (1216)

Jacques de Vitry (c. 1170–1240) is one of the important commentators on the religious life of the early thirteenth century. Before being made Cardinal Bishop of Tusculum in 1228, he was Bishop of Acre for twelve years and had made numerous journeys throughout Europe and the Middle East which he described in his Historia orientalis et occidentalis. The second part of that work devotes considerable attention to the religious movements present in Western Europe at the time and describes in particular his impressions of the Beguines, the Humiliati, and the Minor Brothers and Sisters. The observations of Jacques de Vitry are all the more important when we consider his intense interest in the feminine religious movements of the early thirteenth century.[1] He was personally influenced by the life of Marie d'Oignies (+ 1213) whose biography he wrote and whom he proposed as a model for women interested in the new religious movements represented by the Beguines.[2]

This excerpt is taken from a letter written by Jacques de Vitry in Genoa, October 1216, to his friends in Liège. It recounts from his personal experiences in the Umbrian Valley where he no doubt encountered the Poor Ladies of San Damiano.[3]

I found one consolation in those parts, nevertheless: many men and women, rich and worldly, after renouncing everything for Christ, fled the world. They are called Lesser Brothers and Lesser Sisters. They are held in great esteem by the Lord Pope and the cardinals. They do not occupy themselves with temporal affairs, but work each day with great desire and

---

[1]For further information on Jacques de Vitry, see E.W. McDonnell, "Jacques de Vitry," *New Catholic Encyclopedia* VII (Washington, D.C., 1967) 798–799. A treatment of his interest in communities of female religious can be found in B.M. Bolton, "Mulieres Sanctae," *Women in Medieval Society,* ed. S.M. Stuard (University of Pennsylvania Press, 1976), 141–159.

[2]Cf. J. de Vitry, *De Maria Oigneacensi in Namurcensi Belgii Diocesi,* ed. D. Paperbroec, *Acta Sanctorum* June 5 (Paris 1867): 542–572, can now be found translated: *The Life of Marie d'Oigniers,* trans. Margaret H. King (Saskatoon, Saskatchewan: Peregrina Publishing Co., 1986).

[3]Original Latin text can be found in R.B.C. Huygens, *Lettres de Jacques de Vitry* (Leyde 1960): pp. 75–76.

enthusiastic zeal to capture those souls that were perishing from the vanities of the world and to bring them along with them. They have already borne much fruit through the grace of God, and have converted many, so that whoever hears them says "Come" (Rev 22:17; Jn 1:46) and one circle of hearers draws another.

They live according to the form of the primitive Church of which it is written: "The multitude of believers was of one heart and one soul . . . " (Acts 3:32).[4] They go into the cities and villages during the day, so that they convert others, giving themselves to active work; but they return to their hermitages or solitary places at night, employing themselves in contemplation.

The women live near the cities in various hospices.[5] They accept nothing, but live from the work of their hands. In fact, they are very much offended and disturbed because they are honored by the clergy and laity more than they deserve.

The men of this Order, with much profit, come together once a year in a determined place to rejoice together in the Lord and to eat together. They draw up and promulgate their holy statutes with the advice of good men and have them confirmed by the Lord Pope. After this they disperse for an entire year throughout Lombardy, Tuscany, Apulia, and Sicily.

---

[4]Whereas other religious movements of this period used this text of Acts as a foundation of their embrace of an apostolic spirituality, neither St. Francis nor St. Clare makes use of it in his or her writings.

[5]"Hospices" refers to simple, poor houses which became the dwelling places for many of the new religious movements of women such as the Beguines and the Poor Ladies. The translation "hospital" was suggested by Paul Sabatier in his edition of the *Mirror of Perfection* (*Speculum perfectionis seu s. Francisci Assisiensis Legenda antiquissima* [Paris 1898], 296) to support his conviction that the Clares were not originally a contemplative order but one given to hospital and manual work. The position has been thoroughly refuted by I. Omaechevarria, *Escritos de Santa Clara y Documentos Complementarios* (Madrid: 1982), 36, n. 2. An excellent discussion of the medieval hospice in the larger religious context can be found in M.W. Labarge, *Women in Medieval Life: A Small Sound of the Trumpet* (London: Hamish Hamilton, 1985), 182–183.

The Canticle
of the Creatures (1225)

The companions of Saint Francis tell us that the Canticle of the Creatures *was composed while he was staying in a small hut next to San Damiano.*[1] *The saint had completed a long and no doubt exhausting preaching tour after his time on LaVerna, August to September, 1224, and spent time convalescing close to Saint Clare and the Poor Ladies. Almost blind and completely helpless, his body racked in agony, Francis lay in a little darkened cell. In those long hours of interior and exterior darkness, he suffered severe temptations of despondency. Yet during one of those moments of discouragement, the Lord assured him that he would enjoy heavenly glory and this inspired this canticle of joy which will always characterize Franciscan spirituality.*

We might wonder what were the intentions of the stigmatized mystic Saint Francis in desiring to spend time at San Damiano. Thomas of Celano and Bonaventure write of his desire to return to his beginnings, that is, to practice once again the patterns of his conversion that first led him to the Lord. No doubt San Damiano was a sentimental favorite in this regard since it was there that the call to rebuild the Lord's house was first made known to him, but it may also be that Francis realized how completely Clare and her sisters had come to live a fuller Trinitarian life.

In any case, this canticle of praise, filled with Francis' vision of a universe mirroring the presence of the Triune God, could only have come from the heart of a mystic.[2] *When seen in the light of San Damiano, filled as it is with images of both saints, Francis and Clare, the* Canticle of the Creatures *becomes a beautiful, meaningful reflection of both.*

1. Most High, all-powerful, good Lord,
   Yours are the praises, the glory, the honor, and all blessing.[3]

---

[1]Cf. *The Assisi Compilation* 43.

[2]For further background, see R.J. Armstrong, I.C. Brady, *Francis and Clare: The Complete Works* (New York: Paulist Press, 1986), 37–39; E. Leclercq, *The Canticle of Creatures: Symbols of Union*, trans. M.J. O'Connell (Chicago: Franciscan Herald Press, 1978).

[3]Cf. Rev 4:9, 11.

2. To You alone, Most High, do they belong,
and no one is worthy to mention Your name.

3. Praised be You, my Lord, with all Your creatures,
especially Sir Brother Sun,
Who is the day and through whom You give us light.
4. And he is beautiful and radiant with great splendor;
and bears a likeness of You, Most High One.

5. Praised be You, my Lord, through Sister Moon and the stars,
in heaven You formed them clear and precious and beautiful.[4]
6. Praised be You, my Lord, through Brother Wind,
and through the air, cloudy and serene, and every kind of weather,
through which You give sustenance to Your creatures.

7. Praised be You, my Lord, through Sister Water,
which is very useful and humble and precious and chaste.

8. Praised be You, my Lord, through Brother Fire,
through whom You light the night
and he is beautiful and playful and robust and strong.

9. Praised be You, my Lord, through our Sister Mother Earth,
who sustains and governs us,
and who produces varied fruits with colored flowers and herbs.[5]

10. Praised be You, my Lord, through those who give pardon for Your love,
and bear infirmity and tribulation.

11. Blessed are those who endure in peace
for by You, Most High, shall they be crowned.[6]

---

[4]Cf. S.P. Coy, "The Problem of 'Per' in the *Cantico di Frate Sole* of Saint Francis," M L N (1976), 1–11; also explanation for this translation provided in R.J. Armstrong, I.C. Brady, *Francis and Clare: The Complete Works* (New York: Paulist Press, 1986), 38–39. The use of the Italian/Latin word "clarite" is thought-provoking here and may well be an allusion to Clare.

[5]The companions of Saint Francis tell of the conclusion of the Canticle at this point; cf. *Scripta Leonis, Rufini et Angeli Sociorum S. Francisci* 43, ed. and trans. R.B. Brooke (Oxford: Oxford at Clarendon Press, 1970), 162–166.

[6]According to the companions these two verses form the second section of the Canticle composed to stimulate peace between the Bishop and Podestà of Assisi; cf. *Scripta Leonis, Rufini et Angeli Sociorum S. Francisci* 44, ed. and trans. R.B. Brooke (Oxford: Oxford at Clarendon Press, 1970), 166–170.

12. Praised be You, my Lord, through our Sister Bodily Death,
from whom no one living can escape.

    13. Woe to those who die in mortal sin.
        Blessed are those whom death will find in Your most holy will,
        for the second death shall do them no harm.[7]

14. Praise and bless my Lord and give Him thanks
and serve Him with great humility.[8]

---

[7]This final section of the Canticle, according to the companions, was composed at the Portiuncula as the saint was dying; cf. Legend of Perugia 100, *Francis of Assisi: Omnibus of Sources*, ed. Marion A. Habig (Chicago: Franciscan Herald Press, 1953), pp. 1075–1076.

[8]The editor wonders if verse 14 may have been a refrain sung at the end of each verse or at the conclusion of each section. Unfortunately, as in the case of the *Canticle of Exhortation*, there is no trace of the melody or musical accompaniment for the *Canticle of the Creatures*.

The Canticle of Exhortation
to Saint Clare and Her Sisters (1225)

The Canticle of Exhortation *belongs to the same literary genre as the* Canticle of the Creatures. *Once again "those who were with him," that is, the companions of Francis, tell us that he composed this piece while convalescing at San Damiano.*[1] *From a purely human and medical point of view, this intensely poetic composition remains a mystery. During an acute viral infection, accompanied as it was by severe headaches and general physical debilitation, a patient easily not only loses his orientation with time and place, but also experiences the loss of personal relationships with his closest associates. The temptation always exists to focus on one's own body and its distress. But this canticle, together with the* Canticle of the Creatures, *suggests that the contrary was true in Francis' case.*

Unfortunately this simple canticle was overlooked for centuries for it can easily be considered a spiritual last will and testament for the Poor Ladies. As the companions tell us, Francis wished to express his mind not only for that occasion but for the future as well. Indeed each stanza contains a reflection on the daily life of the Poor Ladies of San Damiano.[2]

1. Listen, little poor ones called by the Lord,
   who have come together from many parts and provinces.[3]

---

[1]Cf. *Legend of Perugia* 45. *Francis of Assisi: Omnibus of Sources*, ed. Marion A. Habig (Chicago: Franciscan Herald Press, 1973).

[2]For further information concerning this work consult: G. Boccalli, "Parole di esortazioni alle 'poverelle' di San Damiano," *Forma Sororum* 14 (1977), 54–70; "Canto di esortazioni di San Francesco," *Collectanea Franciscana* 48 (1978), 5–29; O. Schmucki, "Das wiederentdeckte 'Audite' des hl. Franziskus für die Armen Frauen von San Damiano," *Fidelis* 68 (1981). Also helpful is I. Baldelli, "La 'Parola' di Francesco e le nuove lingue d'Europa," *Francesco, Il Francescanesimo e la cultura della nuova Europa*, ed. I. Baldelli and A.M. Romanini (Roma Istituto della Enciclopedia Italiana, 1986), 13–16.

[3]"Little poor ones," *poverelle* in the Italian original, contains an echo of what Francis himself was called: "*Il Poverello.*" No doubt Francis saw proof of the role of grace in that within the twelve years following Clare's embrace of religious life, candidates from various parts of Italy entered San Damiano.

2. Live always in truth,
   that you may die in obedience.[4]
3. Do not look at the life without,
   for that of the Spirit is better.[5]
4. I beg you through great love,
   to use with discretion
   the alms which the Lord gives you.
5. Those who are weighed down by sickness
   and the others who are wearied because of them,
   all of you: bear it in peace.[6]
6. For you will sell this fatigue at a very high price
   and each one [of you] will be crowned queen
   in heaven with the Virgin Mary.[7]

---

[4]Cf. Jn 17:17; 2 Jn 4; 3 Jn 3; also SalVirt 3, EpOrd 46. The phrase implies living in "truthfulness" or "sincerity" rather than living in doctrinal orthodoxy. In this sense obedience, frequently seen as expressing the whole of Franciscan life (e.g. RegNB II 9), may well refer to attentiveness to the prompting of the Spirit (cf. SalVirt 14–15) and the never-ending desire to do God's will (RegNB XXII 9).

[5]This may be seen as paralleling Francis' counsel in his Later Rule (RegB II 13): the gospel image of the plowman who is distracted from giving his full attention to his work and looks backward. In this instance, it is an interior openness to the promptings of the Spirit, not the physical enclosure as such, that is contrasted with "the life outside."

[6]This passage becomes more meaningful in light of the difficult, constricted quarters of San Damiano, the poor diet and rigorous fasting of the Poor Ladies, and the inevitable sicknesses, especially tuberculosis and malaria, to which they were susceptible. For excellent background, cf. K. Haines, "The Death of St. Francis of Assisi," *Franziskanische Studien* 58 (1976) 27–46; also cf. the bibliography provided by O. Schmucki, "Infermità," *Dizionario Francescano* (Padova, 1983), 769–770.

[7]Two interpretations of this passage have been offered: (a) the present one which follows that of O. Schmucki; cf. "Das wiederentdeckte 'Audite' des hl.Franziskus für die Armen Frauen von San Damiano," *Fidelis* 68 (1981); and that of G. Boccali, "Parole di esortazioni alle 'poverelle' di San Damiano," *Forma Sororum* 14 (1977), 54–70; "Canto di esortazioni di San Francesco," *Collectanea Franciscana* 48 (1978), 5–29. The latter offers "You will see that such fatigue is precious."

The imagery of selling can also be found in Thomas of Celano's Second Life 12 in which Francis met his brother, Angelo, who could not understand his spiritual ways and sarcastically remarked to a companion: "Tell Francis to sell you a penny's worth of sweat." To which Francis replied: "Indeed, I will sell my sweat more dearly to my Lord."

The Last Will
Written for Saint Clare
and the Poor Ladies
of San Damiano (1226)

Once again Saint Clare is the source of this writing. She inserted it in her Rule (VI 7–9) to reinforce her dedication to the pursuit of poverty that she learned from her spiritual father. The companions of Saint Francis, however, place this brief message in the context of the serious illnesses of both saints and thereby suggest a certain urgency to its message. Their insight certainly confirms the impression that this embrace of poverty was uppermost in the mind of Saint Francis at the time of his death. We might wonder if Francis realized that after his death others, including the Pope himself, would encourage the Poor Ladies to depart from the path he had indicated to them. Were that so, then this writing must have been a great source of strength to them as they struggled to preserve the great heritage entrusted to them.

1. I, brother Francis, the little one, wish to follow the life and poverty of our most high Lord Jesus Christ and of His most holy mother and to persevere in this until the end,[1] 2. and I ask and counsel you, my ladies, to live always in this most holy life and in poverty.[2] 3. And keep most careful watch that you never depart from this by reason of the teaching or advice of anyone.[3]

---

[1]Cf. II EpFid 5: "Though He was rich beyond all other things (cf. 2 Cor 8:9), in this world, He, together with the most blessed Virgin, His mother, willed to choose poverty."

[2]When this counsel is seen in light of the *Canticle of Exhortation* 2, we have a further indication of Francis' wish that the Poor Ladies "live always in truth." Did he intend to make "this most holy life (the Gospel) and poverty" synonymous with "the truth"? There can be little doubt that Francis saw the danger of riches in obscuring the truth; cf. RegNB XXII 16.

[3]Clare echoes this advice in her *Second Letter to Agnes of Prague* 17–18.

The Witness
of Thomas of Celano (1228)

Brother Thomas was born in the small city of Celano nestled in the Abruzzi mountains of southern Italy. Nothing is known of his early life until Thomas himself alludes to his entrance into the primitive fraternity in his First Life of Saint Francis 57: "Not long after [Francis] had returned to the church of St. Mary of the Portiuncula, some educated and noble men very gratifyingly joined him." Brother Jordan of Giano tells us in his Chronicle that Thomas was among the brothers who made the second and more successful attempt to move into Germany where in 1222 he was chosen custodian of Mainz, Worms, Cologne, and Speyer. The exact date of his return to Italy is difficult to determine, but his description of the canonization of Saint Francis in the First Life suggests that he was an actual eye-witness.

The First Life of Saint Francis was commissioned, as Thomas himself tells us, by the newly elected Gregory IX, the former Cardinal Hugolino and friend of the saint. After its approval on February 25, 1229, Thomas seems to have spent the rest of his life in Tagliacozzo, a small city not far from Rome. He was called upon on at least three other occasions to devote his literary talents to writing of Saint Francis. The Legend for Use in Choir was written in 1230. The Second Life of Saint Francis, subtitled A Remembrance in the Desire of a Soul, was commissioned by the brothers in 1244 and completed by Thomas in 1247. Finally, The Treatise on the Miracles of Saint Francis was written between 1250 and 1253 when John of Parma, at the urging of the brothers, asked Thomas to complete his recording of the saint's miracles.

It is thought that Thomas died sometime after 1260, although there is no evidence to determine the precise date of his death. He was buried at first in the monastery of the Poor Ladies of Saint Clare in Tagliacozzo to whom he had ministered for many years. In 1476 the brothers acquired the monastery and reverently cared for the remains of their literary predecessor. Thomas' body can be found there to this date with the following inscription marking his grave: "Blessed Thomas of Celano, Disciple of Saint Francis, Author, Chronicler of Saint Francis and of the Sequence of the Dead."[1]

---

[1]Further details concerning the life and writings of Thomas of Celano can be found in

First Life of Saint Francis, Part I (18–20)

When Thomas wrote the following passage of the First Life of Saint Francis, Clare and her sisters had been living in San Damiano for at least fifteen years. We can easily imagine their embarrassment at the lavish praise with which the author extolled their hidden life in this place where Saint Francis heard the call of the Crucified to rebuild His house which was falling to pieces. Yet it is clear that Thomas, writing this First Life in the context of a theology of ecclesial reform, perceived the fulfillment of that call in the life of the Poor Ladies.[2] Indeed, Clare is portrayed in an obviously ecclesial context and called "the most precious and firmest stone of the entire structure" and its "foundation" upon whom "a noble structure arose."

Thomas' description of the life of the Poor Ladies indicates that at this early period he perceived as one of their salient qualities "that excelling virtue of mutual and continual charity," a characteristic later extolled by Innocent IV and Alexander IV. In his seven part schema he places humility in second place, placing mutual charity in the first position. He, therefore, deviates from an earlier tradition that placed humility as the foundation for holiness. The pursuit of the contemplative ideal, the seventh and final quality described by the author, is built firmly upon one of the outstanding strengths of the Poor Ladies, their pursuit of mutual charity and unity. In doing so, Thomas accentuates one of the important contributions of the Poor Ladies to Franciscan spirituality.

18. The first work that blessed Francis undertook,
after he had gained his freedom from the hand of his carnally-minded
father,
was to build a house of God.
He did not try to build a new one,
but he repaired an old one,
restored an ancient one.
He did not tear out the foundation,
but he built upon it,

M. Bihl, "Disquisitiones Celanenses," *Archivum Franciscanum Historicum* 21 (1928) 3–54, 161–205; idem, "Praefatio," *Analecta Franciscana* (Ad Aquas Claras, Florence, 1926–1946) X, iii–xlii; L. Dubois, "Thomas of Celano, The Historian of St. Francis", *Catholic University Bulletin*, XIII (1907) 250–268; P. Hermann, "Introduction to First and Second Life of St. Francis with Selections from Treatise on the Miracles of Bl. Francis," *St. Francis of Assisi: Omnibus of Sources* (Chicago: Franciscan Herald Press, 1972) 179–212
    [2]Further information concerning the ecclesial reform aspect of the works of Thomas of Celano can be found in E. Peters, "Restoring the Church and the Churches: Event and Image in Franciscan Biography," *Franziscanische Studien* (1987), pp. 213–236.

always reserving to Christ his prerogative,
although he was unaware of it,
for no one can lay another foundation,
but that which has been laid,
which is Jesus Christ.[3]

When he had returned to the place where,
as has·been said,
the church of San Damiano had been built in ancient times,
he repaired it zealously within a short time
with the help of the grace of the Most High.[4]

This is the blessed and holy place
where the glorious religion and most excellent Order
of Poor Ladies and poor virgins
had its joyful origin,
about six years after the conversion of the blessed Francis
and through that same blessed man.[5]

The Lady Clare,
a native of the city of Assisi,
the most precious and the strongest stone of the whole structure,
was its foundation.[6]

For,
after the beginning of the order of brothers,
when the said lady was converted to God
through the counsel of the holy man,
she lived for the advantage of many
and as an example to countless others.

---

[3] 1 Cor 3:11.

[4] Cf. 1 Cel 8: "When he neared the city of Assisi, [Francis] came upon a certain church along the way that had been built in ancient times in honor of Saint Damian but which was threatened by its exceeding age."

[5] Cf. II Cel 13: "Most fervently [Francis] stirred up everyone for the work of that church [San Damiano] and speaking in a loud voice in French, he prophesied before all that there would be a monastery there of holy virgins of Christ."

[6] This could well be allusions to 1 Kgs 7:9–10 and Rev 21:19 which describe the temple of the historical and the heavenly Jerusalem.

She was of noble lineage,
but she was more noble by grace;
she was a virgin in body,
most chaste in mind;
a youth in age,
but mature in spirit.

[She was]
steadfast in purpose and most eager in her desire for divine love;
endowed with wisdom and excelling in humility;
bright by name,
brilliant by life,
most brilliant by character.[7]

19. A noble structure of the most precious pearls arose above her,
whose praise comes not from men but from God,[8]
since our limited understanding is not sufficient to imagine it,
nor our scanty vocabulary to utter it.

Above everything else
that excelling virtue of mutual and continual charity
that so binds our wills together
flourishes among them,
that forty or fifty of them dwell together in one place,
agreement in likes and dislikes molds one spirit in them out of many.[9]

Secondly,
the gem of humility,
which so preserves the good things bestowed by heaven
that they merit other virtues as well,
glows in each one.[10]

---

[7]This is the earliest instance of the play on the name Clare or Chiara which is awkwardly translated as "bright."

[8]Rom 2:29.

[9]"*Idem velle atque idem nolle, ea demum firma amicitia est* (For agreement in likes and dislikes—this, and this only, is what constitutes a firm friendship)." This is a proverbial saying that Sallust places in the mouth of Cataline as he urges his fellow conspirators in the name of friendship to join him in revolt; cf. C.C. Sallust, *Bellum Catilinarium*, XX 4 (The Loab Classical Library), pp. 33–34.

[10]The earlier monastic tradition presented humility as the foundation of all virtue, e.g., Bernard of Clairvaux, *Sermo I in Nativitate Domini* (PL 183:115): "Be eager to humble yourselves, for [humility] is the foundation and guardian of the virtues." Thomas, however, places it in the second place in the life of the Poor Ladies even though he echoes the earlier approach in suggesting that humility "preserves the good things bestowed by heaven" and enables them to "merit other virtues as well."

Thirdly,
the lily of virginity and chastity
diffuses such a wondrous odor among them
that they forget earthly thoughts
and desire to meditate on only heavenly things;
and so great a love of their eternal Spouse arises in their hearts
that the integrity of that holy feeling keeps them
from every habit of their former life.

Fourthly,
all of them have become so conspicuous
by the title of the highest poverty
that their food and clothing
never or hardly at all
come together to satisfy extreme necessity.

20. Fifthly,
they have so attained that unique grace
of abstinence and silence
that they do scarcely need to exert any effort
to check the movements of the flesh
and to restrain their tongues.

Sixthly,
they were so adorned with the virtue of patience
in all these things,
that the adversity of tribulation
or the injury of vexation
never breaks or changes their spirit.

Seventhly,
and finally,
they have so merited the height of contemplation
that they learn in it everything they should do or avoid,
and they know with joy how to leave the mind for God,
persevering night and day
in praising Him and in praying to Him.

For the moment
let this suffice
concerning these virgins dedicated to God
and the most devout servants of Christ,

for their wondrous life and their glorious institutions,
which they have received from the Lord Pope Gregory,
at that time the Bishop of Ostia,
requires a work of its own
and the leisure in which to write it.

First Life of Saint Francis, Part II (116–117)

These passages, like so many others of the First Life, reveal the influence of Sulpicius Severus' Life of St. Martin of Tours on Thomas of Celano. At almost every turn in the world of medieval hagiography the figure of the ideal missionary and miracle-worker, Martin of Tours, appears.[11] *A comparison of the texts, particularly the more simple description of the Poor Ladies' reverence for the remains of Saint Francis presented by his companions, shows how much Thomas borrowed from this source.*[12] *The first biographer, then, was simply following the literary style of his time, which is not surprising since he was responding to a commission given him by the Holy See. Nonetheless these passages are among the most beautiful in the First Life and show the author's masterful knowledge and use of Scripture as well as the testimonies of those present at this moving journey from Our Lady of the Portiuncula to the Church of San Giorgio in Assisi by way of San Damiano.*

116. The brothers and sons, therefore, who gathered together with *a great crowd of people* (Ez 27:33) from the neighboring cities and rejoiced to be present at such great solemnities, spent the entire night during which the holy father had died singing the praises of God, so much so that, because of the charm of the jubilation and the brightness of the lights, it seems to be a wake of the angels. *But when morning had come* (Jn 21:4), *a great crowd* (Acts 2:6) from the city of Assisi re-assembled with all the clergy, took the sacred body from the place where Francis had died, and carried it amid great honor to the city, with hymns and praises and *the sound of trumpets* (Jos 6:20). *They took up branches of* olive *trees* (Jn 12:13; Mt 21:8) and of other trees, and carrying out the funeral rites with solemnity, they fulfilled their duties of praise with many lights and with loud voices.[13]

When, with the sons carrying their father and the flock following their shepherd (cf. 2 Sam 7:8; Am 7:15) who was hastening to meet *the Shepherd of all* (Ez 37:24), they came to the place where he himself had planted the

---

[11]Cf. H. Delehaye, *The Legend of the Saints* (Notre Dame, 1961).

[12]Cf. infra, p. 259.

[13]A reference to the liturgical hymn, *Gloria, laus et honor,* sung during the procession of Palm Sunday. Throughout Italy olive branches are frequently used for these processions.

religion and order of poor ladies and holy virgins, they placed him in the church of San Damiano.[14] They paused there, and the little window— through which the servants of Christ were accustomed to receive the sacrament of the Body of the Lord *at the appointed time* (2 Sam 24:15)—was opened. The coffin was opened, in which a treasure of supercelestial virtues lay hidden and in which he who was accustomed to bear many was being borne by a few (cf. Is 46:4). Behold, the Lady Clare, who was truly most brilliant by the holiness of her merits and was the first mother of the others since she was the very first plant of this holy Order, came with the rest of her daughters to see their father who would no longer speak to them or return to them for he was hastening elsewhere.

117. Redoubling their sighs and looking upon him *with* great *sorrow of heart* (Ps 37:9) and many tears, *they began to proclaim* (Jos 3:3) in a restrained voice: "Father, father, what shall we do? Why do you abandon us in our misery? or to whom do you leave us who are so desolate?[15] Why did you not send us rejoicing ahead of you to the place where you are going—us whom you leave in prison, us whom you will never again visit as you used to? All our consolation departs with you and no solace like it remains for us who are buried to the world! Who will comfort us in our great poverty, no less of merits than of goods? *O Father of the poor* (Job 29:16), lover of poverty! Who will strengthen us in temptation, you who experienced innumerable temptations and who knew how to overcome them? Who will console us in our trials, you who were our *helper in the troubles that excessively come upon us* (Ps 45:2)? O most bitter separation, O hostile departure! O most dreadful death that slays thousands of sons and daughters deprived of so great a father, by hastening to remove him through whom *our efforts* (Jer 7:3, 5), such as they were, greatly flourished!"

Their virginal modesty restrained them, however, *from weeping over him* (Zech 12:10). It was not proper to mourn too much for him for whose passing a host of the army of angels had come together and *the citizens with the saints and members of God's household* (Eph 2:19) rejoiced.[16] So, divided be-

---

[14]Cf. Sulpicius Severus, *Epistola III*, n. 19 (PL 20, 183): "He conducted himself before them as a pastor before his sheep."

[15]This is the first of four passages taken from Sulpicius Severus' *Vita S. Martini*. In the first, before the death of Saint Martin, his monks cried: "Father, why have you abandoned us? or to whom do you leave us who are so desolate?" Cf. Sulpicius Severus, *Vita S. Martini*, c.n.10 (PL 20). In the second, he states: "through his example . . . so many shoots have borne fruit." Cf. *ibid.*, n. 18 (PL 20). The third passage states: "then the choir of virgins, held back their weeping out of a sense of propriety. They disguised it with a holy joy, because it was hurting them." Cf. *ibid.*, n. 19 (PL 20). Finally, the author writes: "O how great was the sorrow of all, how especially great were the lamentations of his monks." Cf. *ibid.*, n. 18 (PL 20).

[16]From the *Office of the Feast of St. Martin:* " . . . at whose passing the assembly of the

tween sorrow and joy, they kissed his most radiant hands, adorned with most precious gems and shining pearls.[17] When he had been taken away, *the door*, which will hardly ever be opened for so great a sorrow, *was closed* (Mt 25:10) to them.

Oh how great was the sorrow of all because of the sad and pitiable outcry of these poor ladies! How especially great were the lamentations of his grieving children! Their special grief was shared by all, so much so that hardly anyone could keep from weeping when *the angels of peace wept so bitterly* (Is 33:7).

---

saints sang, the choir of the angels exulted, and the host of all the heavenly powers ran singing psalms."

[17]A blending of two passages from the Office of the Feast of Saint Agnes (Responsory II and Antiphon III of Third Nocturn): "adorned with indescribable pearls . . . and shining, precious gems." This is clearly a reference to the stigmata of Saint Francis.

Witness of the "Anonymous of Perugia," John of Perugia (1240–1241)

The enigmatic author of these early recollections of the primitive fraternity is generally agreed to be John of Perugia, a companion of Brother Giles, and one of the earliest companions of Saint Francis. Although there is still discussion concerning the date of the composition of this work, most historians maintain that it was written sometime between 1240 and 1241 and forms a basis for the later Legend of the Three Companions. *This early text, the* Anonymous of Perugia *41b, c, then, provides us with a most important source concerned with the origins of the Poor Ladies.*[1]

According to the demands of the time, the Lord gave [the brothers] His word and Spirit to carry most sharp, penetrating words to the hearts of many listeners, especially those of the young rather than those of the old. After they left father and mother and all their belongings, they followed them and assumed the habit of the holy Order. At that time, then, the word of the Lord in the Gospel was greatly fulfilled in the Gospel: "I did not come to send peace upon the earth but the sword; for I have come to set a man against his father and a daughter against her mother" (Mt 10:34–35). Those whom the brothers received were brought to the blessed Francis that he might invest them.

In the same way many women, virgins and those not having husbands, after hearing their preaching, came to them with sorrowful hearts and said: "What shall we do? We cannot be with you. Tell us, therefore, how we can save our souls." For this reason they established monasteries of recluses for doing penance in every city in which they could. They also appointed one of the brothers to be their visitator and corrector.

---

[1]A concise introduction by Bill Hugo, O.F.M. Cap., and the translation of Eric Kahn, O.F.M., can be found in *The New Round Table* 36 (1983) 29–52.

Legend of the
Three Companions (c.1246)

Discussions concerning the author and dating of this work continue to occupy Franciscan scholars. Most authors accede to its basis in the earlier Anonymous of Perugia *and its publication in 1246.*[1] *However the publication of a critical edition of the text as well as its analysis by a computer study prompts speculation that there were a number of different redactions of this work beginning in 1241 and continuing until some time after the acceptance of St. Bonaventure's biographies in 1266.*[2]

The following passage (24) is not contained in the Anonymous of Perugia *and seems to come from the witness of Saint Clare herself since it is similar to her* Testament *(12–14). When both testimonies are put together, it appears that St. Francis was more certain at that early period of helping to establish a monastery of women than a religious order of men.*

24. While he was continuing with some other workers in that project mentioned above (rebuilding San Damiano), [Francis] used to call with a loud voice in the joy of the Spirit to those living near or passing by the church and would say to them in French: "Come and help me in [this] project for the church of San Damiano which will be in the future a monastery of women by whose fame and life our heavenly Father will be glorified throughout the entire Church."[3]

In that way, filled with the spirit of prophecy, he actually predicted the future. For this is that sacred place in which the glorious religion and

---

[1] A concise discussion on this work in the context of the *Anonymous of Perugia* can be found in *The New Round Table* 36 (1983) 29–31.

[2] Cf. T. Desbonnets, "Legenda trium Sociorum: Edition critique," *Archivum Franciscanum Historicum* 64 (1974), 38–144; J. Godet, G. Mailleux, *Corpus des Sources Franciscaines* III (Louvain, 1976).

[3] It is curious that St. Clare simply quotes St. Francis as saying: "Come and help me in [this] project for the monastery of San Damiano, because there will again be women there by whose fame and way of life our heavenly Father will be glorified through His entire holy Church." Cf. *TestCl* 13–14. We must speculate with Marino Bigaroni if there was not an earlier monastery at San Damiano prior to that of the Poor Ladies, cf. M. Bigaroni, "San Damiano-Assisi: La Chiesa prima di San Francesco," *Atti Accademia Properziana del Subasio*, VI (1983) 49–87.

most excellent order of Poor Ladies and sacred virgins had its joyful origin because of Blessed Francis, scarcely six years after his conversion. Its wonderful life and glorious institution was fully approved by Lord Pope Gregory IX of happy memory, at that time Bishop of Ostia, and by the authority of the Apostolic See.

The Assisi Compilation (c. 1246)

This work is made up of testimonies sent to the Minister General of the Friars, Crescentius d'Iesi, in response to his request of 1244 for further information on the life of Saint Francis. It has had many titles: "The Legend of Perugia," "The Writings of Leo, Rufino and Angelo, Companions of St. Francis," or "The Assisi Compilation," and has been published in varying ways. Nonetheless, this collection represents the impressions and recollections of those companions of Saint Francis who, as they described themselves, "were always with him." There is little doubt that Thomas of Celano was familiar with and used much of this material in his Second Life of Saint Francis. However, the basic text of 1246 seems to have been supplemented and revised at later periods so that it is difficult to determine the historical accuracy or objectivity of all that it contains.[1]

The following passages touch on the life of Saint Clare and the Poor Ladies of San Damiano and provide us with insights overlooked by the earlier biographies. They undoubtedly come from eye-witnesses who were the close companions of Saint Francis during the last years of his life and who, more than likely, knew Saint Clare herself.

The Assisi Compilation 45

An earlier passage of this collection describes St. Francis' presence at San Damiano while suffering from a painful affliction of his eyes.[2] During this period, Spring 1225, the saint composed the first two stanzas of the Canticle of the Creatures and the work described in this passage, the Canticle of Exhortation for the Poor Ladies.[3] Thus the companions of Saint Francis and possibly the Ladies of San Damiano provide the background for two

---

[1] An excellent introduction to the *Assisi Compilation* can be found in *Scripta Leonis, Rufini et Angeli Sociorum S. Francisci (The Writings of Leo, Rufino and Angelo Companions of St. Francis)*, ed. and trans., Rosalind B. Brooke (Oxford, 1970), 1–78.

[2] Cf. *Scripta Leonis, Rufini et Angeli Sociorum S. Francisci*, nn. 42–43, ed. and trans. R.B. Brooke (Oxford: Oxford at Clarendon Press, 1970), pp. 162–167 For the nature of this affliction, cf. K. Haines, "The Death of St. Francis of Assisi," *Franzikanische Studien* 58 (1976): 27–46.

[3] Cf. supra p. 247–249 for background and text the *Canticle of the Creatures* and supra p. 250–251 for that of the *Canticle of Exhortation for the Poor Ladies*.

works flowing from the depths of his contemplative soul. While some modern authors have suggested Saint Clare and the Poor Ladies as part of the inspiration for the Canticle of the Creatures, *there is no doubt that they were the sole motivation for the beautiful* Canticle of Exhortation.

During those days and in the same place, after Saint Francis had composed the *Praises of the Lord for His Creatures,* he also composed some holy words with a melody for the greater consolation of the Poor Ladies of the monastery of San Damiano, especially since he knew that they were very grieved at his illness.[4] Since he could not visit or comfort them personally because of his illness, he wanted those words passed on to them by his companions.

In composing them he wanted, then and forever, to make known to them with brevity his will: how they should be of one mind and live together in charity, because, when there were still only a few brothers, they had been converted to Christ by his example and preaching. Their conversion and way of life was not only the joy and edification of the Order of brothers, whose little plant they were, but also of God's universal church. When Saint Francis knew that from the very beginning they had led and were still leading, both by choice and by necessity, a very hard and poor life, his spirit was always stirred with compassion toward them. Therefore, since the Lord had gathered them together from many parts into one congregation dedicated to holy charity, holy poverty, and holy obedience, he asked them in his message to always live and to die in those virtues.[5] [He asked them] in particular to provide for their bodies, out of the alms that God gave them, with wisdom, cheerfulness, and thankfulness. Most of all, [he encouraged them] to see that those who were well were patient in the labors they bore for their sick sisters and the sick patients in their sickness and in the unavoidable suffering they had to bear.

The Assisi Compilation 109

The companions of Saint Francis are extremely helpful in providing us with knowledge of the seriousness of Saint Clare's illness.[6] Unfortunately the letter written by Saint Francis to console her has been lost; this is our only source for knowing its contents.

---

[4]Unfortunately there is no score preserved of the melody provided by Saint Francis for this canticle.

[5]It is helpful to note the substitution of "charity" for "chastity" in this passage. This reflects the more tradition expression of dedicating one's self to "chaste charity" rather than simply "chastity."

[6]Cf. infra p. 133 n. 17 for information on the precise illness of Saint Clare.

During the week in which Saint Francis died, the lady Clare, who was the first little plant of the Order of Sisters, abbess of the Poor Sisters of the monastery of San Damiano in Assisi and emulator of Saint Francis in preserving always the poverty of the Son of God, was herself very ill and feared she would die before Saint Francis. She wept in bitterness of spirit and could not be consoled because she was not able to see before her death her only father before God, that is to say, Saint Francis, her comforter in soul and body, who had established her in God's grace—which had been granted both before his conversion and during his life in religion. Saint Francis was told this by one of the brothers. Since he loved her and her sisters with a fatherly affection because of their holy life, Saint Francis, when he heard this, was moved to pity, especially because it was only a few years after he began to have brothers that, with God's help, his advice converted her to God. Her conversion was edifying not only to the Order of brothers, but also to the universal church of God.

When Saint Francis pondered that what she desired, that is, to see him, was impossible at that time since both of them were gravely ill, he wrote his blessing in a letter to comfort her and he also absolved her of all failings, if she had any, in obeying his commands and wishes and those of the Son of God. Moreover, that she might put away all grief and be consoled in the Lord, he told the brother whom she had sent to him—yet the Spirit of God, not himself, spoke through him—"Go and take this letter to Lady Clare and tell her to put aside all sorrow and sadness because she cannot see me at this moment. But let her know that before she dies both she and her sisters will see me and have the greatest consolation from me."

It so happened that shortly afterwards, at dawn, since Saint Francis had died during the night, the whole population of the city of Assisi, men and women, with all the clergy, brought his holy body [singing] hymns and [songs of] praise from the place of his death. Everyone took branches from the trees and carried [the body] to San Damiano that, by God's will, the word spoken by God through his servant would be fulfilled for the consolation of his daughters and servants. The iron grating through which God's servants used to communicate and at times hear the word of God was removed. The brothers took the holy body from its bed and, for a good hour, held it at the window in their arms. Meanwhile the Lady Clare and her sisters received the greatest consolation from him, even though they were full of tears and afflicted with sorrow since, after God, he was their only consolation in this world.[7]

---

[7]This passage is a much simpler rendition of that contained in the *First Life of Saint Francis* (116) of Thomas of Celano. It does not contain the biblical allusions which embellish Thomas' text but presents details that add significantly to our knowledge of this poignant scene.

Witness of Thomas of Celano (1246)

The prologue of Thomas of Celano's Second Life of Saint Francis *presents two almost independent approaches. "Our memory, dulled as it is by length of time, like that of the untrained," the first paragraph laments, "cannot reach the flight of agile words. . . . " It was clearly Thomas' task to write down those events and insights of the first followers of Francis that were not contained in his* First Life. *But we must wonder at his profuse modesty which belies his literary expertise. The Prologue's second paragraph, however, offers another perspective maintaining that the Second Life was written "to declare with careful zeal what was the good, acceptable and perfect will of our most holy Father [Francis] both for himself and his followers." Thus the work contains more than new hagiographical material; it also attempts a synthetic presentation of the spiritual theology of the saint. If Thomas'* First Life *was built upon the strong foundation of an ecclesial theology of reform, the Second Life relied on the same basic principles of reform to strengthen the life of the Order of Friars Minor as the fraternity faced the developmental crises of its first decades.*

It is clear that Thomas used those memoirs and documents sent to the Minister General, Crescentius d'Iesi, upon the request of the General Chapter of 1244, and wove them into his own tapestry.

The Second Life of Saint Francis (13)

The following paragraph can be found in Book One of the Second Life. *It represents the initial intention of Thomas, i.e., to write down those yet unknown recollections of the saint's first followers. This incident of Francis' embarrassment at begging before his fellow citizens of Assisi, which is not contained in the* First Life, *prompts the mention of his prophetic vision of the role of San Damiano and "the holy virgins" who would live there. None of the eloquence found in Thomas' earlier work can be seen here; there is, instead, a rather plain, matter-of-fact presentation of Francis' realization of the importance of his task.*

One day the man of God went through Assisi to beg oil to light up the lamps of the church of San Damiano which he was repairing at that time. He saw a large group of men playing before the house he wanted to enter and was filled with shame and retraced his steps. But after he had directed his noble spirit to heaven, he chastised himself for his cowardice and *passed judgment on himself* (Jas 3:1). He immediately returned to the house and freely explained the reason for his shame. *In a kind of spiritual intoxication* (Jer 23:9), he begged in French for oil and got it.

He most enthusiastically stirred up everyone for the work of that church and, in a loud voice, prophesied *before all* (Gen 23:10) that it would be a monastery for holy virgins of Christ. For when he was filled with the *ardor of the* Holy *Spirit* (cf. Is 4:4), he always burst into French *to express his* ardent *words* (cf. Ps 44:1), knowing beforehand that people would honor him and have a special veneration of him.

The Second Life of Saint Francis (204–207)

Thomas returns in these paragraphs to his lofty vision of San Damiano and the Poor Ladies who are living there. We see him repeating once more an appreciation for the role of Saint Clare and her sisters in fulfilling the mission of Saint Francis in repairing this little church. Moreover, we cannot overlook Thomas' understanding of the much wider and more profound implications of the life of the Poor Ladies of San Damiano. Their presence in that sacred place, symbolic in Thomas' mind of so many aspects of Francis' call, was a continuing reminder of the ecclesial dimensions of the Franciscan vocation. Therefore, Thomas does not let the opportunity pass in his articulation of the virtues that should animate a disciple of Saint Francis, thus understanding the obligation of care and respect that should be shown to the Poor Ladies. In so doing, however, he delicately uses various recollections of Francis' first followers to describe the qualities that this ministry to the Poor Ladies should assume.

204. It would not be proper to pass over
the memory *of the spiritual edifice,*[1]
a much nobler edifice than that earthly building,
which Francis,
under the guidance of the Holy Spirit,[2]
founded in that place
after he had repaired that material building.

It should not be thought
that it was to repair a church
that would perish and was falling down

---

[1]Cf. 1 Pet 2:5.
[2]Cf. Is 63:14.

that Christ spoke to him from the wood of the cross
in a manner so stupendous
that *it filled* those who heard of it *with fear* and sorrow.[3]

But,
as the Holy Spirit had once foretold,[4]
the order of the holy virgins was established there,
which,
like a polished mass *of living stones,*[5]
was one day to be brought there
for the restoration of a heavenly house.

In fact,
after *the virgins of Christ*[6]
began to come together in that place,
gathered there from various parts of the world,
they professed the greatest perfection
in observing *the highest poverty*[7]
and *in adorning themselves with all virtues*[8]

Though their father gradually withdrew
his *bodily presence* from them,[9]
he nevertheless gave them his affection
in the Holy Spirit[10]
by caring for them.

For when the saint recognized
by many signs of the highest perfection
that they had been proved
and were ready to make every sacrifice *for Christ*[11]
and to endure every difficulty
without ever wanting *to depart from* Christ's holy *commandments*[12]

---

[3]Cf. 2 Mac 12:12.
[4]Cf. Acts 1:16.
[5]Cf. 1 Pet 2:5.
[6]Cf. 2 Cor 11:2.
[7]Cf. 2 Cor 8:2.
[8]Cf. Jud 10:4.
[9]Cf. 2 Cor 10:10; Col 2:5.
[10]Mt 3:11.
[11]Cf. Phil 1:29.
[12]Cf. Ps 118:21.

he firmly promised them
and others who would profess poverty in a similar way of life
that he would always give them his help and counsel
and that of his brothers.

As long as he lived
he always carried this out with eagerness,
and when he was close to death
he emphatically commanded that it should be always so,
saying that *one and the same spirit*[13]
had led the brothers and the poor ladies
out of the world.[14]

205. The brothers wondered at times why Francis did not visit the holy servants of Christ with *corporal presence* (cf. 2 Cor 10:10) more frequently. He would reply: "Do not believe, dearest brothers, that I do not love them perfectly. For if it were a fault to cherish them in Christ, would it not have been a greater fault to have united them to Christ? In fact, not to have called them would have been wrong; not to care for them once they have been called would be the greatest unkindness. But I must give *you an example, that, as I have done to you, so you should also do* (Jn 13:15). I do not want anyone to offer himself of his own accord to visit them, but I command that the unwilling and most reluctant brothers be appointed to take care of them, provided they be *spiritual men* (cf. Hos 9:7) proven by a worthy and long religious life."

206. Once when a certain brother, who had two daughters of perfect life in a certain monastery, said he would willingly take some poor little gift to that place for the saint, Francis rebuked him very severely, saying things that should not now be repeated. So he sent the little gift by another brother who had refused to go but had not persisted obstinately in his refusal.

Another brother went in the winter to a certain monastery on an errand of sympathy, not knowing the saint's strong will about not going on such visits. After the fact had become known to the saint, he made the brother walk several miles naked in the cold and deep snow.

207. Repeatedly asked by his vicar to preach *the word of God* (cf. Jn 3:34) to his daughters when he stopped for a short while at San Damiano, Saint Francis was finally overcome by his insistence and consented. But when, according to their custom, the nuns had come together *to hear the*

---

[13]1 Cor 12:11.
[14]Gal 1:4.

word of God (cf. Jn 8:47), though no less to see their father as well, Francis raised *his eyes to heaven, where his heart* always was (cf. Is 51:6; Mt 6:21), and began to pray to Christ. He then commanded ashes to be brought to him and he made a circle with them around himself on the pavement and *sprinkled* the rest of them *on his head* (cf. 1 Mc 3:47; Jud 9:1). But when they waited for him to begin and the blessed father remained standing in the circle of silence, no small astonishment arose in their hearts. The saint suddenly arose and to the amazement of the nuns recited the *Miserere mei, Deus* (Ps 51) in place of a sermon. When he had finished, *he* quickly *left* (cf. Ps 40:7). The servants of God were so filled with contrition because of the power of this symbolic sermon that their tears flowed in abundance and they could scarcely restrain their hands from inflicting punishment on themselves. He taught them by his actions to regard themselves *as ashes* (cf. Gen 18:27; Eccl 10:9) and that there was nothing in his heart concerning them *but what was fitting* this consideration (cf. Ez 6:11).

This was the way he acted toward these holy women.

His visits to them were very useful,
but they were forced upon him and rare.

And this was his will for his brothers:
he wanted them to serve these women
in such a way *for Christ, whom they served,*
that, like them,
they would have wings
that would always guard *against*
the snare laid out for them.[15]

---

[15]Cf. Prov 1:17.

Letter of Saint Bonaventure, Minister General, to the Abbess and Sisters of the Monastery of Saint Clare in Assisi (1259)

It is unlikely that Saint Bonaventure ever met Saint Clare. But this letter written within two years of his election as Minister General of the Order of Friars Minor shows his appreciation for the religious life established by her. Her place in the life of Saint Francis certainly becomes clear in the Major Life of Saint Francis *written by the Seraphic Doctor shortly thereafter.*

This letter was written by Saint Bonaventure during his lengthy, decisive period of prayer on Monte LaVerna in 1259. In his Soul's Journey into God, *which was inspired at this same time, he wrote of his search for a place of quiet and his desire to find there peace of spirit. Both writings suggest Bonaventure's wish to deepen his understanding of the ideals of Saint Francis that he would more effectively care for the fraternity entrusted to him. That he achieved this can be seen by the profoundly mystical approach to Franciscan life that characterizes his writings from this point.*

There are no sources indicating the reasons for the composition of this letter to the Poor Ladies. The mention of Br. Leo's name, however, might well hint at his influence in reminding the newly elected Minister General of his responsibility of caring for these women of the Second Order of Saint Francis. When it is placed beside Bonaventure's treatment of Saint Clare and the Poor Ladies in his Major Life of Saint Francis, *it is clear that from this point he became aware of their prominent place in the unfolding of the Franciscan ideals.*

1. To his beloved daughters in Jesus Christ, the abbess of the Poor Ladies of Assisi in the monastery of Saint Clare, and to all its Sisters, Brother Bonaventure, Minister General and servant of the Order of Friars Minor, sends his greeting and [wish that you], together with the holy virgins, follow the Lamb as His attendants wherever He goes.

2. Dear daughters in the Lord, I have recently learned from our dear

Brother Leo, once a companion of our holy Father, how eager you are, as spouses of the eternal King, to serve the poor crucified Christ in total purity. I was filled with a very great joy at this, so that I now wish, through this letter, to encourage your devotion and your generous following of the virtuous footprints of your holy Mother, who, by means of the little poor man Francis, was taught by the Holy Spirit.

"May you desire to have nothing else under heaven," except what that Mother taught, that is, Jesus Christ and Him Crucified. My dear daughters, may you run after the fragrance of His blood according to the example of your mother. May you strongly hold onto the mirror of poverty, the pattern of humility, the shield of patience, the insignia of obedience. And, inflamed by the fire of divine love, may you totally give your heart to Him Who on the cross offered Himself to God the Father for us. Thus you will be clothed with the light of your Mother's example and on fire with the delightful burning flames that last forever. Imbued with the fragrance of all the virtues, you will be the perfume of Christ, the Virgin's Son and the Spouse of the prudent virgins, among those who have been saved and those who are perishing.

3. Be so attentive in continuing your affections and fervent in the spirit of devotion that when the cry is raised, "The Bridegroom is coming," you will be able to meet him with faithfulness and with the lamps of your souls filled with the oil of charity and joy. While the foolish virgins are left outside, you will go in with Him to the wedding of eternal happiness. Christ will have His spouses sit down there with His angels and chosen ones, will minister to them, and offer them the bread of life and the meat of the Lamb that was slain, roasted fish cooked on the cross upon the fire of love, that burning love with which He loved you. Then He will give you a cup of spiced wine, that is, of His humanity and divinity, from which His friends drink and His dearly beloved, while miraculously maintaining their sobriety, drink deeply. While enjoying that abundance of sweetness reserved for those who fear Him, you will gaze upon Him Who is not only the most beautiful of all children but also of all the thousands of angels. It is upon Him, moreover, that the angels desire to look, for He is the brightness of eternal light, the unspotted mirror of God's majesty and the radiance of the glory of paradise.

4. Therefore, dearly beloved daughters, as you continue to cling to Him Who is our everlasting good and when He has done good things for you, commend a sinful person as me to His indescribable kindness. Keep up your prayers that, for the glory and honor of His wonderful name, He will be good enough to guide my steps mercifully in caring for the poor little flock of Christ entrusted to me.

The Major Life of Saint Francis
by Saint Bonaventure (1260)

The Chapter of Narbonne in 1260 commissioned Saint Bonaventure to compile new lives of Saint Francis based on the existing ones of Thomas of Celano and Julian of Speyer. The results were his Major Life (Legend), which was intended as table reading, and Minor Life (Legend), written as nine lessons for the liturgical office for the feast of Saint Francis.

The following brief passage comes almost entirely from the pen of the Seraphic Doctor. He takes only Thomas' description of Saint Clare as the "first tender sprout," thus giving us wonderfully new titles with which to consider her.[1] Moreover, Bonaventure continues to develop Thomas' appreciation of Saint Clare and the Poor Ladies' role in the Church by placing this description in the context of the Order's progress and its confirmation by the Pope.

The Major Life of Saint Francis, IV 6

Young women, too, were drawn to perpetual chastity, among whom was the maiden Clare, who was especially dear to God.

She was the first tender sprout
among these
and gave forth fragrance
like a bright white flower
that blossoms in springtime,
and she shone like a radiant star.
Now she is glorified
in heaven
and venerated in a fitting manner
by the Church on earth,
she who was the daughter in Christ
of our holy father Francis, the little poor man,
and the mother of the Poor Ladies.

---

[1] This phrase comes from Thomas' *Second Life* (109).

The Major Life of Saint Francis XII 2

*With the exception of the second sentence, the following section of St.
Bonaventure's account cannot be found in any of the earlier biographies of
Saint Francis.*[2] *It appears in the consideration of the saint's preaching ministry and his struggle to discern a call to a more eremetical way of life.
While the passage is not concerned directly with Saint Clare, it does provide a further insight into her role in helping Saint Francis shape the direction of his life.*

[Francis] was not ashamed
to ask advice in small matters
from those under him,
true Friar Minor that he was,
though he had learned great things
from the supreme Teacher.
He was accustomed
to search out with special eagerness
how and in what way
he could serve God more perfectly
according to God's good pleasure.
As long as he lived
this was his supreme philosophy,
this his supreme desire,
to inquire from the wise and the simple,
the perfect and the imperfect,
the young and the old,
how he could more effectively reach
the summit of perfection.

Choosing, therefore, two of the friars, he sent them to Brother Sylvester—who had seen the cross coming out from his mouth and in those days
spent his time in continuous prayer on the mountain above Assisi—that
Sylvester might ask God to resolve his doubt over this matter (of a life totally given to prayer) and send him the answer in God's name. He also
asked the holy virgin Clare to consult with the purest and simplest of the
virgins living under her rule and to pray herself with the other sisters in
order to seek *the Lord's will* (Lk 12:47) in this matter. Through the miraculous revelation of the Holy Spirit, the venerable priest and the virgin dedicated to God came to the same conclusion: that it was God's good pleasure

---

[2]This second sentence is taken from the *First Life* (91) of Thomas of Celano.

that Francis should preach as the herald of Christ. When the two friars returned and told him God's will as they had received it, he at once rose, *girded himself* (Jn 21:7) and without the slightest delay took to the roads. He went with such fervor to carry out the divine command and he ran along so swiftly that *the hand of the Lord seemed to be upon him* (4 Kgs 3:15), giving him new strength from heaven.

INDICES

Abbreviations

PART I:
THE WRITINGS OF SAINT CLARE

1LAg	The First Letter to Blessed Agnes of Prague (1234)
2LAg	The Second Letter to Blessed Agnes of Prague (1235)
3LAg	The Third Letter to Blessed Agnes of Prague (1238)
4LAg	The Fourth Letter to Blessed Agnes of Prague (1253)
LEr	The Letter to Ermentrude of Bruges
RCl	The Rule (1253)
TestC	The Testament (1247–1253)
BCl	The Blessing

PART II:
THE WRITINGS THAT CONCERN CLARE ALONE AND THE POOR LADIES

1PrPov	The Privilege of Poverty of Pope Innocent III (1216)
LHon	The Letter of Pope Honorius III to Cardinal Hugolino (1217)
RHug	The Rule of Cardinal Hugolino (1219)
LHug	The Letter of Cardinal Hugolino (1220)
LGreg	The Letter of Pope Gregory IX (1228)
LRay	The Letter of Cardinal Raynaldus (1228)
2PrPov	The Privilege of Poverty of Pope Gregory IX (1228)
LAgA	The Letter of Saint Agnes of Assisi (1230)
Mand	The Mandate (1238)
RInn	The Rule of Pope Innocent IV (1247)
Not	The Notification of the Death of Saint Clare (1253)
Proc	The Acts of the Process of Canonization (1253)
BC	The Bull of Canonization (1254)
LegCl	The Legend of Saint Clare (1254–1255)

PART III:
THE WRITINGS THAT CONCERN CLARE, THE POOR LADIES, AND FRANCIS AND HIS BROTHERS

FormViv	The Form of Life Given by Saint Francis (1212/1213)

279

JdV   The Witness of Jacques de Vitry (1216)
CantSol   The Canticle of the Creatures of Saint Francis (1225)
CantExh   The Canticle of Exhortation of Saint Francis (1225)
UltVol   The Last Will of Saint Francis Written for the Poor Ladies
             (1226)
1 Cel   The First Witness of Thomas of Celano (1228)
AP   The Witness of the 'Anonymous of Perugia' (1240–1241)
L3S   The Legend of the Three Companions (1246)
AC   The Assisi Compilation (1246)
2 Cel   The Second Witness of Thomas of Celano (1246)
LBon   The Letter of Saint Bonaventure to the Sisters of Saint Clare
             (1259)
LegMaj   The Major Life of Saint Francis by Saint Bonaventure (1260–
             1263)

Index to Foreword, Preface, Introductions and Notes

Index to
Part I:

THE WRITINGS
OF
SAINT CLARE

I. Index of Scripture References and Allusions

287

Romans		
8:17	2 LAg 21	
12:1	2 LAg 10	
	3 LAg 41	
14:13	2 LAg 14	
15:30	1 LAg 33	
16:3	3 LAg 8	

1 Corinthians	
1:26	TestC 4
2:9	3 LAg 14
3:6–7	TestC 78
3:9	3 LAg 8
12:26	2 LAg 21
15:10	2 LAg 25
16:22	LEr 11

2 Corinthians	
1:3	TestC 2
	TestC 58
	BCl 12
2:15	TestC 58
3:3	4 LAg 34
3:18	3 LAg 13
5:18	1 LAg 14
8:2	RCl Prol
	RCl VIII 4
8:6	TestC 78
8:9	1 LAg 19
	RCl VIII 3
8:11	TestC 78
11:2	1 LAg 12
	1 LAg 24
	3 LAg 1
	4 LAg 4
	4 LAg 8
	4 LAg 15
13:11	BCl 16

Galatians	
2:20	3 LAg 15
4:19–20	RCl VIII 16
6:2	LEr 17

Ephesians	
1:3	BCl 12
3:14	TestC 77

Philippians	
1:8	1 LAg 31
3:14	3 LAg 3
	TestC 23
4:1	3 LAg 11
4:3	2 LAg 22
4:4	3 LAg 10
4:8–9	3 LAg 2

Colossians	
1:13	1 LAg 14
1:23	RCl XII 13
3:14	RCl X 7
3:17	TestC 1
4:6	3 LAg 41

1 Thessalonians	
1:6	4 LAg 7
1:8	1 LAg 3
2:7	RCl VIII 16
4:17	BCl 16
5:19	RCl 7:2
5:25	1 LAg 35
	4 LAg 39

1 Timothy	
3:15	TestC 38
4:12	TestC 5
6:15	2 LAg 1

2 Timothy	
2:11–12	2 LAg 21
4:5	LEr 13
	LEr 14

Titus	
2:13	4 LAg 39

Hebrews	
1:3	3 LAg 12
	3 LAg 13
	4 LAg 14
2:10	3 LAg 2
12:2	1 LAg 14
13:17	RCl IV 8

II. Analytical Index

291

III. Index of Proper Names

Adam, first parent:
  –1 LAg 14
Agnes:
  –saint Agnes, martyr: 4 LAg 8
  –of Assisi, sister of Clare: 4 LAg 38
  –of Prague: 1 LAg; 2 LAg; 3 LAg; 4 LAg
Apostles:
  –Peter and Paul: 3 LAg 36; RCl Epil

Bonagura (Brother):
  –4 LAg 40

Clare:
  –Lady: RCl Prol
  –Sister Clare: RCl I 5; BLC 6
  –servant-handmaid: 1 LAg 2, 33; 2 LAg 2; 3 LAg 2; 4 LAg 2; RCl I 3
  –mother: 4 LAg 33; TestC 79; BlC 6
  –abbess of San Damiano RCl Prol
  –little plant of St. Francis: RCl I 3; TestC 37, 49; BlC 6; cf. Abbess, Mother, Servant-Handmaid, Sister

Elias (Brother)
  –2 LAg 15

Francis:
  –brother: RCl VI 7
  –father: TestC 18; glorious: 3 LAg 30; blessed: TestC 42; holy: TestC 37–38, 40; holy saint: RCl Prol; I 3; VI 1–2; TestC 5, 7, 17,

24, 30, 36, 46–48, 50, 52, 57, 75, 77, 79,
  –blessed: 3 LAg 36; RCl Prol; I 1, 4–5; VI 10; XII 7; TestC 27
  –saint: RCl III 14; TestC 9, 16, 31

Innocent III:
  –RCL I 3; TestC 42
Innocent IV:
  –RCL Prol; Epil

Michael (Saint):
  –his intercession: BlC 7

Peter and Paul:
  –RCL Epil; cf. Apostle
Pope:
  –grants Privilege of Poverty: TestC 42
  –gives Cardinal Protector: RCl XII 12
  –grants rite to enter monastery: RCl XI 7
  –Clare promises reverence: RCl I 3; recommends to sisters: TestC 44; cf. Gregorio IX, Innocent III, Innocent IV

Rachel:
  –2 LAg 11
Raynaldus:
  –RCL Prol

IV. Index of Names of Places

Index to
Part II:

THE WRITINGS
CONCERNING SAINT CLARE
AND
THE POOR LADIES

I. Index to Scripture References and Allusions

II. Analytical Index

Abbess:
–elected freely by community RInn 12;
–and the enclosure: RHug 10–11; 13; RInn 6, 7, 9;
–and silence: RHug 6; RInn3;
–and canonical visitation: RInn 8;
–and administration of goods: RInn 11;
–and care of sick: RHug 7, 8;
–and religious garb: RHug 12: RInn 5;
–and young: RInn 4;
–and studies: RInn 5; RInn 2

Abstinence:
–time and form: RHug 7;
–observed by Clare: Proc I 8; III 5; IV 5;
–excessive in her: Proc I 7; VII 11; XIII 4;
–cause of illness: Proc 1:8

Admission:
–conditions: RHug 4, 10; RInn 1;
–of serving sisters: RInn 5

Alms:
–received with confidence: LegCl 14, 20, 30

Asperges:
–hours of: Proc XIV 8;
–in receiving Lord: Proc XIV 8

Austerity:
–in community: Proc I 8; III 5; IV 5; VI 5, 7; VIII 4, 11; XI 5; XII 6; XIII 4; BC 11; LegCl 18;
–in clothing: Proc II 4–7; III 4; IV 6; VI 5; VII 4; XI 5; XII 6; XIII 4; BC 11; LegCl 17;
–in bedding: Proc I 7; IV 6; VII 4; XII 6; BC 11; LegCl 17

Bed, dormitory:
–poor and humble: RHug 9

Behavior of seculars:
–conditions: RHug 6; RInn 3

Blessing:
–of God for Poor Ladies: LegCl 45;
–of Raynaldus for Clare: LRay 4;

Bloodletting:
–RInn 4

Body:
–enemy of soul: BC 11;
–changed into temple of God: LegCl 6;
–overcome by penance: LegCl 39.

Canonization of Clare:
–waiting for: LegCl 62;
–initiation of process: LegCl 62;
–for her miracles: LegCl 62;
–approval of: LegCl 62;
–by Alexander: IX BC 19; LegCl 62

Canticle of Creatures:
–composition in San Damiano: AC 83, 84

Cardinal Protector:
–of Poor Ladies: RegHuh 10; LRay 2;
–welcome into monastery: RHug 10;
–visit to Clare: Not 5; LegCl 44

Chaplain:
–of Poor Ladies, qualities and duties: RInn 6, 11; RInn 7, 12; entrance into enclosure: RHug 11; RInn 7;
–obligations of: Reg 12;
–object of visit: RInn 8.

Christ:
–one foundation: RHug 3;
–true nourishment: LegCl 44; I PrPov 2; II PrPov 2;
–one dedication: LegCl 24;

311

III. Index of Proper Names

IV. Index of Names of Places

Index to
Part III:

THE WRITINGS
CONCERNING SAINT CLARE,
THE POOR LADIES
AND
THEIR RELATIONSHIP WITH
SAINT FRANCIS
AND
HIS BROTHERS

I. Index to Scripture References and Allusions

II. Analytical Index

Canticle of Creatures:
–composed at San Damiano: AC 83, 84
Canticle of Exhortation:
–composed at San Damiano: AC 45
Charity:
–mutual and continuing: 1 Cel 19
Chastity:
–among Poor Ladies: 1 Cel 19
Christ:
–adored Spouse: LBon 2–3
–only foundation: I Cel 18
–only dedication: I Cel 18; LBon 2–4
–serving: 2 Cel 207
Church:
–form of primitive: JdV
–rebuilding of: L3C 24; 2 Cel 204
–venerates Clare: LegMaj IV 6
Clare, Saint:
–model of all virtues: 1 Cel 19–20
Commandments:
–observance of: 2 Cel 204
Contemplation, contemplative life:
–merit height of: 1 Cel 20
–excellence of: LBon 2–3

Death:
–of Francis: 1 Cel 106; AC 109;
–reaching Spouse: LBon 3
Discretion:
–use alms with: CantExh 4

Following:
–of Christ in poverty: FormVit
–of poor and humble Christ: LBon 2
–of Clare: LBon 2
Form of Life:
–given by St. Francis: FormVit

Francis of Assisi:
–founder of Poor Ladies: 1 Cel 18
–their guide: 1 Cel 113
–their visitator: FormVit; 2 Cel 204–205
Friars Minor:
–and Poor Ladies: JdV
–care of Poor Ladies: FormVit
Funeral:
–of St. Francis: 1 Cel 116; AC 109

Glory:
–of Poor Ladies in heaven: LBon 3
God:
–confidence in: 1 Cel 18
–protects Order: 1 Cel 18
–sole interest in: LBon 2
Gospel:
–perfection of: FormVit
Growth of Poor Ladies:
–JdV; 1 Cel 18

Heaven:
–joined to Spouse in: LBon 3
Humility:
–of Poor Ladies: 1 Cel 19

Love:
–of Christ poor and crucified: 1 Cel 19

Mother of God:
–and poverty: UltVol

Obedience:
–die in: CantExh 2

III. Index of Proper Names

IV. Index of Names of Places

Bibliography

PRIMARY SOURCES:

Anonymous. *Anonymus Peruginus.* Edited by Lorenzo DiFonzo. *Miscellanea Franciscana*, 72 (1972): 117–483.

———. "Legenda trium sociorum: Édition critique." *Archivum Franciscanum Historicum* 64 (1974): 38–144.

———. *Scripta Leonis, Rufini et Angeli Sociorum S. Francisci.* Edited and translated by R. B. Brooke (Oxford: Oxford at Clarendon Press, 1970).

Bonaventure of Bagnoregio, Saint. "Legenda major S. Francisci," *Analecta Franciscana.* Vol. X. Quaracchi: Collegium S. Bonaventurae, 1926–1941.

Clare of Assisi, Saint. *Claire D'Assise: Écrits.* Edited and translated by Marie-France Becker, Jean-François Godet, Thaddée Matura. Paris: Les Éditions du Cerf, 1985.

Francis of Assisi, Saint. *Die Opuscula des Hl. Franziskus von Assisi.* Edited by Kajetan Esser. Grottaferrata: Collegium S. Bonaventurae, 1976.

———. *Opuscula Sancti Patris Francisci Assisiensis.* Edited by Kajetan Esser. Grottaferrata: Collegio S. Bonaventurae, 1978.

Jacques de Vitry. *Lettres de Jacques de Vitry.* Edited by R. B. C. Huygens. Leyde, 1960.

Lazzeri, Z. "De processu canonizationis S. Clarae," *Archivum Franciscanum Historicum* V (1912).

———. "Il processo di canonizzazione di S. Chiara d'Assisi," *Archivum Franciscanum Historicum* XIII (1920).

Mailleux, Georges and Jean-François Godet, eds. *Corpus des Sources Franciscaines.* Volumes I–V. Louvain: Centre de Traitement Électronique des Documents de L'Université Catholique de Louvain, 1974–1976.

Omaechevarria, Ignacio, ed. *Escritos de Santa Clara y Documentos Contemporaneos*, 2nd ed. Madrid: Biblioteca de Autores Cristianos, 1982.

Schmucki, Ocktavian. "Das wiederentdeckte 'Audite' des hl. Franziskus für die Armen Frauen von San Damiano," *Fidelis* 68 (1981).

Thomas of Celano. "Vita Prima S. Francisci." *Analecta Franciscana.* Vol. X. Quaracchi: Collegium S. Bonaventurae, 1926–1941.

———. "Vita Secunda S. Francisci." *Analecta Franciscana.* Vol. X. Quaracchi: Collegium S. Bonaventurae, 1926–1941.

SECONDARY SOURCES:

Medieval Women and Religious Life

Baker, Derek. *Medieval Women.* Oxford: Basil Blackwell, 1978.

Bynum, Caroline Walker. *Jesus as Mother: Studies in the Spirituality of the High Middle Ages.* Berkeley: University of California, 1982.

————. *Holy Feast and Holy Fast: The Religious Significance of Food to Medieval Women.* Berkeley: University of California, 1985.

Dridenthal, Renata, and Claudia Koonz. *Becoming Visible: Women in European History.* Boston: Houghton-Mifflin, 1977.

Dronke, Peter. *Women Writers of the Middle Ages: A Critical Study of Texts from Perpetua (d. 203) to Marguerite Porete (d. 1310).* Cambridge: Cambridge University Press, 1984.

Erickson, Carolly. *The Medieval Vision: Essays in History and Perception.* New York: Oxford University Press, 1976.

Herlihy, David. *Women in Medieval Society.* (B. K. Smith Lecture Series). Houston: University of St. Thomas, 1971.

Kirshner, Julius, and Suzanne Wemple, eds. *Women of the Medieval World: Studies in Honor of John H. Mundy.* Oxford: Basil Blackwell, Ltd., 1985.

Labarge, Margaret Wade. *Medieval Women: A Small Sound of the Trumpet.* London: Hamish Hamilton, 1986.

Morewedge, Rosemarie Thee, ed. *The Role of Women in the Middle Ages.* Albany: State University of New York, 1975.

Nichols, John A., and Lillian Thomas Shank, eds. *Distant Echos: Medieval Religious Women.* Volume I. Cistercian Studies Series, 71. Kalamazoo: Cistercian Publications, 1984.

————. *Peace Weavers: Medieval Religious Women.* Volume II. Cistercian Studies Series, 72. Kalamazoo: Cistercian Publications, 1987.

Power, Eileen. *Medieval Women.* Cambridge: Cambridge University Press, 1975.

Southern, Richard W. *Western Society and the Church in the Middle Ages.* New York: Viking-Penguin Publications, 1967.

Stuard, Susan Mosher. *Women in Medieval Society.* Philadelphia: University of Pennsylvania Press, 1976.

————. (ed). *Women in Medieval History and Historiography.* Philadelphia: University of Pennsylvania Press, 1987.

Tavormina, M. Teresa. "Of Maidenhood and Maternity: Liturgical Hagiography and the Medieval Ideal of Virginity," *American Benedictine Review* 31 (December 1980): 384–399.

Weinstein, Donald, and Rudolph M. Bell. *Saints and Society: The Two Worlds of Western Christendom, 1000–1700.* Chicago: University of Chicago Press, 1982.

Saint Clare and the Poor Ladies

Armstrong, Regis J. "Clare of Assisi. The Mirror Mystic." *The Cord* 35 (July–August 1985): 195–202.

Asseldonk, Optatus van. "The Holy Spirit in the Writings and Life of St. Clare." *Greyfriars Review* I (1987): 93–104.

Bartoli, Marco. "Analisi storica e interpretazione psicoananalitica di una visione di santa Chiara d'Assisi," *Archivum Franciscanum Historicum* 73 (1980): 449–472.

Carney, Margaret. *The Rule of St. Clare of Assisi and The Feminine Incarnation of the Franciscan Ideal.* Unpublished Doctoral Dissertation. Pontifio Atheneo "Antonianum," 1988.

DeRobeck, Nesta. *St. Clare of Assisi.* Milwaukee, Bruce Publishers, 1951; reprinted, Chicago: Franciscan Herald Press, 1981.

Fortini, Arnaldo. "Saint Clare, Lady of Light." In *Francis of Assisi*, trans. Helen Moak. New York: Crossroad, 1981.

Gilliat-Smith, Ernest. *Saint Clare of Assisi: Her Life and Legislation.* New York: E. P. Dutton & Co., 1914.

Godet, Jean-François. "Lettura della Forma di Vita." *Vita Minorum* 3 (Maggio-Giugno 1980).

Iriarte, Lazaro. "The Order of Poor Clares." In *Franciscan History: The Three Orders of St. Francis of Assisi*, trans. Patricia Ross. Chicago: Franciscan Herald Press, 1979.

Lainati, Chiara Augusta. "The Enclosure of St. Clare and the First Poor Clare in Canonical Legislation and Practice." *The Cord* 28 (1978): 4–15, 47–60.

Leeuwev, Peter van. "Clare's Rule," *Greyfriars Review* I (September 1987), 65–77.

Marie Aimée du Christ, Sister. "The Charism of St. Clare: A Prophecy for Women of Every Age." *Greyfriars Review* I (1987): 77–93.

Roggen, Heribert. *The Spirit of Saint Clare.* Chicago: Franciscan Herald Press, 1971.

Società Internazionale di Studi Francescani. *Movimento religioso femminile e francescanesimo nel secolo XIII.* Assisi: Società Internazionale di Studi Francescani, 1980.

Concordance of
Major Translations and the
Corpus des Sources Franciscaines

In recent years several translations of the writings of Saint Clare have appeared. Unfortunately, these translations have shown little or no consistency in the numbering of sentences, so that a scholar or student finds difficulty in finding and citing texts.

At the same time, *the Corpus des Sources Franciscaines,* a computerized concordance of the texts and a valuable research tool, leaves something to be desired in its system of numbering. Whereas it uses the system of the legislative editions for the *Rule* and *Testament,* for the letters to Blessed Agnes of Prague it adopts the cumbersome numbering of Walter W. Seton's *Archivum Franciscanum Historicum* edition of 1924. Moreover, it presents no concordance to the letter to Ermentrude of Bruges.

Most recently the bilingual French/Latin edition of the writings of Saint Clare in the *Sources Chrétiennes* has offered what most experts hope will be considered "a critical edition" and definite numbering of the text. We have adopted this numbering for the present volume.

The editor offers the following concordance to simplify the student's path through the various translations and editions:

CA = CLARE OF ASSISI: EARLY DOCUMENTS
   Claire D'Assise: Écrits. Edited and translated by Marie-France Becker, Jean-François Godet, Thaddée Matura. Paris: Les Éditions du Cerf, 1985.

FC = FRANCIS AND CLARE: COMPLETE WORKS
   R. J. Armstrong, I. C. Brady, *Francis and Clare: The Complete Works* (Paulist Press: New York, 1982).

CSF = CORPUS DES SOURCES FRANCISCAINES
   Mailleux, Georges and Jean-François Godet, eds. *Corpus des Sources Franciscaines.* Volume V. Louvain: Centre de Traitement Électronique des Documents de L'Université Catholique de Louvain, 1976.

LETTERS TO AGNES OF PRAGUE
Letter One

CA/FC	CSF
1	1, 2
2	2–5
3	6–8
4	8–10
5	10–12
6	12–14
7	14–16
8	16–17
9	17–21
10	19–21
11	21–23
12	23–24
13	24–27
14	27–29
15	30–31
16	31–33
17	33–35
18	35–37
19	37–39
20	39–41
21	41–42
22	42–44
23	44–46
24	46–47
25	48–50
26	50–52
27	52–53
28	53–55
29	55–58
30	59–61
31	61–63
32	64–65
33	66–69
34	69–70
35	71

Letter Two

CA/FC	CSF
1	1–2
2	2–4
3	5–7
4	7–9
5	10–11
6	11–12
7	12–14
8	14–16
9	16–17
10	17–19
11	19–21
12	21–22
13	22–23
14	23–26
15	26–28
16	28–29
17	29–32
18	32
19	32–34
20	34–37
21	37–40
22	40–41
23	41–43
24	44
25	45–47
26	47

Letter Three

CA/FC	CSF
1	1–3
2	3–5
3	6–8
4	8–10
5	11–12
6	12–15
7	15–18
8	18–20
9	20–21
10	21–22
11	22–23
12	23–24
13	24–26
14	26–28
15	28–30
16	30–32
17	32–33
18	33–34
19	34–35
20	35–37
21	38–39
22	39–41

Concordance of the
Acts of the Process of Canonization
and the *Legend of Saint Clare*

The passages in **bold print** are unique
to *Acts of Process of Canonization.*

Legend (Number)	*Outline of Life*	*Process* (Witness)
1	Clare: from Assisi,	I 2
	location of house	I 2
	noble, rich, knightly family	I 4; XVI 1; XVIII 4; XIX 1; XX 2–3;
	name of her father, ancestors	I 4; XVI 1; XIX 1; XX 2
	Mother Ortulana, pilgrimage; later Sister Ortulana	I 4–5
2	Prophecy about Clare's birth	III 28; VI 12
3	Clare's virtue while still in world	I 1–3
	compassion for poor	I 3; XVII 1, 2, 4; XVII 1; XX 3
	sends money for workers at **Portiuncula**	XVII 7
4	A "Rosary" of pebbles	
	Wears hairshirt	XX 4
	Sends Bona on pilgrimage	XVII 6
	"Beautiful face"	XVIII 2
	They want to marry her	XVIII 2; XIX 2
	Fame of her virtues	I 3; II 2; III 2; IV 2; XII 1; XVII 4
5	Conversation with Francis, **Filippo**	XVII 3
	vision at breast of Francis	III 29; VI 13
6	Moved by example, exhortations of Francis	III 1; IV 2; VI 1; XII 2; XVI 3, 6; XX 6
	Sees Francis in a dream	III 29; VI 13

341

7	Palm Sunday	
	Departure from home	XIII 1
	Clare's age at that moment	II 2; XIII 1
8	Gives herself to Christ at Portiuncula	XII 4; XVI 6; XVII 5; XVIII 3; XX 6
	Goes to San Paolo delle Abbedesse	XVII 5; XVIII 3; XX 6
9	Struggles with family at San Paolo	XII 4; XVIII 3; XX 6
10	At Sant'Angelo di Panzo	XII 5
	At San Damiano	XII 5; XX 7
	Fame of her virtues	XVI 2; XVII 8
11	Multiplication of monasteries	
12	Title of Abbess	I 6
	Her humility	I 10; II 1–3; III 9; VI 2; X 6
	Prefers to serve than command	I 10
	Serves the sisters	I 12; II 3; III 9
	Washes mattresses	I 12, II 1; VI 7
	Washes feet of sisters	I 12; II 3; III 9; X 6, 11
13	Sells inheritance for sake of poor	II 22; III 31; XII 3; XIII 11
	and part of Beatrice's	XII 3
	Enamored of poverty	I 13; III 3
14	Privilege of Poverty	III 13; 32; III 14
	Refuses possessions	I 13; II 22; III 14
	Prefers pieces of bread, not whole	III 13
15	Multiplication of bread	VI 16
16	Miracle of oil	I 15; II 14
17	Habit and mantle are poorest	II 4; III 4
	Cords	II 5; III 4
	Borrowed Cords	II 7; X 1
	Her bed	I 7; III 4; X 7
	Straw mat prescribed by Francis	X 7
18	Fasts	I 8; II 8; III 5; IV 5
	Sisters suffer because of her fasts	I 7
	Prohibition from Francis and Bishop	I 8; II 8; IV 5
	Happiness of Clare	III 6; VI 4
19	Prolonged prayer after Compline	X 3
	Prolonged prayer during night	I 7; X 3
	Gift of tears	III 7; VI 4
	Attempts of devil to dissuade her	

20	Returning from prayer	I 9; IV 4; VI 3
	Calls Sisters for Matins	II 9; X 3
21	Efficacy of her prayer	VI 11
21–22	Saracens	II 20; III 18; IV 14; IX 2; X 9; XII 8; XIV 3; XVIII 6
23	Vitale d'Aversa	III 19; IX 3; XIII 9; XIV 3; XVIII 6
24–26	Conversion of her sister Agnes	– – –
27	Woman from Pisa delivered from demons	IV 20; VII 14
	Letters from Gregory IX to Clare	– – –
28	**Corporals blessed by Bishop distributed to churches**	I 11; II 12; VI 14; IX 9
	When she confessed	II 11
	Fervor when going to Eucharist	II 11; III 7
29	Christmas vision of 1252	III 30; IV 16; VII 9
30	Devotion to Passion of Christ	X 10
	Teaching it to novices	XI 2
	Special prayer at Sext	X 3
	Beaten by devils	– – –
	Prayer to Five Wounds	X 10
	Office of the Cross	– – –
	Cord with thirteen knots	– – –
	Desire for martyrdom	VI 6; VII 2; XII 6
31	Ecstasy on Good Friday	III 25
32	The power of the sign of the Cross	I 18; III 6; VI 9
	Illness of Brother Stephen	II 15
33	The boy with pebble in his nose	II 18
	Another boy with film on his eye	IV 11
34	Sr. Benvenuta (fistula)	II 16; III 10; IV 8; X 1; XIV 5
	Sr. Amata (dropsy, fever, cough)	III 11; IV 7
35	Sr. Benvenuta of Perugia (voice)	II 13; VII 7
	Sr. Cristiana (deafness)	III 17; IV 10; V 1
	Healing of five Sisters	I 16–19
	Healing of Sister Blavina	VII 12–13
	Healing of Sister Cecilia	IV 9; VI 8
	A boy with fever	III 15; IX 6

	Prophecy concerning five sisters	VI 15
	Prophecy concerning abandoned woman	XVI 4

36	Daily instruction of sisters	I 9, 14; II 10; III 3; VI 2; VIII 3; XI 2
	Admonitions of serving sisters	XIV 9
	"Vidi aquam"	XIV 8

37	The preaching of Br. Filippo	X 8
	Vision of Child Jesus	IX 4; X 8
	Another during Communion	IX 10
	Prohibition of Pope Gregory IX	– – –
	Light from her place of prayer	II 17

38	Charity toward her Sisters	– – –
	Covers those sleeping	II 3
	Discerning with weak	II 6
	Consoles those tempted	X 5
	Response of the Sisters	Cf. III 2 ff.
	Washes feet of Sisters	X 11

39	Sick for 29 years	I 17; cf. XIV 2
	Miracle of door	V 5; VI 17; XIV 6; XV 2
	Towel and cat	IX 8

40	Visit of Cardinal of Ostia	– – –

41	Visit of Pope	III 24
	Kisses foot of Pope	– – –

42	Asks for absolution	– – –
	Rejoices at double blessing	III 24
	Receives Rule with papal seal	III 32

43	Response to her sister Agnes	– – –

44	Last words: Brother Raynaldus	– – –

45	Brs. Juniper, Angelo and Leo	– – –
	Mourning of sisters	– – –
	Last confession	III 23
	Last prayer	X 10

46	"I am speaking to my blessed soul"	III 20–21; XI 3; XIV 7
	"I see the King of Glory"	IV 19
	Vision of the Virgin	IX 4
	Last words	X 10
	Sister healed at her death	IX 7
	Her death	III 32; XI 4

47–48	Funeral	– – –

MIRACLES

49	Miracles prove her sanctity	– – –
50–51	Freeing from demons	– – –
52	Young Frenchman	XX 9
59	Sister Andrea	II 23; III 16